The World Economy

D1458586

Horst Siebert

London and New York

First published in 1999 by Routledge
11 New Fetter Lane, London EC4P 4EE

Simultaneously published in the USA and Canada
by Routledge
29 West 35th Street, New York, NY 10001

Reprinted 2000

Routledge is an imprint of the Taylor & Francis Group

Typeset in Baskerville by
J&L Composition Ltd, Filey, North Yorkshire
Printed and bound in Great Britain by
Biddles Ltd, www.biddles.co.uk

British Library Cataloguing in Publication Data
A catalogue record for this book is available from the British Library

Library of Congress Cataloguing in Publication Data
A catalogue record for this book has been requested

ISBN 0–415–21725–3 (hbk)
ISBN 0–415–21726–1 (pbk)

Contents

Figures

Tables

Preface

The topic of this book is the world economy. It provides an analysis of the global economic structures and processes in the world. It looks at the economy of the planet Earth as if the world were observed from outer space. In a time when the communication system is organized globally, when we can communicate from Buenos Aires to Kiel over the Internet and when huge quantities of data can be interchanged between Cambridge and Hangzhou, when CNN broadcasts news worldwide, when transport costs are becoming less and less important and when more and more people are becoming accustomed to finding their jobs in all parts of the world, such a world view of the economic processes and structures appears to be imperative.

In this book, we study the world's product, its composition by sectors and the main components of world aggregate demand. We look at economic growth, including some historical evidence. We analyze the world markets for goods, the adjustments to disturbances of equilibria on the commodity markets and the role of trade. Moreover, the world market for factors for production, for labor and capital, are examined.

Specific issues are the world monetary and financial markets. A global monetary equilibrium with different monies and exchange rates is discussed, including approaches explaining the exchange rate in the long and the short run. Purchasing power parity, interest rate parity, exchange rate overshooting, optimal asset portfolios, financial bubbles and recent currency crises are the topics. The volatility of financial and currency markets has an impact on the real sphere of the economy, and a crisis may jump from one country to another. An important issue is how financial crises can be prevented and what role the IMF should play.

In a further step, the book looks at the regional dimension of the world economy, namely at developing countries and the new market economies (transformation countries). It also analyzes approaches to regional integration in the world including the European Union.

The book also addresses potential conflicts between the national interest and global concerns. This relates to national protectionism versus free trade. It also refers to the concept of locational competition which means that the immobile factors of production, that is labor, compete for the mobile factors, that is capital and technological knowledge. Locational competition is competition between governments, including competition in taxation, in the supply of public goods and in the institutional design of countries. Using the national and the global environment can be interpreted as another area where national and global interests can clash. In order to prevent strategic (i.e. non-cooperative) behavior, an institutional order is required for the world economy for the international division of labor.

The book has developed from my regular lecture on the world economy at the University of Kiel, from my research at the Kiel Institute of World Economics and from the discussions with my research colleagues. If one works at a research institute like the Kiel Institute of World Economics where many ideas are floating around, one is permanently exposed to a shifting frontier of knowledge. New areas of problems have to be recognized quickly. Many international visitors stimulate imagination and require answers to pressing problems. Moreover, I had to present the Kiel ideas in international conferences, in lectures at Zhejiang University in Hangzhou, China, and at the Instituto Universitario Banco Patricio in Buenos Aires, at the Fundación Mediterránea, at Córdoba in Argentina, the Uruguay–German Chamber of Commerce in Montevideo and at the UN Commission for Latin America and the Caribbean in Santiago de Chile. Some of the paragraphs of this book have been written in these and other parts of the world, often of necessity ignoring the tourist attractions.

This book has grown out of my German book *Weltwirtschaft* (1997). Helge Barlen, Björn-Ole Böttcher, Jens Mundhenke and Mark Oosterlinck have prepared a preliminary translation of the original text; they also helped with tables, diagrams and documentation. I have then rewritten the text from scratch adding the new Part II on 'Monetary and Financial Markets' and a new chapter on the European Union. The other chapters have been extended widely, new material having been added.

I am grateful to many who have criticized the manuscript in its different stages and who have influenced my thoughts. Karsten Junius, Michael Koop and Oliver Lorz read the complete manuscript and have suggested many corrections. Daniel Piazolo has gone through chapter 14, Juergen Stehn through chapter 10, Markus Schlie has criticized the section on the ECB, with Claudia Buch I have discussed capital flows. I have continuously discussed the topic of the international division of labor with my colleagues at the Kiel Institute, especially with Gernot Klepper, Henning Klodt, Rolf J. Langhammer, Klaus-Werner Schatz, Joachim Scheide, Rüdiger Soltwedel, Harmen Lehment, with my colleagues at the Economics Faculty of Kiel University, especially Gerd Hansen, Horst Herberg and Manfred Willms, and with my colleagues at the German Council of Economic Advisors, Juergen B. Donges, Wolfgang Franz, Herbert Hax and Rolf Peffekoven who have sharpened my grasp of economic problems and of approaches to problem solving. Last but not least, my students at Kiel, and also at the Universities of Konstanz and Mannheim where I had taught before, have been a permanent challenge to presenting the fascinating issues, avoiding the boring and not to hesitating to state the obvious.

A manuscript like this one is born slowly, and under pain with many round-about processes which, unfortunately, are not always productive. In typing the manuscript, Nicole Petersohn has accompanied this process of creative destruction with composure and professionalism.

I also acknowledge the following for permission to reprint illustrations used in the book: the World Bank for figures from the *World Development Report 1995*, 'Workers in an Integrating World', pp. 51 and 121; the Centre for International Economics and Dr Andrew Stoeckel for a table from *Western Trade Blocs*, 1990, p. 69; dtv (Deutscher Taschenbuchverlag) and Charles P. Kindleberger for a figure from *The World in Depression, 1929–1939*, 1973, p. 172. Routledge, London and New York, and Bernhard Heitger and Leonard Waverman for figures from *German unification and the international economy*, 1993, pp. 76–77.

Horst Siebert

The global view

The world economy is an exciting topic. The collapse of the centrally planned economies, the oil crisis, the Great Depression in the 1930s, the failure of Latin America in the lost decade of the 1980s and the success of the Asian 'tigers' in spite of the temporary financial disturbance in 1997/98 – these are all fascinating issues (section 1.1). The world economy is becoming more global. The segmentation of markets is being reduced; new regions, which have until recently scarcely been involved in world trade, are pushing into the international division of labor (section 1.2). The reader will be familiarized with the most important variables of the world economy, notably world product and its composition from the production and the expenditure side as well as its regional structure (section 1.3). The world economy is in a process of continuous change. Thus, the newly industrializing countries have succeeded in becoming much more integrated into the international division of labor (section 1.4). Meanwhile some of them have reached remarkable places in the ranking of competitiveness (section 1.5). For these and other problems we have to take a global view, as if the world is being analyzed from outer space (section 1.6).

1.1 Seven pictures of the world economy

Picture 1

Let us turn back the clock some 140 years. At that time, Japan was a closed economy without significant international relations in either the economic or the cultural field. During the Meiji revolution in 1868 Japan opened itself consciously to the outside world. For the early periods of the opening process and of its development, it is reported that Japan started to produce spokes for imported bicycles and in this way pursued a policy of import substitution. At the end of the 1920s, Japan had become an important exporting country with a share of the world export volume of approximately 3 percent. After Japan's breakdown due to the Second World War, Japan had to start building the economy up again. In 1950, Japan had a relatively insignificant position in the world economy; its share of the world export volume was 1 percent. Today, Japan provides nearly one tenth of the world export volume, and its efficient industry is, in spite of some problems in the 1990s, challenging North America as well as Europe.

How does a country manage to integrate itself successfully into the international division of labor? How does an open country efficiently use its resources so that it reaches a maximum of welfare gains from trade? Which mechanisms cause an economy to produce those export goods that are demanded in the world? What does a policy concept with a consistent international orientation look like? Where are the limits of the process of economic growth through trade? Does continuing success with export goods mean that worldwide demand for the currency of the country is growing considerably, eventually culminating in an appreciation so that price competitiveness is partly eaten away? Has Japan run into structural problems in the 1990s that will severely affect its growth potential? What experience on catching up do we have for other countries?

Picture 2

After 1945, the centrally planned economies of Eastern Europe could not reduce their development gap to the US. Whereas during the 1950s and the 1960s relatively high real growth rates of the communist countries could still be recorded, the 1970s are characterized by very low growth rates. During the 1980s, the communist systems collapsed. They could not adequately provide their citizens with goods. In Figure 1.1, the relative distance to the US level of GDP per capita is denoted on the horizontal axis, growth rates are depicted on the vertical axis. High growth rates in a decade would move a country to an improved relative

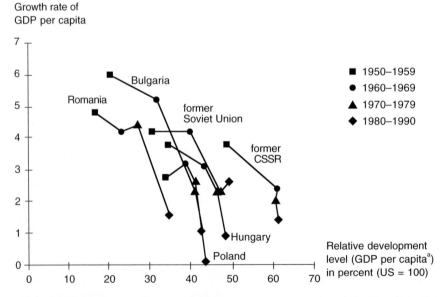

Figure 1.1 Economic growth in the centrally planned economies of Eastern Europe, 1950–1990

[a]Calculated with purchasing power parity

Source: Heitger (1993), according to data from Summers and Heston (1988, 1991) position to the US. Note that purchasing power parities are used; nevertheless comparisons may be distorted.

What are the reasons for this failure of the communist system? Apart from an inefficient planning system, lacking property rights and setting wrong incentives, how important was the so-called 'division of labor planned from above' for the miscarriage? How relevant was the attempt of the centrally planned socialist economies in the COMECON (Council of Mutual Economic Assistance) in Eastern Europe to exploit economies of scale in production by an explicit process of specialization? Buses for the COMECON countries were produced in Hungary, tramcars in former Czechoslovakia, and railway cars in former East Germany. This specialization, planned from above, eliminated competition between the COMECON economies which were exempted from international competition anyway.

How can we explain how economies do not catch up, cannot keep up their prosperity level or even suffer a self-inflicted erosion of their economic competitiveness relative to other countries? How long can governments conceal such processes from their population? When do people, drawing comparisons with other countries, become aware of their deteriorated economic situation? How can the post-communist reform countries be integrated into the international division of labor? Under what conditions will countries fall behind?

Picture 3

The story of economic growth of different regions of the world is told in Figure 1.2. Latin America recorded weak economic growth in the five decades from 1950 until 1997 and had a negative growth rate in the 1980s, its 'lost decade'. It pursued an economic policy that was not successful. By means of an import substitution policy, it partly excluded itself from the international division of labor. Imports were hindered, and domestic sectors were not exposed to international competition. Until the 1980s, for example, Mexico had a system of import licenses where, as a rule, an import license was linked to a stronger peso in a system of split exchange rates. In this way, license holders could buy imported goods at a preferential price. This system was governed by a bureaucracy which made it possible for the politicians in charge to exert political power. Mexico did not give up this policy until the 1980s and joined the GATT only in 1986. The positive growth rates of Latin American countries in the 1950s, 1960s, 1970s and 1990s were not sufficient to reduce the income gap relative to the US, where the growth rate was higher.

The development of the Asian countries on the Pacific rim took a different course. They were basically characterized by an international orientation of their economic policy and exposed their economies to competition from abroad. On average, discrimination in favor of the domestic relative to the external sector was not prevalent. Until the Asian financial crisis of 1997/98, the four 'tigers' (Hong Kong, South Korea, Taiwan, Singapore) had real growth rates of 6 percent (and higher) for five decades.

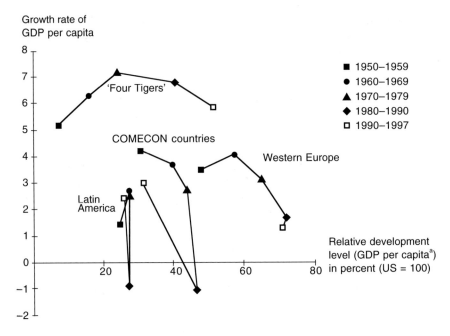

Figure 1.2 Economic growth in selected regions of the world, 1950–1997
ᵃCalculated with purchasing power parity
Source: Heitger (1993), according to data from Summers and Heston (1988, 1991), updated with data
from World Bank, *World Development Indicators* CD-ROM (1998)

The COMECON countries had negative growth rates in the 1980s. On average they have fallen back in their income position relative to the US. In the
1990s, this result is especially influenced by Russia, Belarus and the Ukraine; the
Eastern European countries have been more successful in the transformation
process.

Western Europe has caught up with the United States in the four decades since
1950, but fell back a little in the 1990s when the growth process in the US economy became stronger again and when capital accumulation proceeded there at a
higher pace than in Western Europe.

What are the necessary ingredients for a successful growth process? Why do
countries stagnate relative to others, why do some fall back? Did those countries
pursuing a policy of import substitution and protection from foreign trade
deprive themselves of possible development prospects and potential welfare
gains? What is the relationship between international orientation and economic
growth? Do open economies experience stronger growth?

Picture 4

At the time of the Great Depression at the beginning of the 1930s, the world economy experienced a massive breakdown. The volume of world trade fell to one third of its former level within four years. The so-called Kindleberger spiral shows how the world import volume of 75 countries, which can be regarded as a world trade indicator, dwindled from month to month (Figure 1.3).

What would be the effects of such a breakdown of world trade today? For instance, the US is exporting 10 percent of its GDP; a fall of its exports to one third would mean a reduction of 3 percent of aggregate demand – a severe recession. Or take Germany which exports about one third of its GDP. Here, a drop in the export volume to one third would represent an 11 percent drop in aggregate demand and a devastating depression. Related questions are: Can monetary and financial crises spread into the real sphere of the economy? Under what conditions can a regional crisis like the Mexican crisis in 1994/95 and the

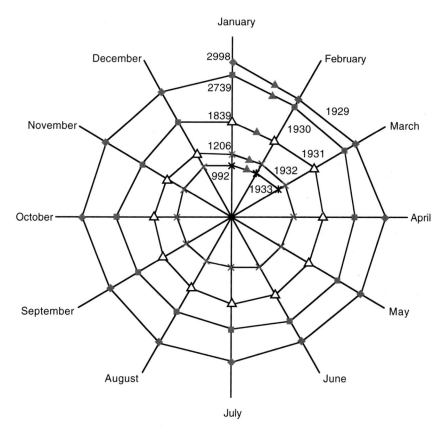

Figure 1.3 The Kindleberger spiral
Note: World import volume in million US gold $
Source: Kindleberger (1973, p. 172)

Asian crisis in 1997/98 be contained? Under what conditions is contagion inevitable?

Picture 5

During the two oil price shocks in the 1970s the oil price increased nearly twentyfold compared to the 1960s (Figure 1.4). Whereas in the 1960s the oil price was significantly below 2 US$ per barrel of crude oil, it increased fivefold to approximately 10 US$ during the first oil crisis in 1973/74. During the second oil price shock in 1979/80 the price per barrel rose from 12 US$ to nearly 40 US$. The reason for this development was that the resource countries claimed the property rights to the crude oil reserves in their soil. In this way the seven big international oil companies were cut off from their supply sources. Under the terms of the concession contracts that were used until then, the oil firms had to pay a given percentage of their proceeds for the extracted amounts of oil (royalty). *De facto*, they were in charge of the oil extraction and also had the right (often for a period of up to 70 years) to tap new oil wells. At the beginning of the 1970s, the oil exploitation rights moved to the resource countries. As a consequence, the world's oil supply could no longer be allocated in the vertical hierarchy of the enterprises (extraction, refinery, transport, distribution). Instead, markets – especially the Rotterdam spot market, but later on also forward markets – increasingly took over the allocation of oil.

The impact of the oil crisis was that the capital stock, geared to the low oil prices of the 1960s, became partly obsolete, especially the machines in the pro-

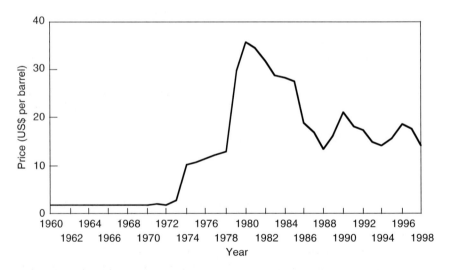

Figure 1.4 The world oil price
Note: Price of Arabian light crude oil
Source: British Petroleum Company, *BP Statistical Review of World Energy 1997*; Datastream 1998, annual averages from monthly data

duction processes and the engines of the means of transport. The productivity of existing capital fell, and this had effects on production, employment and growth. At the same time, a redistribution of real income in favor of the oil-producing countries took place. The countries without oil resources, particularly the industrialized nations, had to give away more export goods per barrel of imported oil than before, their terms of trade deteriorated. In the end, the oil-producing countries had considerable petro-dollar earnings at their disposal which could not be completely absorbed by their imports. A petro-dollar recycling took place which later became the germ cell of the debt crisis of the developing countries.

How does the world economy cope with such a sudden shortage of a production factor? What adjustment processes have to take place? Are economies that depend strongly on the import of a natural resource able to reduce their demand for this resource in the middle and long run? Is it possible at least partially to substitute by other production factors those resource inputs which become more expensive? Is import demand inelastic? How is the income distribution between the production factors affected by such an adjustment process? How does the political process of a country deal with such a shortage?

Picture 6

Since the 1960s consciousness concerning scarcity in the environment has been growing, especially in the industrialized nations. In contrast to the oil crisis, this has not induced a sudden cutback of the supply of a resource but the beginning of a long-term and lengthy process in which countries change the framework for using the environment by defining new property rights. The environment is not only a national factor of endowment requiring national policy approaches; some aspects of the environment represent an international public good where worldwide user rights have to be developed.

What effects does such a long-term redefinition of the institutional framework for environmental use have on the international division of labor? Do particular countries lose competitiveness in specific economic branches? Do other countries gain comparative price advantages? How are trade flows and capital flows adjusted to environmental scarcity? What solutions are offered for global environmental activities like the protection of the ozone layer?

Picture 7

After the opening up of Central and Eastern Europe and with the integration of China into the international division of labor, a huge and radical change is taking place in the world economy. Countries well endowed with the production factor of labor are starting to participate in the international division of labor. The integration of China alone, with 1.2 billion people, means that the effective supply in the world labor market increases by one fifth.

What impact does such an increase in the effective labor supply have on the world economy? Is it true that prices of labor-intensively produced goods will have to fall? Will the incomes of workers that have produced these goods in industrialized countries up to now have to fall as well? Will countries now take refuge in protection? To what extent will the regions being newly integrated into the world economy represent attractive markets? What stimulating effects will originate from these additional markets? Are these stimulating effects strong enough to compensate the industrialized countries which may lose in labor-intensive goods? Will the industrialized countries as a whole gain or lose?

The common element of these seven pictures is that change is taking place in the world economy. This could be a sudden shock for the world economy, like the oil price shock or the collapse of world trade and production in the Great Depression of the 1930s. But change can also be a long-term, 'historical' process that develops gradually such as the gradual decline of the economies in Eastern Europe, the poor performance of Latin America in the decades from 1950 until 1990 and the slowly increasing awareness of the environmental problem.

1.2 What does globalization mean?

In the 1990s, globalization has become a key word. By 'globalization' we mean a reduction of market segmentations and an increasing interdependence of national markets. We shall now look at the catalysts for globalization and at its impact.

Reasons for globalization

In the world economy we can observe a whole string of tendencies that lead to globalization:

- Transport and communication costs have fallen significantly in recent decades. This holds for the traditional costs of covering distances by sea and air (which have been reduced to approximately one fifth since the 1920s and 1930s respectively) as well as for the costs of telecommunication (Figure 1.5). For instance, a three-minute telephone call from New York to London in 1930 cost 250 US$ (in constant prices of 1990), in 1950 it was 50 US$ and in 1990 just 3.32 US$; the price for processing information fell from 1 US$ per instruction per second in 1975 to one cent in 1994 (World Bank, *World Development Report 1995*, p. 45). The costs of using satellites have also fallen dramatically.
- In information technology the world is experiencing a revolution. The World Wide Web represents a powerful global information network. In 1998, 180 million Internet stations participated in this worldwide network. According to industry estimates, it will probably increase to half a billion in 2002.
- The reduction of political tensions (e.g. the Cold War, apartheid in South Africa), regional efforts towards integration, for example in Europe, and

Figure 1.5 Costs of transport and communication
Source: World Bank, *World Development Report 1995*, p. 51

the strengthening of multilateral trade agreements also have eliminated impediments to trade.

- The radical change in the former centrally planned economies of Central and Eastern Europe and the opening of China have integrated important regions of the world into the international division of labor. Taking India into account as well, a historical process is taking place, in which more than 40 percent of the world's population is additionally integrated into the world economy. This implies that the limitation of the size of markets, which was a possible barrier for the extension of the international division of labor in the past, will be less important in the future.

- Most developing and newly industrializing countries have changed their strategies for development and foreign trade and are now much more open. Forty-four countries have joined GATT/WTO from 1986 to 1998. As of 1999, 30 countries want to become members of the WTO.

● Apart from measures which explicitly restrict trade, national regulations are increasingly being reviewed. They are continuously adjusted in a process of institutional competition, thus resulting in less impediments as well.

The impact of globalization

Globalization means that market segmentations in product and factor markets are reduced and that national markets become more interdependent. The allocation mechanism is working globally, so that international differences in prices will lead to arbitrage. Globalization means that differences in supply and demand conditions of different countries can be leveled out more easily by international exchange. Market participants have to adjust to this global mechanism of allocation. Firms maximizing their profits have to consider essential repercussions in worldwide markets.

Globalization of markets must not be confused with the centralization of decision processes. The increasing interdependence does not imply a centralization of decisions. Decisions are still, or even more so, made in a decentralized way. The globalization of markets and the decentralization of decisions are supported and stimulated by new technologies for organization and communication, e.g. CAD (computer-aided design), CIM (computer-integrated manufacturing), by software that allows immediate control of the decentralized units, by groupware that can be used by several users simultaneously. But decisions now have to be made under different restrictions, because the options of globalized markets and of a high mobility of factors of production have to be taken into account. A highly integrated world economy, above all the decreasing costs for transport and communication, increases the possibility of a fragmentation of production. An increasing fragmentation of production also means that locations can be changed more easily.

In combination with the fragmentation of production, the increasingly global orientation of firms will go hand in hand with growing intra-firm trade. Direct investment (see below) as a predecessor of future trade flows will gain importance.

The reduction of market segmentations will not only strengthen the commodity arbitrage between different supply conditions in the traditional sense of intersectoral trade, but it will also allow different product preferences of consumers to come into play. Product variety is an important aspect of trade. In this respect, intra-sectoral trade will become more important.

Services

The increasing integration of the world economy changes the conditions for the trade in services. By 'trade in services' we mean several quite diverse phenomena: a service like an international telephone call may actually cross a border ('cross-border supply'), consumers or firms of one country may use the service in another country ('consumption abroad'), a service may be supplied in another country ('commercial presence') or individuals may travel to supply their service in another country ('presence of natural persons'). The diversity of services becomes apparent by the WTO classification list with 7 main categories (and 62 subcategories), namely distribution services, education services, communication services (including telecommunication services, audio-visual services such as motion picture production and distribution, radio and television services), health-care services, professional services (including legal services, accounting services, data processing, business consultancy, advertising services, architecture, engineering), transportation services, and travel and tourism services. In addition, there are also other areas such as financial services (bank services, trade in stocks and shares, the insurance business).

A major distinction of service categories is between border-crossing and local services, analogous to tradable and non-tradable goods. Applying these categories, another distinction becomes relevant, namely between 'person-disembodied' and 'person-embodied' services (Bhagwati 1984; Klodt *et al.* 1994). Disembodied services, like detail engineering using computer programs, the development of software or accounting data processing are not 'embodied' in persons. They do not require business partners to meet locally when the service is carried out. For the international trading order, these services (cross-border supply) are not very different from tangible goods. Just as commodities are carried by the transport system, disembodied services cross national borders by means of communication media.

The increased importance of trade in services has not been observed for the last twenty years (Siebert and Klodt 1999). Although approximately 20 percent of world trade is trade in services, this ratio has stagnated since 1975. However, the new communication technologies are likely to make trade in disembodied services grow ever more intensively. The stronger the tertiarization processes are in the industrialized nations, i.e. the increase of the share of services in GNP, the more important international trade in services is going to be. Moreover, extending the WTO rule system to services should be favorable to the trade in services.

Increasing interdependence of factor markets

The reduction of impediments to international mobility not only refers to commodity markets but also to factor markets. In particular, capital mobility is becoming more important, and foreign direct investment plays an important role for capital movements across borders. Different motives are relevant. For example, it may be desirable to be present in an expanding market, to avoid transaction costs or to circumvent the political segmentation of markets due to foreign trade policy. But direct investment also follows comparative cost advantages, where expected locational advantages are anticipated. In this respect, direct investment today is the predecessor of trade in commodities tomorrow.

Since the 1980s, foreign direct investment has grown considerably faster than world trade (Figure 1.6, Table 1.1) and, if one neglects recessions, world trade measured in real terms has grown considerably stronger than world production. World industrial production increased with a real growth rate of approximately 2 percent per year from 1985 until 1997 and the world trade volume by 6 percent, as measured by the real world export volume. Foreign direct investment, though extremely volatile, rose by 13 percent. These figures indicate a growing interdependence in the world.

Labor markets are becoming increasingly more global for those with high qualifications, e.g. management. Apart from this, for the most part labor markets remain nationally segmented. But this does not imply that there is no international competition between workplaces. Interdependence has an indirect effect, for instance, via trade flows and capital mobility.

International interdependence of financial markets

Besides foreign direct investment, portfolio capital has become extremely mobile; it now can be moved immediately worldwide from one financial market to another.

1.3 **World gross product**

The world gross product amounted to approximately 28 trillion US$ in 1997 (World Bank, *World Development Report* 1997, Table 12). With respect to the term

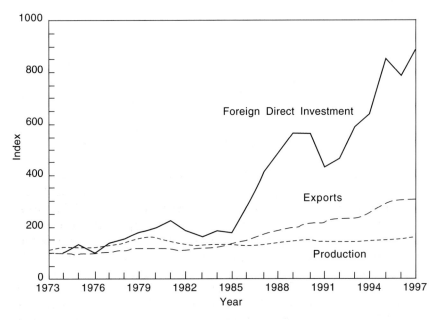

Figure 1.6 World industrial production, world trade and foreign direct investment, 1973–1997[a]

[a]Indices; 1973 = 100. Exports without services. Foreign direct investments adjusted with the US industrial goods price index; 1997 index figure for foreign direct investment contains estimates for some smaller countries

Source: IMF, *International Financial Statistics* CD-ROM July 1998; IMF, *Balance of Payments Statistics*, current volumes; own calculations

Table 1.1 Growth rates of world industrial production, world trade and foreign direct investments, 1985–1997[a]

Year	World industrial production	World trade[b]	Foreign direct investment
1985	3.0	1.3	−2.8
1986	1.3	14.2	57.1
1987	3.4	14.6	49.6
1988	5.8	10.2	16.2
1989	3.6	3.5	18.3
1990	1.7	9.8	0.0
1991	−0.3	2.1	−24.0
1992	−0.9	6.1	0.0
1993	−1.4	−1.4	27.3
1994	4.0	12.3	8.7
1995	3.8	15.1	34.1
1996	1.7	2.4	−7.9
1997	4.0	3.1	12.2

Source: IMF, *International Financial Statistics* CD-ROM July 1998; IMF, *Balance of Payments Statistics*, current volumes; own calculations

Notes
a   All rates measured in percent. The foreign direct investment growth figure for 1997 contains estimates for some smaller countries.
b   Exports

'world gross product', a note to the reader is required. When we look at a single country, we distinguish between two concepts: gross domestic product (GDP) and gross national product (GNP). Gross domestic product is the product generated by the factors of production located in a country including foreigners working in the country and capital in the country even if owned by foreigners. Gross national product is the income accruing to all citizens of a country including income from work (for instance of expatriates) and capital income earned in foreign countries.

On the world scale, GDP and GNP yield the same total when summed up over all countries, as (at least so far) no factor of production is active far outside the planet Earth. In this regard we could use the term 'world product'. However, since we have become used to the term 'GDP' (gross domestic product) and since we will continuously be comparing the country view to the world view in this book, we will use the term 'world gross domestic product', or 'world GDP'. Where GDP data are not available, GNP data will be applied.

Viewed from the production side, services, with a share of 62 percent, are the most important sector of the world domestic product. The industrial sector contributes 33 percent and agriculture 5 percent (Table 1.2). Countries with a lower per capita income (according to the World Bank classification those countries with a per capita income of less than 785 US$ per year) are heavily specialized in agriculture. Countries with a medium or high income (9556 US$ or more per year) have a relatively large share in services.

From the expenditure side, private consumption contributes the biggest share

Table 1.2 World domestic product, production approach by sectors (1997), in percent of
the world domestic product

	Agriculture	Industry	Services
Countries with lower income	31	27	42
Countries with medium income	12	38	50
Countries with higher income (1995)	2	33	65
World (1995)	5	33	62

Source: World Bank, *World Development Report 1997* and *1998*, Table 12

to the world gross domestic product, with more than 60 percent. Gross investment is at about 22 percent and government consumption at 15 percent (Table
1.3). Countries with a lower income show a higher share in gross investment.
Because this share does not completely correspond to gross savings in all
countries, investment must be partly financed from abroad, but mainly it is still
financed from domestic savings. The balance of payments is negative for the
countries with a lower income (−4 percent in relation to the gross domestic
product).

The regional structure of the world domestic product is shown in Figure 1.7:
the gross domestic products of the economies with a lower, medium or higher
income are 0.7 trillion, 5.2 trillion and 22.3 trillion US$, respectively. The US
contributes 28 percent to the world domestic product, Japan 15, Germany 7 percent. The share of the other OECD countries is of a similar dimension to that of
the US (31 percent – without Germany and Japan). China accounts for 3 percent
of the world domestic product.

With its 7 trillion US$ economy, the United States is the largest country of the
world measured in terms of gross national product. China is the largest country
measured in terms of population (Table 1.4).

Table 1.3 World domestic product, expenditure approach (1997), in percent of the world
domestic product

	Government consumption	Private consumption	Gross investments	Gross savings	Balance of payments
Countries with lower income	11	71	22	18	−4
Countries with medium income	13	62	25	25	0
Countries with higher income	16	63	21	21	0
World	15	63	22	22	1

Source: World Bank, *World Development Report 1998*, Table 13

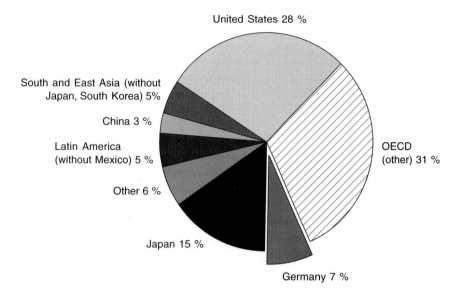

Figure 1.7 Regional structure of the world's gross domestic product 1997
Source: World Bank, *World Development Report 1998*

1.4 Economic change in the world economy

The world economy is in a process of permanent change. Since 1980, economic growth has been roughly at 3 percent per year, in the 1990s it was at 2 (Table 1.5). Quite a few of the developing countries are growing at a higher rate, for instance, the four Asian 'tigers' (Hong Kong, Korea, Malaysia, Singapore) at 6 percent and more before the financial crisis of 1997/98 (Figure 1.8). The industrialized countries have a lower growth rate of 2–3 percent. The transformation countries in Central and Eastern Europe have experienced negative growth rates during the

Table 1.4 The ten largest countries of the world

	GNP (billions of US$, 1997)			Population (millions, 1998)	
1	United States	7690	1	China	1237
2	Japan	4772	2	India	984
3	Germany	2320	3	United States	270
4	France	1526	4	Indonesia	213
5	Italy	1220	5	Brazil	170
6	United Kingdom	1155	6	Russia	147
7	China	1055	7	Pakistan	135
8	Brazil	773	8	Japan	126
9	Spain	584	9	Bangladesh	125
10	Canada	570	10	Nigeria	111

Source: World Bank, *World Development Report 1998*; US Census Bureau, *International Data Base 1998*

Table 1.5 GDP growth rates, 1980–1997

	1980–1990	*1990–1997*
World	3.1	2.3
Low income countries	4.3	4.2
Middle income countries	2.8	2.5
High income countries	3.2	2.1

Source: World Bank, *World Development Report 1988/89*, Table 11

period of transformation. Russia still has negative growth rates. Note that the process of economic growth in the world economy is influenced by the business cycle.

Since 1970 the developing and newly industrializing countries as a whole have succeeded in integrating themselves into the international division of labor. Their contribution to world trade has grown from 18 percent in 1975 to 29 percent in 1997 (Figure 1.9). Especially the newly industrializing countries of Asia on the Pacific rim managed to realize high gains. They significantly increased the share of industry products in their exports, e.g. Singapore from 34 percent (1965) to 84 percent (1996). The world market share of the four 'tigers' (Hong Kong, Singapore, South Korea and Taiwan) grew from approximately 3 percent in 1975 to approximately 10 percent in 1997 (Figure 1.10). In comparison, the African continent south of the Sahara, with a world market share below 2 percent, remains the poorhouse of the world for the time being.

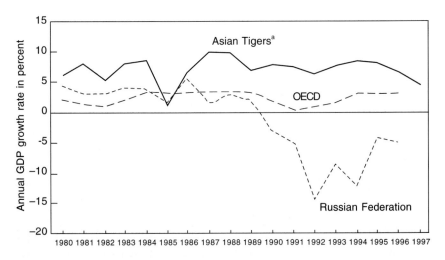

Figure 1.8 Growth in the world economy, 1980–1997
[a]Hong Kong, Singapore, South Korea and Taiwan
Source: World Bank, *World Development Indicators*, CD-ROM 1998; *World Development Report 1998/99*

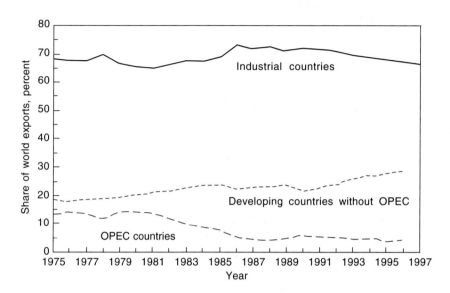

Figure 1.9 Shares of world export: industrial countries and developing countries
Source: IMF, *International Financial Statistics*, CD-ROM, July 1998

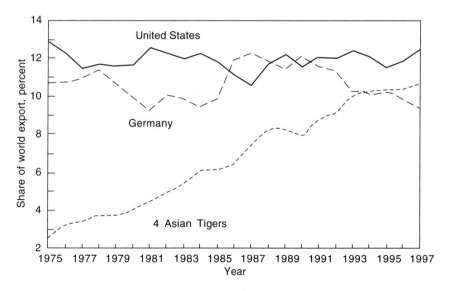

Figure 1.10 Shares of world export: United States, Germany, Asian 'tigers'[a]
[a]Hong Kong, Singapore, South Korea and Taiwan
Source: IMF, *International Financial Statistics*, CD-ROM, July 1998

1.5 A ranking of competitiveness

Several organizations compile rankings of competitiveness for all countries of the world. For instance, the World Economic Forum (1998) has developed a ranking of competitiveness for 49 countries from surveys and statistical information. This index takes into account the openness of a country, the role of the government, the efficiency of the national financial markets, the quality of infrastructure, technology and management, the flexibility of the national labor markets and the institutional framework. In this context, the growth potential of a country is essential. The small open economies are positioned at especially high places. It is somewhat surprising to find Germany ranked only at position 24 (Figure 1.11).

1.6 The global dimension

The subject of this book is the world economy. The book does not concentrate on a single open economy, i.e. an economy linked to other countries through trade or capital flows. Instead, it provides a global analysis of the structures and processes in the world economy, as if the world were looked at from outer space. In a time when the communication system is organized globally, when we can communicate from Buenos Aires to Kiel over the Internet and when huge quantities of data can be interchanged between Cambridge and Hangzhou, when CNN broadcasts news worldwide, when transport costs become less and less important and when more and more people become accustomed to finding their jobs in all parts of the world, such a world view of the economic processes and structures appears to be imperative.

Thus, the paradigm prevailing here is an analysis of the world as a whole. The world is first of all interpreted as an entity. This is true for the macroeconomic aggregates of the world economy, like the world's domestic product and the main components of world aggregate demand. It also refers to macroeconomic approaches to explain processes in the world economy, like cyclical movements or economic growth. In contrast to such a macroeconomic view other aspects are rather microeconomic, for instance, an analysis of the world markets for goods, including adjustments to disturbances of equilibria on the commodity markets. In a similar way, this also holds for the world market's factors of production. A specific issue is the world money market and the financial markets. The volatility of financial and currency markets has an impact on the real sphere of the economy, and a crisis may jump from one country to another. An important issue is how a financial crisis can be prevented. In a further step, this global view can be abandoned to analyze different regions of the world, like developing countries and the new market economies (transformation countries). In a more disaggregated outlook, processes of regional integration, including that in the European Union, are also of interest. Finally, it is interesting to examine the role which is left for national economic policy in the world economy today, to look at potential conflicts between the national interest and global concerns and to study the institutional arrangements which should be developed for the world economy.

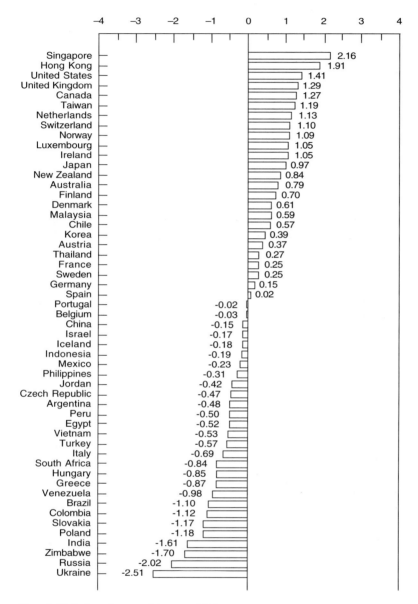

Figure 1.11 Index of competitiveness, 1998
Source: World Economic Forum, *The Global Competitiveness Report 1998*

Part I

The world goods and factor markets and economic growth

Being interested in the world economy, we have to answer the question how the division of labor is carried out and how development and growth processes can be explained. We first analyze the division of labor under static conditions. In a paradigm of allocation, markets are important, notably commodity markets (chapter 2) and factor markets (chapter 3). Second, we study how the division of labor in the world changes over time and how the process of economic growth can be explained (chapter 4).

2 The world product markets

The reduced costs of economic distance and the integration of the newly industrializing countries as well as of the new market economies have changed the equilibrium of the world commodity markets. The supply of commodities has increased and at the same time new markets have arisen. In order to examine these effects, we first look at the world market equilibrium on the commodity markets (section 2.1). Then the effects of the reduction of trade barriers and the rising labor supply will be discussed (sections 2.2 and 2.3). The impact of a labor supply increase on factor income and on employment is a major point (section 2.4). The most important theorems on the international division of labor will be briefly summarized (section 2.5). Shifts of demand and a changed demarcation line between tradable and non-tradable goods also play their role (sections 2.6 and 2.7). Some world markets are characterized by imperfect competition (section 2.8); imperfect competition is associated with intra-sectoral trade (section 2.9). The question is raised whether markets are contestable when economies of scale exist and different preferences have to be taken into account (section 2.10). Finally, markets and vertical hierarchy are discussed as different approaches to the international division of labor (sections 2.11 and 2.12).

2.1 The world market equilibrium

The concept of the world market equilibrium

The world product markets are in equilibrium if there is no excess demand. The prices on the markets must adjust in such a way that this condition is satisfied. We express this condition with

$$E_i^w = C_i^w - Q_i^w = 0 \tag{2.1}$$

Excess demand (E_i^w), that is the difference between demand (C_i^w) and supply (Q_i^w), must be equal to zero for each good i. Then, the world market is cleared. When supply or demand conditions on a world market change, the price has to change as well.

As an example of a world good market, the world crude oil market with the observed prices for a barrel of oil and the traded quantities is shown in Figure 2.1. In the 1960s, supply expanded and the price remained nearly constant. In the two oil crises of 1973/74 and 1979/80, supply remained constant and even

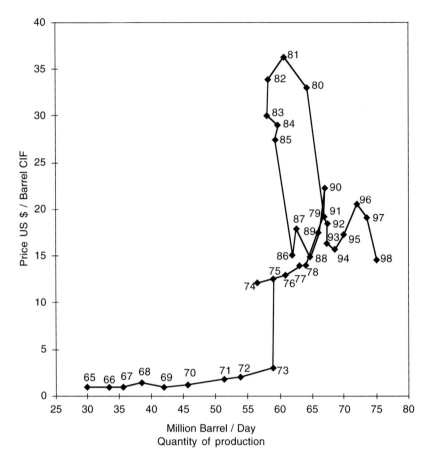

Figure 2.1 World oil market
Source: OECD *Economic Outlook 1998*

declined, whereas prices jumped. Figure 2.2 shows another example of a world
product market, the long term world supply curve for hard coal. On the horizontal axis the mining capacity is shown. The mining costs vary significantly
between different suppliers from 12 US$ per (metric) ton in China to 195 US$
per ton in Germany. In this context, we have to distinguish between extraction
costs for open-pit mining (o) and for underground mining (u). The supply curve
shown comprises 85 percent of the worldwide mining capacity.

   In a world market equilibrium not only has the excess demand for a commodity to be equal to zero. In addition, it must hold that firms have found their
profit maximum with their supply and households their utility maximum with
their demand. For firms, this condition is fulfilled if the commodity price ratio
corresponds to the marginal costs ratio. To clarify this, we introduce the concept
of the world transformation curve (curve VWX in Figure 2.3). It indicates – for a

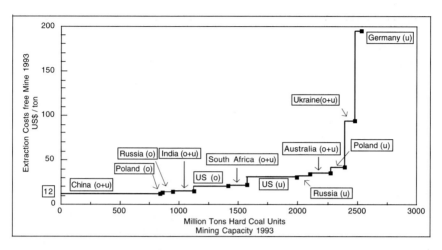

o = open-cast mining, u = underground mining

Figure 2.2 World supply curve for hard coal
Source: Bundesanstalt für Geowissenschaften und Rohstoffe (1995)

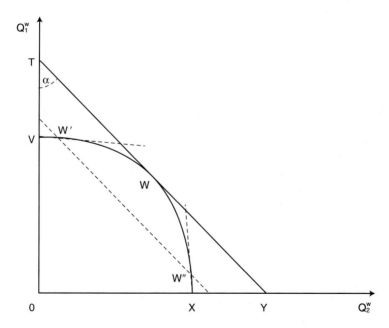

Figure 2.3 World transformation curve and world market equilibrium

given factor endowment and technology – the maximum production quantity of good 1 for a given production quantity of good 2. The marginal rate of transformation (slope of the transformation curve) dQ_2/dQ_1 indicates the opportunity costs of producing an additional unit of good 1, measured in units of good 2 forgone. It shows to what extent it is possible from the production side to produce more of a good by means of diverting the factors of production away from the other good. The marginal rate of transformation corresponds to the ratio of marginal costs. The commodity price ratio p also indicates the relative valuation of the two goods by the households. From the supply side of the economy an equilibrium exists if the commodity price ratio corresponds to the inverse ratio of the marginal rate of transformation $p = p_1/p_2 = |dQ_2/dQ_1|$. In Figure 2.3, the commodity price ratio p is given by a straight line with the angle α. It corresponds to the quantity ratio Q_2/Q_1 (where Q^i denotes units of good i), in this way indicating how many units of good 2 can be exchanged for one unit of good 1.

The quantities of the two goods produced at point W amount to the world domestic product. Valued with the relative price p and measured in units of good 1, the world domestic product is given by the distance OT. Measured in units of good 2, the world domestic product is shown by the distance OY.

The point of production on the world transformation curve depends on the demand conditions, because demand and supply together determine the relative price that clears the market in accordance with equation 2.1. The relative price of the equilibrium can be determined with the usual demand–supply diagram or with the help of the Marshall–Mill offer curves.

Demand–supply diagram

In Figure 2.4a, the relative price $p = p_1/p_2$ is shown on the vertical axis in the usual market diagram. The quantity of good 1 is depicted on the horizontal axis. If the relative price p is high the demand for good 1 is low; with the relative price going down demand for good 1 increases (demand curve $C_1^w(p)$). The supply curve can be derived graphically from Figure 2.3. The point of the maximum production of good 1 corresponds to the point V' (point V of the transformation curve in Figure 2.3); the point of zero production of good 1 corresponds to the point X' (point X in Figure 2.3). The positive slope of the supply curve represents the increasing marginal rate of transformation, that is the increasing marginal costs of the production of good 1. The movement along the supply curve corresponds to the movement along the transformation curve. The relative price of the equilibrium is determined by point W at the intersection of the supply and the demand curve. In Figure 2.4b, the excess demand for good 1 is derived from the horizontal difference between quantities demanded and supplied.

Offer curves

The world market equilibrium can also be described by the Marshall–Mill offer curves. For this analysis, the world market is divided into two regions, home and

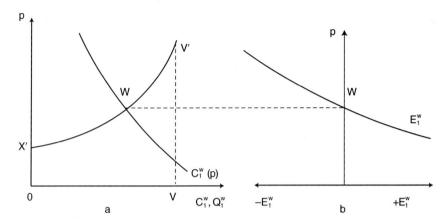

Figure 2.4 Relative price of the equilibrium

foreign. In Figure 2.5 the home and foreign offer curves are shown (in this context good 1 is the home export good and good 2 the foreign export good). The offer curve of a country indicates how many units of the import good have to be offered to a country in exchange for its export good. The shape of the offer curve of a country is explained by the following:

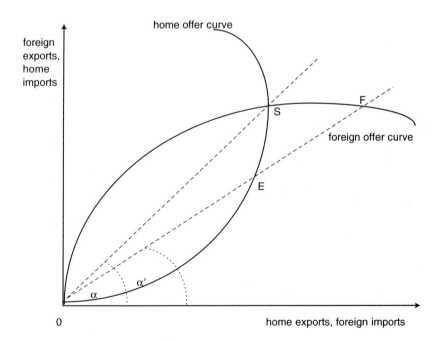

Figure 2.5 Equilibrium with the Marshall–Mill offer curves

- The increasing marginal production costs of a good: the increasing marginal rate of transformation when moving along the transformation curve of a country indicates that the opportunity costs of a good become higher the more is produced. Therefore, the offer curve is upward-sloping.
- The substitution effect: with an increasing relative price of a good (the export good) demand for this good decreases and demand for the other good (the import good) rises correspondingly. This effect also causes a positive slope of the offer curve.
- The income effect: the rising relative price p means an increase in real income for the home country, because it gets more units of the import good for one unit of its export good, i.e. its terms of trade improve. With higher income, demand for each of the two goods increases. In this way, the income effect runs contrary to the substitution effect.

The equilibrium is reached at point S with a relative price p that is given by the tangent of the angle α. At point S, excess supply of the export good of the home country and excess demand of the import demand of the foreign country are identical. The market is cleared. Along the straight line with the gradient α', however, the points E and F signal that at the given relative price the home country's trade offer does not correspond to the offer of the foreign country. There is excess demand for good 1 and excess supply of good 2. Consequently, the relative price p must rise.

The law of one price

The world market is characterized by the law of one price. If no trade barriers exist and if transport costs equal zero, that is if markets are not segmented, the same price must be observed everywhere for a homogeneous good. This is a significant simplification, of course, but it helps to make an important aspect perfectly clear, namely spatial arbitrage. As long as there are price differentials it is worthwhile to arbitrage them away by moving goods from one location to another.

2.2 The reduction of trade barriers and the world market equilibrium

The reduction of trade barriers, for example as a result of lower transport and communication costs, means that arbitrage is intensified and that the efficiency gains rise. The world transformation curve moves outward.

The world transformation curve results from the transformation curves of each individual country. Figure 2.6 shows the special case of two countries. In order to keep the argument simple we assume that initially both countries are in autarky. Alternatively, the initial situation may be interpreted as having some trade, but the level of trade can be expanded if market segmentations are reduced. The transformation curves are drawn in such a way that the production points A and

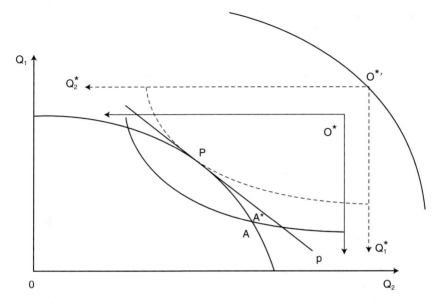

Figure 2.6 Trade barriers and world transformation curve

A* of the two countries coincide in one point. In this case, world production is given by point O*. But the states of autarky A, A* in the two countries do not represent a world market equilibrium, because relative prices differ and because without trade barriers it is worthwhile for the home country to produce more of good 1 (moving in the direction of an increasing production of good Q_1 on its transformation curve). At the same time, it is worthwhile for the foreign country to produce more of good 2 until the price ratios in the two countries are brought in line with each other. This is the case at point P in Figure 2.6. The marginal rates of transformation in the two countries correspond to each other, and they correspond to the uniform price ratio in the world economy (straight line p). Point P means a higher output in the world economy (O*'). In this way the world as a whole gains from the transition from autarky (or from a low level of trade) to trade (or to more trade).

The world as a whole gains from the more intensive arbitrage that is made possible by the reduction of market segmentations. It can also be shown that each country gains from the higher level of trade. Take the home country and compare its budget space in the initial situation A and in the new situation P. In autarky, the home country has no other choice but to consume in point A. With free trade, the home country consumes on a point along line p. Its budget space has increased; it enjoys a higher welfare. Trade is an option to supply or demand goods at the given world market price. It offers welfare gains. Otherwise, a country could always choose the state of autarky. Gains from trade will even occur if the other country behaves in a protectionist way (Free Trade for One theorem).

After the most important characteristics of the world market equilibrium have been discussed, it will be explained in the following how the world market equilibrium adjusts to disruptions.

2.3 Increase of labor supply and world market equilibrium

World market equilibrium will be disturbed, if the supply of a production factor changes. Factor abundance may also change gradually, for example, if the pollution of the environment is increasingly taken into account. Another relevant case is that the world labor supply increases. That is the situation nowadays with the integration of China and the former centrally planned economies into the world economy. Then, the world transformation curve shifts outward more in favor of the labor-intensively produced good 2 than in favor of good 1 (Figure 2.7). Consequently, more of this good can be produced. Let us conduct a thought experiment. Assume that the relative price p between the two goods remains constant for the moment; the world market equilibrium then moves from point W to point W''. The production of good 1 falls, the production of good 2 increases. If consumers associate an increase of good 2 with a lower marginal utility of a unit of good 2 and a decrease of good 1 with a higher marginal utility of a unit of good 1, then the relative price of the initial position will not be a market equilibrium. In other words, at the old price there is an excess supply of good 2 and an excess demand for good 1. The price of good 2 must fall (by a little), the price of good 1 must rise (by a little). The relative price p has to rise and in this way a new

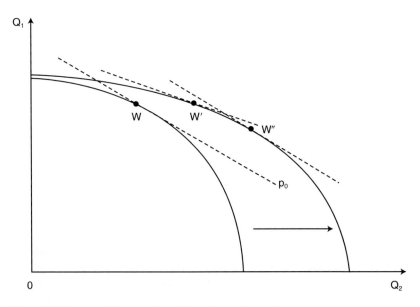

Figure 2.7 Increased labor supply and world transformation curve

point of equilibrium W′ will be realized. This point must be situated to the right of the initial equilibrium W if the transformation curve moves in favor of good 2. (If homothetic preferences are assumed, the quantity ratio $Q_1 : Q_2$ decreases compared to the initial position.)

In the demand–supply diagram, the increased labor supply can be expressed by a downward shift of the supply curve of the labor-intensive good, in relation to the relative price of this good (Figure 2.8). The relative price of the labor-intensive good 2 is $p_2/p_1 = 1/p$, which is the reciprocal value of the relative price of good 1 which has been used as a numeraire. With a given relative price 0W there is an excess supply TW of good 2. Therefore, this cannot be an equilibrium and the relative price $1/p$ must fall to OW′. When determining the new equilibrium point W′ it must be taken into account that besides the additional supply or production effect an income effect is relevant as well. The income effect results from the rise in world domestic product. This means that income increases and that the demand for good 2 rises (the demand curve moves upwards). Assuming that the production effect dominates the income effect, the excess demand curve moves downwards and relative price changes to the disadvantage of the labor-intensively produced good and in favor of the non-labor-intensively produced good.

In order to show the adjustment process in the separate regions of the world economy, let us divide the world into relatively capital-abundant industrialized countries and newly industrializing countries with relative labor abundance. According to their comparative advantage, the industrial countries export the capital-intensively produced good 1 and import good 2. For the representative industrialized country the increased labor supply means that its terms of trade improve (p rises).

The industrial country specializes even further in the production of the capital-intensive good. The point of production moves from P to P′ (Figure 2.9a).

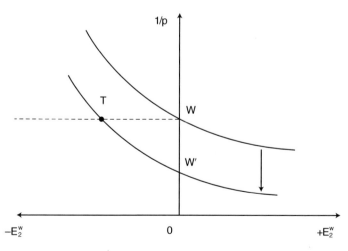

Figure 2.8 Increased labor supply and relative price

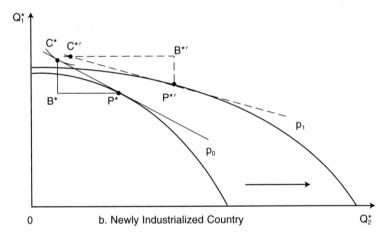

Figure 2.9 Increased labor supply and welfare in industrialized and newly industrializing
        countries

The new trade triangle indicates the more favorable terms of trade. The country
reaches a higher utility level (the indifference curve in point C′ is further away
from the origin than the indifference curve in point C). The situation analyzed
here differs from the oil crisis. There is not a shortage of an important foreign
production factor, with the supply deficit negatively affecting the terms of trade
of the industrialized country. Instead labor supply increases.

   The terms of trade of the representative newly industrializing country
decrease. If we only take this effect into consideration, then the newly industrializing country loses. But the additional production due to the increased labor
supply moves its transformation curve outward, which allows the country to real-

ize a higher welfare level (Figure 2.9b). It remains open whether the terms of trade effect or the volume effect dominates for the newly industrializing country.

If we do not only look at an isolated labor supply increase, other factors can improve the real income position of the newly industrializing countries, for example if there is technological progress in the production of the export good 2 or if demand for the export good of the newly industrializing countries increases strongly due to world economic growth.

2.4 Increase of labor supply and factor income

Globalization does not only mean that segmentations of commodity markets are reduced and that the law of one price holds for goods. In addition, the factor markets are also moving closer together. At any rate, this is valid for production factors that are mobile internationally, but it can be shown that the law of one price is also valid for the immobile factors including labor.

Adjustment of production quantities and factor demand

Given a set of assumptions, factor prices will be brought into line with each other by trade, even if the factors are internationally immobile. Again, we start with the assumption that important population-abundant regions of the world are integrated into the international division of labor. This is equivalent to an increase of the world factor supply. In Figure 2.10, the rectangle OCO′B characterizes

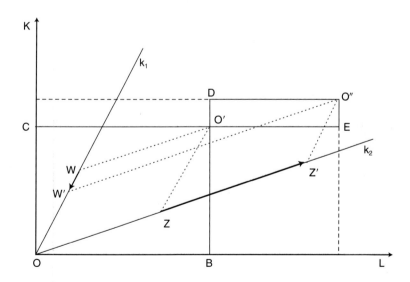

Figure 2.10 A change in factor endowment

the factor endowment of the world (industrialized countries plus developing countries) before the integration of Central and Eastern Europe and China. In this endowment box (Edgeworth box), the slopes of the lines k_1 and k_2 show the capital intensities of the two sectors 1 and 2. The capital intensity defines how many units of capital are used per unit of labor in the production of a good. These factor intensities are determined by the wage–interest ratio, that is by the factor price ratio. The lengths of the lines (OW and OZ) are proportional to the production volumes of the two goods.

By integrating new regions into the world economy the factor endowment box of the world is enlarged by the rectangle O'DO"E. If we assume that the wage–interest ratio – and along with it the factor intensities – remains constant, then the additional labor supply causes an extension of the production of good 2 from Z to Z'. The production of the capital-intensive good is reduced from point W to W'. If we only take an increase of the labor supply into account (and not an increase of the capital supply as well), then, if a constant relative price of the goods is assumed, the production of the capital-intensive good will clearly decrease. This is the Rybczinski theorem. If the regions that have newly been integrated into the world economy possess a capital stock in addition to their labor supply, the change in the production of good 1 is not clear if a constant relative price of the goods is assumed. However, as the newly integrated region is relatively labor-abundant compared to the rest of the world, the relative production $Q_1 : Q_2$ falls (from OW : OZ to OW' : OZ').

Adjustment of relative factor prices

Until now our argument has followed the Rybczinski theorem and assumed that the wage–interest ratio remains constant. This implies that the capital intensities in both sectors remain constant, too. However, as shown above, an increase in the world labor supply results in an increase in the supply of the labor-intensive good 2. As a consequence, the price of good 2 must fall and the relative price p must rise. As the relative commodity price and the factor price ratio are connected with each other this means that the wage-interest ratio must fall (if good 2 is the labor-intensive good).

We can explain this relationship with the help of the Harrod–Johnson diagram which is based on the Heckscher–Ohlin model (Figure 2.11). Let us assume perfect competition and a linear-homogeneous production function. Then the capital intensity rises with an increasing wage–interest ratio. Labor will be replaced by capital with an increasing wage–interest ratio. This relationship is valid for both sectors. In Figure 2.11, sector 1 is more capital-intensive than sector 2. Let us assume that the wage–interest ratio rises. Then, the relative production costs for the labor-intensively produced good 2 increase. Consequently, the relative price p falls.

We can also argue in another way: let us assume that demand changes in favor of good 2. This increases the incentive to produce more of the labor-intensive good 2. Demand for labor increases and the wage–interest ratio rises. Therefore,

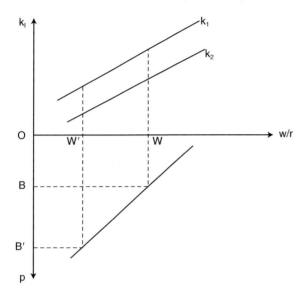

Figure 2.11 Commodity price ratio and factor price ratio

the Harrod–Johnson diagram has the shape that is shown in the lower part of Figure 2.11. These relationships are valid in both countries, because we assume that the same technology is used everywhere.

The distance OW in Figure 2.11 characterizes the wage–interest ratio in the world economy in the initial position. This wage–interest ratio corresponds to the commodity price ratio OB. If the labor supply in the world increases when labor-abundant countries are integrated into the international division of labor, the labor-abundant countries find it favorable to produce more of the labor-intensive good. For the capital-abundant country it is favorable to specialize more strongly in the production of the capital-intensive good. On balance, the wage–interest ratio must fall to OW′. The relative price p rises to OB′, that is the labor-intensively produced good becomes relatively cheaper.

If the world market equilibrium is disturbed by an increase of the labor supply the system will adjust until a new equilibrium is found. With the new uniform relative price, the world consumption point and the world production point on the world transformation curve are determined. It is further determined which commodities are traded between the different regions of the world, in this way evening out the differences in the factor endowments. The relative price is determined on the commodity markets. The new factor price ratio is found as well, and the factor intensities that characterize production in the world are determined (Figure 2.12). In this way we have a new 'integrated' world market equilibrium.

Figure 2.12 Chain of effects of an increased labor supply

Important aspects in economic reality

In reality, there will never be a perfect equalization of commodity prices and factor prices. There will always remain some arbitrage possibilities, because not all segmentations of markets will be eliminated. However, there is a process in which relative prices tend to become more equal. Besides remaining segmentations, other aspects have to be taken into consideration which are not included in the very simplified Heckscher–Ohlin model that is used here. This is true for the assumption of the same technology in the two regions of the world as well as for the assumption of homogeneous production factors. In the real world, countries have different technologies (embodied in the capital stock). Moreover, labor is not homogeneous, because in the real world labor represents different levels of technological knowledge (human capital). Therefore labor productivity, for example, in the industrialized countries is higher than elsewhere. Consequently, there cannot be a perfect wage equalization.

The approach used here only looks at a comparative-static change of an increased labor supply. Other approaches have to complement this picture. For example, the newly industrializing countries could succeed in building up a capital stock and in attracting capital and technology from abroad, which improves the productivity of labor, if they pursue a suitable policy. Then a growth process starts and, as a consequence, real income and real wages in the newly industrialized countries rise. This is in addition to the effect of the increased demand for labor due to specialization in the newly industrialized countries. As empirical surveys show real wages in these countries rise (World Bank 1995, *World Development Report*, Figure 2.2).

Finally, the Heckscher–Ohlin approach merely explains the inter-sectoral division of labor. Under comparative-static conditions, one sector of a country expands, whereas the same sector of the other country shrinks. According to the paradigm of intra-industry trade, this need not be the case (see below).

Quantity adjustment with rigid factor prices

If the factor price ratio does not react to the changed scarcity conditions, the factor quantities, particularly employment (and unemployment), have to adapt. This is the 'European' model of the labor market (or the 'Continental' model, as it applies especially in France, Germany and Italy) with relatively rigid factor prices. As a simplification, we look at only three regions of the world: (i) the labor-abundant countries that are newly taking part in the international division of labor, where the wage rate rises due to the specialization in labor-intensive products; (ii) the US, where wages adapt flexibly so that full employment is achieved; (iii) Continental Europe with its inflexible labor markets and a rigid relative factor price, where as a consequence the adjustment process is carried out via employment changes.

If there is an excess supply on the world labor market, this imbalance is 'corrected' by the quantity effects in Europe. Figure 2.13a shows the European endowment box. The factor price ratio and therefore the factor intensities remain constant. Europe has to reduce the production of the labor-intensive product 2

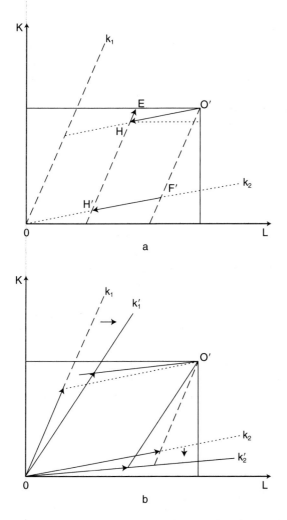

Figure 2.13 The European model of unemployment and the American model of employment

by H'F'. If at the same time the capital-intensive production is expanded by HE, then this results in unemployment EO'.

In contrast to the European model, the relative factor price adjusts in the American model (Figure 2.13b). Here, the wage–interest ratio (w/r) falls (in reality the wage of the less qualified goes down relatively). The capital intensity in the two sectors falls from $k_1(k_2)$ to $k_1'(k_2')$ and full employment is reached.

2.5 The most important theorems

The adjustment process in the world economy can be summarized by the following theorems. Originally, these theorems were related to the transition from autarky to trade; in our context we apply the theorems to the change from an initial position with foreign trade to a new situation where an increased labor supply is integrated into the world economy. It is assumed that full employment is reached by flexible factor prices.

- *Jevon's law of one price. If transaction costs are left out of consideration, then there will be a uniform price for one good in the world market.* The characteristic of the world market equilibrium is that the product markets are in equilibrium and that therefore the profit-maximum product supply corresponds to the utility-maximum product demand. This equilibrium is established by a uniform relative price ratio.

- *Heckscher–Ohlin theorem. A country has a comparative advantage to export the good the production of which is factor-intensive with respect to the relatively abundant production factor.* An increased labor supply in a labor-abundant region of the world means that this region exports the labor-intensive good and expands the production of this good; the capital-abundant region exports the capital-intensive good and expands the production of that good relative to the labor-intensive good.

- *Rybczynski theorem. With given relative product prices, the increase of a factor supply leads to an increase in the production of the good whose production is relatively intensive in that factor.* This result illustrates one aspect of the Heckscher–Ohlin theorem. The incidence of an exogenous increase of a production factor is described by a partial equilibrium analysis.

- *Stolper–Samuelson theorem. The rise of the relative price of one good results in an increase of the real price of the factor that is used intensively in the production of the good. The real price of the other factor falls.* In the labor-abundant region of the world, the demand for labor increases and the wage rate rises. In the capital-abundant industrialized nations, the real interest rate rises and the real wage falls. The income share of labor in the labor-abundant region rises. In the typical industrialized country, the income share of capital increases.

- *Factor price equalization theorem. Trade of final products leads to a complete equalization of the factor price ratio. The real factor prices adjust as well.* Relative product prices adjust. The factor prices adjust as well. The labor-abundant country exports more labor-intensive products and this drives up wages. The capital-

abundant country exports more capital intensive products and this drives up
the interest rate.

2.6 Demand shifts and world market equilibrium

If the preferences in the world move in favor of good 1, this will have an impact
on the trade equilibrium. Let us assume that a change in preferences in favor of
good 1 disturbs the old equilibrium at point G (Figure 2.14). At the old relative
price $(p : 0G)$, excess demand in the world for good 1 is positive, the market is not
cleared. Point G', reflecting the increased preferences, cannot be realized. Since
there is a positive excess demand $E_1^w(p) > 0$ in G', the relative price must change.
The relative price of good 1 must rise in order to reduce demand for good 1 and
increase the production incentive for this good. A new equilibrium will be realized at point G".

This new equilibrium means a higher relative price p. If we assume good 1 to
be the capital-intensively produced good, then the wage–interest ratio must fall
correspondingly. The income share of labor declines.

2.7 Globalization of commodity markets and non-tradable goods

Apart from internationally tradable goods there are non-tradable goods. These
are goods that, by definition, must be produced in the country where they are
consumed. For these goods there can only be a national (or regional) market equilibrium; world excess demand or world excess supply do not represent feasible

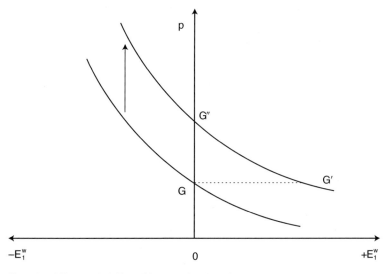

Figure 2.14 Demand shift and international trade

equilibria. If we combine the export goods and the import substitutes of a country into a composite tradable good (which is possible if the relative price between the export goods and the import substitutes remains constant), then an economy can produce tradable (Q_T) and non-tradable (Q_{NT}) goods (transformation curve TT in Figure 2.15). If the relative price p_T/p_{NT} between tradable and non-tradable goods is given (by tan α), then the point of production P is determined. The market equilibrium for non-tradable goods requires that the quantity supplied (OB) correspond to the quantity demanded. This is the case for the straight line BD in Figure 2.15. If the country obtains a credit PD from abroad (budget line p') it can realize a higher point of consumption on the straight line BD. Note that in this diagram a trade triangle cannot be drawn.

Globalization only applies to the goods that are tradable. Globalization is not valid for the non-tradable goods that are produced for purely national (or regional) demand. Here international competition can only have indirect effects; in fact, there are two relationships. First: non-tradable goods define the opportunity costs of the tradable goods, because they need production factors that could otherwise be used for the production of the tradable goods. If the preference for non-tradable goods increases, the production point P moves to the right, and therefore less production factors are available for tradable goods. Depending on the factor intensity of the non-tradable goods, there are effects on the comparative advantages of the country. Second: due to decreasing transport costs and declining barriers to trade more non-tradable goods turn into tradable goods; thus goods that were previously non-tradable can be exported due to lower transport and communication costs. This is even the case for a whole lot of disembodied services (like engineering services). Therefore globalization means that the line of distinction between tradable and non-tradable goods is shifted. This implies that the transformation curve is moved outward

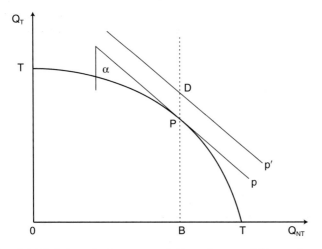

Figure 2.15 Relative price between tradable and non-tradable goods

with a bias: the area of Q_{NT} shrinks and the area of Q_T expands (this effect is not shown in Figure 2.15).

2.8 Imperfect competition

Until now the analysis has been characterized by the assumption of perfect competition: market participants on the world commodity markets are so numerous that the individual firm in a country cannot influence the price and must accept it as given. This premise gets doubtful if the average costs of production fall with an increased quantity of production and if product preferences bring about specific market segments.

Increasing returns to scale

Constant average costs are the result of constant returns to scale, i.e. of a linear-homogeneous production function. By multiplying the use of all production factors by a factor λ (for example by 2), the production result is also multiplied by λ (by 2). If the production activity is compared to putting a flower in a flowerpot, then any number of flowerpots can be put side by side, and the production is multiplied according to the number of flowerpots. Adding an identical second factory to an existing factory therefore leads to a doubling of output. This relationship no longer holds if there are increasing returns to scale, i.e. if $Q\lambda^\alpha = F(\lambda K, \lambda L)$ with $\alpha > 1$. Then a doubling of the inputs multiplies output by more than 2. Therefore, in the case of increasing returns to scale the production becomes less costly if the quantity produced increases. The firm moves downwards along the falling average costs curve (Figure 2.16).

Increasing returns to scale or falling average costs can be explained for example by a learning curve (learning by doing). Empirical studies, e.g. for the construction of large airplanes, show a learning rate of 0.2, which means that unit costs are reduced by 20 percent if the accumulated output is doubled. But falling average costs are also caused by production processes requiring a

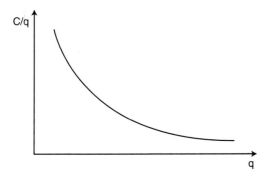

Figure 2.16 Falling average costs

minimum input of production factors, for example, because the input of capital must exceed a minimum size due to the characteristics of the production process. In all these cases, there are fixed costs of production which are more profitably spread over the units of output with an increased production quantity. Falling average costs may apply to specific production units (shop level) or they may appear on the plant level because with several shops it is possible to fragment the production process or to have a better risk-spreading. Finally, increasing returns to scale can be linked to the firm level; minimum advertising budgets or better liquidity can be mentioned as examples.

Increasing returns to scale can also be explained by positive spillovers. Let K^j, L^j represent factor inputs of firm j. Then output Q^j of firm j may also depend on the capital stock K of the industry (of all the firms) with $Q^j = F^j(K^j, L^j) \cdot K^\xi$ where K may represent the capital stock as a measure of accumulated experience from learning by doing or knowledge capital. ξ indicates the impact of the industry's capital stock. Whereas the part F^j of the production function may be linear-homogeneous, the function as a whole can exhibit economies of scale. The marginal productivity of capital in firm j then also depends on the industry factor K with $F^j_K(K^j, K)$.

The spatial dimension of knowledge capital is an important question. (i) If it is industry-specific, each firm of an industry in a country benefits from the knowledge capital of other firms in the same industry. (ii) If it is localized, then firms in a region benefit from the knowledge capital accumulated in the region, but knowledge capital may extend to many sectors. An example is a qualified regional labor pool that may be used in different countries. (iii) Spillovers may also occur worldwide. Then K relates to knowledge capital existing in the whole world.

Increasing returns to scale and of falling average costs imply that perfect competition changes into imperfect competition: a firm may become a monopolist or an oligopolistic structure may arise.

The limits of increasing returns to scale

The argument of increasing returns to scale should not be overestimated. It should not be forgotten that central planning in Eastern Europe was based on the supposed relevance of increasing returns to scale, but in the end the strategy to make use of increasing returns to scale failed. There are quite a few reasons why increasing returns to scale do not grow without limit. With larger organizational units, flexibility will be lost and management costs will rise. Moreover, important restrictions can weaken the advantages of large dimensions, for example missing opportunities to expand at the actual location or lack of employees with the necessary qualifications. In the end, missing competition leads to a loss of efficiency.

Different product preferences

Apart from increasing returns to scale, product preferences are a second reason why world markets can be imperfect. People do not have the same preferences everywhere. They do not all want the same homogeneous product. These product preferences mean that market segments are defined by households with a preference for a specific product. Consumers are prepared to pay a relatively higher price for the specific good they want best ('ideal variety'). Arrange households a–h along a commodity axis indicating proximity or distance between goods according to individual preferences (Figure 2.17). Assume all households have the same income. Then the continuum a–h indicates the demand side of a market with different product preferences. Consider two firms x and y which produce goods c and g. Firm x may also cater for preferences a, b, d, e and f, but it cannot produce these goods with the same quality c; it may compete with firm y with respect to products d, e and f. Depending on the average cost curve of firms and on distance costs in terms of product quality, firms may serve a larger or a smaller market segment. In reality, preferences of consumers may be concentrated on some goods. Also, goods with similar characteristics may be easily substituted against each other so that they form a cluster of relatively similar goods. On the commodity axis, there may be substitution gaps between groups of goods; according to preferences, goods may not be sufficient substitutes. Consequently, the market form of imperfect competition prevails under such conditions.

2.9 Intra-sectoral trade

The combined effect of economies of scale and preferences for different goods on the size of markets is ambiguous. Economies of scale pull in the direction of large markets because average costs fall; preferences for different products pull in the other direction working towards market niches for specific products and for market segmentation. This means that large production units are not necessarily the outcome of both forces. This also has implications for location and trade.

While increasing returns to scale work towards a situation where the production would be concentrated at a few places or even at one single spot, product preferences have the consequence that market segments are defined and that these market segments limit the exploitation of increasing returns to scale. Product preferences thus prevent production from concentrating in a single spot; on the contrary, product preferences of consumers spread production over many firms and thus over a wide area. Then, intra-sectoral trade takes place because the individual firms, each filling a certain market segment, produce for their own

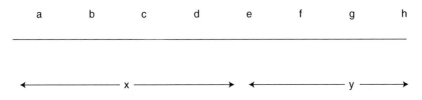

Figure 2.17 Commodity axis and firms

country as well as for abroad. Exploiting increasing returns to scale is limited by the demand for different product varieties and distance costs.

A significant part of the product flows between countries with a high per capita income is not an exchange of products between different sectors, but exchange within the same sector. Italians import German cars and Germans import Italian cars. Increasing returns to scale and product preferences are two reasons why we can observe such intra-industry or intra-sectoral trade.

More than half of the trade between the industrialized nations is intra-sectoral trade. With a wide delimitation of sectors on the two-digit level, intra-industry trade reaches nearly 70 percent for the US and slightly more for Germany (Table 2.1). Historically, intra-industry trade has grown strongly. In regional integrations an increasing importance of the intra-industry trade can be observed.

Two different approaches to explaining trade

Consequently, there are two very different approaches to explaining the international exchange of goods. The hypothesis of the inter-industry trade in the sense of the Heckscher–Ohlin approach explains the exchange of different goods, the exchange of wine and cloth, or of crude oil and machines, that is the trade between sectors. Trade is therefore predominantly dependent on the differences in the production conditions, especially the factor endowments. The hypothesis of intra-industry trade, on the other hand, emphasizes the exchange of similar products, for example the exchange of cars for cars or of wine for wine. Here, trade is based on increasing returns to scale and on differences in product preferences.

The perspective of intra-industry trade increases the acceptance of the international division of labor: while in inter-industry approaches countries can only gain advantage from the international division of labor by allowing sectors with a relative price disadvantage in the country to shrink, intra-industry trade means that the same sector can expand in different countries due to an intensified division of labor. Although single branches must also shrink in this approach, other branches of the same sector can grow. This makes adjustments less painful.

Table 2.1 Intra-industry trade[a]

	1961	1966	1971	1976	1981	1986	1991	1996
Germany	0.4102	0.4868	0.5735	0.5631	0.6115	0.6597	0.7500	0.7277
Japan	0.2453[b]	0.2319	0.2743	0.2025	0.2010	0.2463	0.3385	0.4310
US	0.4695	0.5295	0.5271	0.5008	0.4953	0.5361	0.6556	0.6721

Source: OECD, *International Trade by Commodities Statistics*

Notes
a   Intra-industry trade of each country with the world, calculated with the Grubel–Lloyd index, two-digit level $GL = [\sum_i [(Ex_i + Im_i) - |Ex_i - Im_i|]/\sum_i (Ex_i + Im_i)]$.
b   1962.

2.10 Contestable markets

Monopolies and international oligopolies

Increasing returns to scale mean that, in theory, large production facilities arise. This implies at the extreme single suppliers (monopolies) or few suppliers (oligopolies). Oligopolistic firms can either be in a Cournot quantity competition (with, as a rule, a homogeneous product) or in a Bertrand price competition (with a heterogeneous product). In this context, the assumptions about the strategy variable of a supplier, especially how he or she reacts to the actions of the other supplier, is relevant. In the Cournot quantity oligopoly, each supplier takes the quantity supplied by the other producer as given and decides on their own supply quantity. In the Bertrand oligopoly, the price of the other suppliers is taken as given and then one decides on one's own price. In a two-stage game, the production capacity is determined first; then price competition starts. Oligopolistic market forms are the starting point for strategic trade policy (chapter 9).

Barriers to market entry

Most of the capital that has been invested in a firm is no longer malleable and cannot be used in any other way. This capital represents sunk costs. Firms that are established on a market have two strategic advantages in comparison with a potential newcomer: as part of their capital used has sunk, they no longer necessarily have to take these capital costs into account in order to calculate their prices. The new entrant, however, must first of all incur these fixed costs before they can actually enter the market. Sunk costs give the established firm a short-term competitive advantage. Apart from sunk costs, the established enterprise can have an advantage because it has gained production experience and has moved downwards on the average costs curve, e.g. due to learning effects. This stresses the advantage of an early start. Enterprises that are established early on the world market have the opportunity to gain experience, to make use of learning effects and to attain lower average costs with their accumulated production.

The contestability of markets

Markets are contestable in the sense that a market entry of a new supplier could be imminent. This limits the maneuvering space of an incumbent firm in its price setting. In Figure 2.18 the position of a monopolistic supplier with a falling average cost curve is shown. If the firm is in a monopolistic position it may produce at point M on its average cost curve with a monopoly profit MF. Point M is determined by marginal revenue (not shown in Figure 2.18) and marginal costs being equal. If a newcomer enters the market, the firm can no longer capture demand alone. For the monopolistic supplier, the demand function rotates downward. If the market is sufficiently contestable, profit will be driven to zero (point S′).

Whereas a new supplier must finance the use of fixed capital whereas the

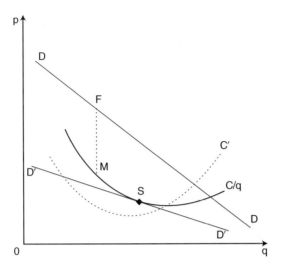

Figure 2.18 The incumbent and the newcomer

established supplier does not have to consider their sunk costs in the short term, there are no sunk costs in the long term. That is because in the long term the established firm must renew its capital. Then it has to decide whether to redirect the earned depreciations to another investment purpose. That means that the renewal of the depreciated capital must pay off. Besides sunk costs, a newcomer must take into account the lower average costs of the incumbent supplier due to the production experience it has gained. But if the established firm exceeds its scope for setting its price, a newcomer can successfully enter the market. Therefore the established enterprise is restricted in the use of its monopoly position by the imminent market entry of a potential competitor. In addition, it is possible for the newcomer to undermine the pre-eminence of the established enterprise with a better technology (for example, Microsoft and other software and PC firms with respect to the dominant player IBM, supplier of telephone services).

It is difficult to come up with examples for monopolistic or oligopolistic world product markets that are actually not contestable. Unambiguously there is an oligopoly with high barriers to enter the market in the construction of large-capacity airplanes with the two suppliers Airbus and Boeing–McDonnell–Douglas (the latter came into existence by a merger in 1996). Other world markets, however, can be characterized as contestable markets, for example the world automobile market or the semiconductor market. It is important to note that the lifespan of the products has decreased significantly, for instance in the semiconductor market. This implies that new entrants get a chance and competition is intensified.

The race for the technological lead

Markets are also contestable if enterprises compete for new knowledge, i.e. if they engage in a research and development race (Grossman and Helpman 1991a). Enterprises of the individual countries try hard to find new products and new production technologies by means of research and development in order to become the market leader in the corresponding markets. Research and development may be interpreted either as an independent industry or as an element of the industrial firms of the high-technology field. The output of the research and development industry, i.e. new products and new technology, can be regarded as an input to the manufacturing industry. The research and development process is driven by the profit prospects in the industry. This means that new technological knowledge is generated in a competitive process. Technological progress is endogenous, being the result of competition.

In such an approach, firms compete with their research and development expenditures for world market shares. This has implications for trade. The manufacturing industry can be subdivided in this context into a high-technology field and a traditional industry. The high-technology industry is characterized by the market form of an international oligopoly with profit prospects due to technological leads or by the market form of monopolistic competition, whereas the traditional industry can be characterized by perfect competition with constant returns to scale. While in the high-technology field in essence intra-industry trade takes place, the traditional industry is the basis for the inter-industry trade. Besides inter-industry and intra-industry trade, international trade also encompasses the exchange of technological knowledge.

2.11 Hierarchy versus markets

Goods and resources can be allocated through markets or within firms. Markets can replace firms, that is there are hierarchies or vertical integrations. The firms can be interpreted as a network of contracts that combines different production factors. A firm can also be defined in the sense of institutional economics as an organizational unit with lower transaction costs than on markets: a transaction will be carried out within a firm if the transaction costs within the firm are lower than on the markets. The dividing line between firms and the market therefore is determined by the level of the transaction costs.

Firms can be integrated vertically by including production levels that precede or follow the production process within the firms. For example, the large crude oil companies (the 'seven sisters') were integrated vertically before the first oil crisis; concession contracts, often for a period of 50 to 70 years, guaranteed their access to the natural resources, also to the undiscovered resources of the resource countries. The firms had transport capacities at their disposal, and they owned refineries and distribution networks in the industrialized countries. In the 1970s, the extraction rights were passed to the resource countries and therefore the vertical integration of the enterprises was broken up. The spot markets (for example in Rotterdam) gained in importance and forward markets were established. Markets replaced vertically integrated firms.

2.12 Shifting comparative advantage and relocation

In the course of time, locational conditions and therefore trade flows change. Different mechanisms are responsible for this effect: some economies, for instance the newly industrializing countries, succeed in improving their factor endowment (acquired comparative advantage instead of natural comparative advantage). For example, the savings rate and the investment rate of some newly industrializing countries of South-East Asia amount to 35 percent or more, which results in a strong increase of the capital stock. Apart from physical capital, also the endowment with human capital can be strengthened in the course of time, by investing in education. As a third factor, the infrastructure can be improved by building new roads, airports and better telephone networks. In addition, the diffusion of new knowledge causes an improvement of the locational conditions in developing countries.

At the same time, processes take place in the industrialized countries that reduce the competitiveness of some sectors. The desire for a higher labor income causes some labor-intensive products to become unprofitable. The extension of the social security systems leads to a rise of labor costs. Moreover, a society can get lethargic: for example people could shy away from taking entrepreneurial risks or from opening the educational system to competition.

3 The factor markets in the world economy

Besides the markets for goods, the factor markets play a decisive role in the paradigm of the world economy. Equilibrium of the world economy also requires the factor markets to be in equilibrium. If this equilibrium is disturbed, the world economy has to adjust. The adjustment processes in the world factor markets are thus of great importance. The world labor market (section 3.1) and the world capital market (section 3.2) are discussed in particular. Important questions are whether national capital markets are segmented and how close is the relation between national investment and national savings (sections 3.3 and 3.4). Historically, some countries have developed from net debtors to net creditors. This is the debt cycle hypothesis (section 3.5). For a given production technology, the prices of the production factors are related to each other and a factor-price frontier exists (section 3.6). Finally, the world market for natural resources and disturbances on the factor markets are dealt with (sections 3.7 and 3.8).

3.1 The world market for labor

Migration and wage equalization

Applying the concept of a world market for labor as a production factor, like we did for goods, we have to compare the world demand for labor and the world supply of labor. A simple interpretation of the world labor market is obtained under the following assumptions. Assume labor to be perfectly mobile internationally and to be homogeneous especially as far as qualifications are concerned. Furthermore, the labor supply is assumed to be exogenously given and constant over time. Under these assumptions, the world market for labor can be represented as shown in Figure 3.1. OO* is the world supply of labor, allocated between the home country, or Home (OC), and foreign countries, or Foreign (O*C). Home's labor demand curve (F_L) shows a higher marginal productivity than the corresponding curve of Foreign (F_L^*). The two markets are assumed to be segmented; the home wage of CA is higher than the foreign wage CB.

If the wage difference BA is sufficiently high, foreign workers find it worthwhile to migrate into the home country. Consequently, world production can be extended. Migration generates additional production represented by the triangle BAG (Harberger triangle). Home's additional production is AGDC, whereas Foreign's production is reduced by BGDC. Due to the migration, the factor

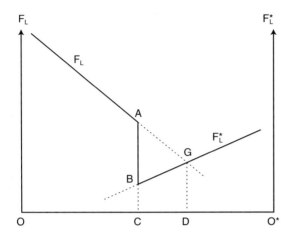

Figure 3.1 The world market for labor

endowments of the two countries change; Home increases its supply of workers, requiring the Home wage to fall. In the new equilibrium (point G), all home workers receive a lower wage. Foreign loses labor, and all foreign workers receive a higher wage.

The world's labor supply curve

The assumption of a homogeneous and perfectly mobile world supply of labor causes difficulties: the demand for workers is spatially concentrated, but workers are – on average – immobile and are not able to satisfy a local demand elsewhere. For the curves of labor demand and supply in the world labor market, we therefore have to take into account that the demand and the supply of labor are spatially fixed. The labor markets of the world will thus be characterized by regional segmentation. Taking this into consideration, a simplified labor supply curve of the world can be developed (Figure 3.2). In this concept, labor supply depends on the annual income in US dollars, the segments of this curve being valid only for particular regions of the world. For each segment, labor is homogeneous, receiving the same real wage. Chinese peasants supply labor for an income of approximately 1,000 dollars; skilled workers in OECD countries supply labor for an income of about 34,000 dollars. The horizontal distance between the particular lines indicates the size of the labor supply of the relevant regions in the overall world labor supply.

Segmentation and wage differences

If workers are spatially immobile internationally and inhomogeneous concerning their qualification, then national labor markets are segmented, and wage differ-

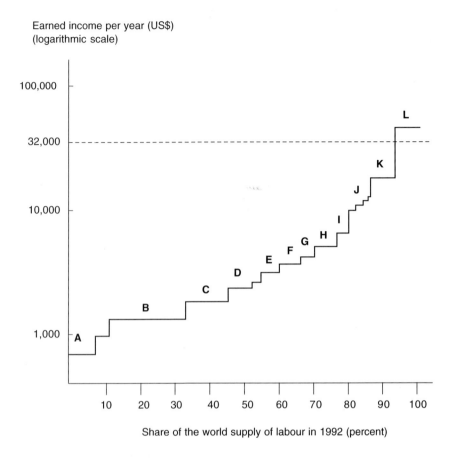

Earned income per year (US$)
(logarithmic scale)

Share of the world supply of labour in 1992 (percent)

A - African peasants	G - Skilled workers (South Asia)
B - Chinese peasants	H - Unskilled (South America)
C - South Asian peasants	I - Skilled workers (China)
D - Unskilled (China)	J - Skilled workers (reform countries)
E - Unskilled (South Asia)	K - Unskilled (OECD)
F - Unskilled (reform countries)	L - Skilled workers (OECD)

Wages logarithmically scaled, in prices of 1995. The share of the labor supply segments is given by the length of the horizontal part. Unlabeled horizontal parts represent labor supplies that make up for less than 2.5 percent of the world supply of labor.

Figure 3.2 The supply curve of the world market for labor. Data for 1992
Source: World Bank, *World Development Report 1995*, Figure 18.1

ences exist. But besides differences in qualification, or human capital, workers in a particular country can also benefit from a better endowment with physical capital or from locally immobile technological knowledge that enables them to be more productive. Such differences of endowment conditions have to be distinguished from policy-induced market segmentations, e.g. immigration laws.

Finally, preferences for a certain location can be so strong that people accept lower wages.

Movement of goods instead of migration

Even if labor is completely immobile internationally, there can be a tendency to equalization of real wages through international trade, with goods assuming the role of migration. The country that is relatively rich in capital specializes in the production of capital-intensive goods, causing the price of capital goods, i.e. the real interest rate, to rise and the real wage to fall. Under appropriate model conditions, a convergence or even a complete equalization of real wages occurs (see chapter 2).

3.2 The world market for capital

On the world capital market, the equilibrium between savings and investments is determined. Savings means abstaining from consumption, investment means accumulating capital. Demand and supply of new capital meet on the world capital market. The share of gross savings and gross investment is approximately 22 percent of the world national product (World Bank, *World Development Report 1998*, Table 13). With a world domestic product of approximately 28.2 trillion US$ (*World Development Report 1998*, Table 12), the world capital market consequently has a volume of about 6.2 trillion US dollars per year. Since we are here looking at savings and investment this sum does not refer to financial markets but to the market for 'real' capital.

The productivity of abstaining from consumption

On the capital supply side, people abstain from consumption, i.e. they save. The demand for capital is determined by production. From the production side, it is possible to produce additional units of goods in period 1 through capital formation in the preceding period 0. Not consuming a cow today means that the cow is still available for consumption tomorrow and that on top of this it has calved as well. As Robinson Crusoe abstains from walking to the remote source of fresh water, and as he produces a bucket during the time, he suffers thirst. But he also spares himself the frequent walk to the water source in the next period and then has more water per unit of time at his disposal. Abstaining from consumption, i.e. investing, has a positive productivity. In the next period, $1 + F_K$ units of a good are available instead of one unit, F_K indicating the marginal productivity of capital (of abstaining from consumption).

In Figure 3.3, the transformation curve shows the possibility of transformation over time. The marginal rate of transformation $|dQ1/dQ0|$ indicates how many additional units of output are possible in the second period (distance HI) if one unit of consumption is abstained from in the first period (distance TH). The marginal rate of transformation in time results, on the one hand, from a unit of a

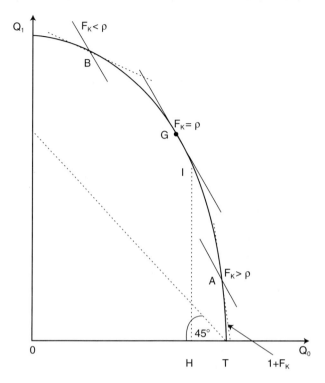

Figure 3.3 Transformation in time

good not consumed today being preserved and being available for consumption in the next period (storing). But, on the other hand, abstaining from consumption is also linked to a productive detour or a roundabout method (Marshall 1890), yielding a positive marginal productivity per unit of consumption abstained from.

The transformation curve ranks all investment projects in the world according to their marginal productivity of capital F_K. Those projects with the highest marginal productivity are located on the lower part of the transformation curve, so that the first unit of capital invested has the highest marginal productivity. The more capital is invested, the lower is the marginal productivity of an additional project. The increasing marginal rate of transformation thus indicates the declining marginal productivity of additional units of capital. The opportunity cost of abstaining from consumption rises.

The rate of return of investment (i.e. of non-consumption) is F_K. Through non-consumption, $1 + F_K$ units of the good are available in the next period. This is the benefit of waiting. The marginal rate of transformation in time $|dQ_1/dQ_0|$ must correspond to the relative price of the two goods in time, p_0/p_1; this relative price is of the dimension Q_1/Q_0. It shows in which quantitative relation a good is intertemporally exchanged on the market. Thus, from the production side of the world economy, $\left|\dfrac{dQ_1}{dQ_0}\right| = 1 + F_K = \dfrac{p_0}{p_1}$ has to hold.

The cost of abstaining from consumption

Abstaining from consumption involves costs of waiting. These opportunity costs are generated by shifting consumption to the future. If the household had only the one unit at its disposal tomorrow that it abstains from today, and if it would it assign the same utility to this situation as to the initial situation, it would have no preference for the present period.[1] But if it values this unit less, because it will be consumed only in the future, the future consumption has to be discounted with the rate of time preference, ρ. The rate of time preference indicates how the future consumption is evaluated in comparison to consumption today. It is the factor used to discount consumption in the future in comparison to consumption today. For the rate of time preference, $\rho = \left|\dfrac{dC_1}{dC_0}\right| - 1$ holds, where $\left|\dfrac{dC_1}{dC_0}\right|$ is the marginal rate of intertemporal substitution. It measures the quantity of consumption necessary in the second period to compensate the household for abstaining from one unit of consumption in the first period.

The time preference rate of consumption ρ is not identical to the utility discount rate δ. The preference rate of consumption in time ρ expresses how the future consumption has to be discounted, whereas the discount rate of utility δ expresses how the future utility has to be discounted. This is the 'impatience'. The discount rate of utility is, as a rule, assumed given as constant over time, whereas the rate of time preference varies with the consumption level. If future consumption is higher than present consumption, an additional unit of consumption yields less satisfaction in the future than it creates in the present.

The rate of time preference ρ is thus determined by two factors. One is the impatience of households. A household generally values future satisfaction of its needs lower than the immediate satisfaction. This impatience is represented by the discount rate of utility δ. The second factor is intertemporal consumption smoothing: because of a diminishing marginal utility of consumption, a household wants to stretch consumption over time. In a long-term growth equilibrium, where consumption does not change anymore, the rate of time preference ρ equals the discount rate of utility δ. Thus (in models where consumption increases over time) the discount rate of utility can be regarded as the lower limit of the rate of time preference. Therefore, the literature often speaks only of the discount rate.

What does this mean for the consumption and saving decision of households? Consumers are indifferent about consuming today or tomorrow if the utility of a unit consumed today and the present value of the utility of a unit consumed tomorrow are equal in their judgement. For households, the relative price has to correspond to the marginal rate of substitution in time and thus be equal to the ratio of the marginal utilities in both periods.[2] The marginal rate of substitution in time thus measures the consumption quantity that is necessary to compensate the household for abstaining from one unit of consumption in the first period. Thus, from the consumption side of an economy, the price ratio between consumption today and consumption tomorrow has to be equal to the marginal rate of substitution $\left|\dfrac{dC_1}{dC_0}\right| = 1 + \rho = \dfrac{U_0'(C_0)(1 + \delta)}{U_1'(C_1)} = \dfrac{p_0}{p_1}.$

Equilibrium between the benefits and the costs of abstaining from consumption

Summing up the conditions for the production and consumption sides, it follows that.

$$\left|\frac{dQ_1}{dQ_0}\right| = 1 + F_K = \frac{p_0}{p_1} = \frac{U_0'(C_0)(1 + \delta)}{U_1'(C_1)} = 1 + \rho = \left|\frac{dC_1}{dC_0}\right|.$$

The marginal rate of transformation (tangent to the transformation curve) and the marginal rate of substitution (tangent to the indifference curve) have to be equal (point G in Figure 3.3; the indifference curve is not shown).

In Figure 3.3, point A cannot be an optimal point, as the marginal productivity of capital is higher than the rate of time preference ρ. The benefit of waiting, i.e. the additional production, is higher than the costs of waiting, i.e. the loss of utility through abstaining from consumption. Analogously, point B is not an optimal point, as the marginal productivity of capital is smaller than the rate of time preference. Here the benefit of waiting is less than the costs of waiting. The optimum is reached in point G.

The position of the optimal point G varies with the rate of time preference. If the rate of time preference ρ is high, abstention from consumption is relatively low. Then, the equilibrium point G moves downward on the transformation curve. If the rate of time preference is low, abstention from consumption is higher. Then, the equilibrium point G moves upward.

Marginal productivity, time preference rate and market interest rate

The marginal productivity indicates how, from the supply side, investing yields a return (through a productive detour or a roundabout process); the time preference rate expresses what, from the consumption side, the consumers demand for abstaining from consumption. The relative price p_0/p_1 for the product in the two periods expresses the intertemporal relative price. For this relative price, $p_0/p_1 = 1 + r$ holds, where r is the market interest rate. The equilibrium for capital formation in the world capital markets thus requires $F_K = \rho = r$.

In equilibrium, the market interest rate r has to be equal to the marginal productivity and the rate of time preference. As we shall see later on, in intertemporal approaches and in models of growth as well, we distinguish between long-term equilibria and adjustment paths to long-term equilibria (chapter 4). The market for capital has to be in equilibrium in the long-term situation as well as during transition.

The demand–supply diagram of the world market for capital

The relationship between the benefits and the costs of waiting can also be illustrated in a different representation of the world capital market (Figure 3.4a). On
the vertical axis, the marginal productivity of capital (F_K), the rate of time
preference ρ and the (real) interest rate r are shown. On the horizontal axis, the
levels of investments (I) and savings (S) are shown. The demand curve for new
capital contains projects with different marginal productivities. Projects with a
particularly high marginal productivity are located in the upper part of the F_K-
curve. When these projects are complete, projects with a lower marginal productivity of capital become worthwhile. The F_K-curve is thus the demand curve for
new capital in the world economy. It results from the demand curves of the individual countries. The curve is obtained by horizontally adding the curves of the
individual economies. Regarding the world market, all feasible projects in
the world are ranked according to their profitability on this curve. It represents
the demand side of the capital market with different investment prospects.

The supply curve shows the abstention from consumption that the households
of the world are ready to accept at different world-market interest rates. One may
also imagine that this supply curve for new capital represents households or countries with different rates of time preference. Countries or households with a low
rate of time preference offer abstention from consumption, i.e. real savings, even
at a very low real interest rate. If the real interest rate rises, more households or
countries supply savings.

The equilibrium lies in point G, where an equilibrium real interest rate is
determined and the demand for new capital equals the supply of new capital.
Investment projects with a lower marginal productivity are not carried out
whereas the investment projects with a higher marginal productivity receive a
capital user (demand-side) surplus. They have a marginal productivity that is

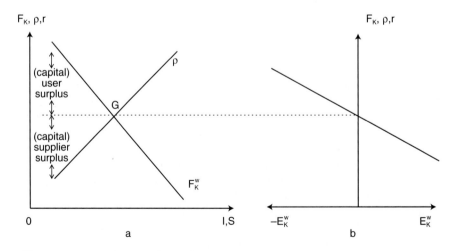

Figure 3.4 The world market for capital

higher than the real interest rate required in the market equilibrium. Concerning the supply curve, the potential savings of households or countries requiring a time preference rate (respectively a discount rate) higher than the market-clearing real interest rate do not become effective. Countries or households with a lower time preference receive a supplier surplus.

These relations can also be represented as a curve of excess demand for new capital depending on the interest rate (Figure 3.4b). At high real interest rates, excess demand is negative, i.e. there is too much abstention from consumption; at low real interest rates, excess demand is positive, i.e. too much capital is demanded.

In Figure 3.4, the flows of a period are taken into account, i.e. the investments, the abstention from consumption, the savings. This figure can also be applied to the aggregated demand for capital over all periods and the aggregated savings over all periods. In this interpretation, the capital stock is indicated on the horizontal axis. If capital already in existence can be employed flexibly, both representations are equivalent.

Tobin's q

Tobin's q represents an evaluation of a country's capital goods (or of its existing stock of capital). In the above model, the stock of capital is determined by the condition $F_K = r$, assuming that capital can be reallocated at negligible costs. In the long run, this may indeed be the case. In the short run, however, adjustment costs arise with the reallocation of capital. This has effects on investment behavior. Consider a firm maximizing its profit over a time period and facing adjustment costs for its capital. Then, the installed capital enters the investment calculation of the firms at a shadow price with adjustment costs playing a role. Tobin's q can be regarded as an expression of this shadow price. It is defined as

$$q = \frac{\text{market value of the capital installed}}{\text{replacement costs of the capital installed}}$$

If $q < 1$, the market value lies below the replacement costs, and it does not pay off to replace the capital good once it is depreciated. It is not worthwhile for a firm to take up new capital from the capital market. The firm reduces its capital stock. If $q > 1$, it is worthwhile to renew a capital good. Then it pays off to use more capital and to attract it from outside.

Tobin's q permits us to link the investment decision to the stock market, as the market value of the capital installed can be indicated by the valuation of shares. The replacement costs of the installed capital are given by the price index for investment goods. Thus the rate of change $\hat{q}$ of Tobin's q is

$$\hat{q} = \text{share index (e.g. Dow Jones) rate of change} -$$
$$\text{rate of change of the price index for investment goods.}$$

If, for example, the share index rises, maybe because optimism spreads in an economy, because of lowered corporate taxes, a technological breakthrough recorded or more favorable export opportunities, the rise of Tobin's q signals better investment opportunities. The formulation with Tobin's q is perfectly compatible with the neoclassical approach of marginal productivity. If the marginal productivity rises through technological progress, the market value of capital will increase, q exceeds 1 and it pays off to invest. With positive expectations, q rises as well. The appeal of the q approach is that the investment behavior of firms is linked to the valuation of the firms through the stock market.

Capital allocation for two countries

An alternative representation of capital accumulation on the world market for capital explicitly considers two regions of the world (two countries; Figure 3.5). It is assumed here that the marginal productivity of the capital stock in the two countries is higher than the discount rate δ (which is relevant in the long run). We assume the two countries to have a uniform discount rate. Figure 3.5 shows the curves for the marginal productivity of capital for the home and foreign countries. It is assumed that due to technological knowledge the home country has a higher marginal productivity of capital. It has accumulated the capital stock OA with the corresponding marginal productivity of capital AX. The foreign country has a less favorable productivity curve, a smaller capital stock OA* and a lower marginal productivity of capital A*X*. The capital productivities of the two countries are higher than their discount rate δ.

The information contained in Figure 3.5a is rearranged in Figure 3.5b. The curve for the marginal productivity of the home country has been duplicated from Figure 3.5a, the home country has realized a marginal productivity according to point X, and it has accumulated the corresponding capital OA. The curve

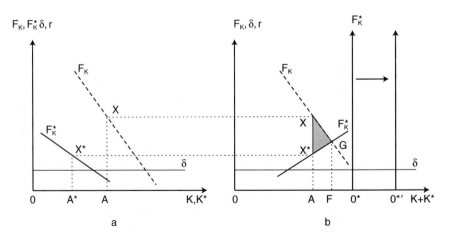

Figure 3.5 Optimal allocation of capital

of marginal productivity for the foreign country is arranged in the 'inverse' direction, originating at point O*. Figure 3.5b is drawn such that the straight line OO* represents the sum of the capital stocks OA of the home country and of the foreign country O*A. With the present capital allocation between the two countries, a gap between their marginal productivities results. The points A and A* can thus not be a world market equilibrium. Similarly to the market for goods, the possibility of arbitrage exists. This is expressed by the Harberger triangle XGX*. It is worthwhile to transfer capital from the foreign country to the home country. The equilibrium point is reached in point G in Figure 3.5b, the foreign country having transferred an amount AF of capital to the home country.

Point G balances the differences in the marginal productivities of capital. It represents, however, only a short-term equilibrium, as the marginal productivity of capital exceeds the discount rate. It is thus worthwhile to accumulate capital. The total stock of capital OO* rises. Capital accumulation can occur in the home country as well as in the foreign country. For simplicity, let us assume that the capital stock rises only in the foreign country, equal to an amount of the straight line O*O*'. Notice that the position of the foreign country's curve of marginal productivity F_k^* moves to the right, along with the point of origin O*'. The equilibrium is attained at the intersection of the curves of marginal productivity on the δ line (not shown in Figure 3.5b). The point of origin O*' moves until the marginal productivity in both countries equals the discount rate δ.

3.3 Global demand for capital interpreted as national excess demands

In the previous analysis, we started out from the assumption of a uniform world market for capital. An alternative concept is to assume that, as a first step, single countries attempt to achieve a balance between the demand for new capital and the abstention from consumption. If there is excess demand for capital in a country, this excess demand then, as a second step, becomes effective on the world market. The world demand for new capital is then the sum of the countries' excess demand for new capital (E_1) and thus $D_1^W = \Sigma E_1^j$ for $E_1^j > 0$. Correspondingly, the supplied savings S_1^W are the sum of all countries' excess supply, and thus $S_1^W = \Sigma E_1^j$ for $E_1^j < 0$.

In principle, this formulation leads to the same result as a uniform view of the world market for capital. The formulation is helpful because it can be specified with the help of the particular countries' current account balances. A current account deficit means that an economy receives more goods, services, property income and unilateral (free) transfers in one period than it gives away. Thus, resources amounting to the level of the current account deficit are transferred into the country. Capital imports take place. A current account surplus means that a country gives away more goods, services and transfers than it receives in one period. Resources are exported. Capital export takes place.

Looking at a current deficit from a financing point of view, a current account deficit means that a country uses more goods than it produces. Absorption exceeds production; this has to be financed from abroad (Siebert 1994, chapter 10). The financing restriction can be explained as follows. Let us start with the equation for national income $Y = C + I + G + X - Im$ (C: consumption, I: investment, G: government expenditure, X: exports, Im: imports). Adding the transfer balance, Tr, on both sides, we have

$$Y + Tr = C + I + G + X - Im + Tr.$$

If taxes T (which are supposed to contain the indirect taxes as well) are subtracted from both sides, it follows that the current account balance $X - Im + Tr$ equals $S - I + (T - G)$. The current account balance thus equals the surplus of savings over investments. Taking into account government savings (i.e. the government budget surplus), we have:

$$S - I + (T - G) = X - Im + Tr.$$

This is the financing restraint of an open economy. The current account balance and the capital account balance are determined simultaneously; they are two sides of the same coin. A country with a current account deficit does not have enough savings to finance its investments. A country with a current account surplus saves more than it intends to invest.

   If the world consists of two countries only, the home country and the foreign country, the balances of the two countries' current accounts must add up to zero in each and every period. If Home has a current account deficit in period 0, meaning that it is not able to fully finance its investments and therefore it has to import capital, indebting itself, Foreign has to have a current account surplus of a corresponding amount in the same period, exporting capital and granting a loan. Let us now introduce the time aspect and assume that there are only two time periods. Then Home has to obtain a current account surplus in period 1 to be able to repay its debt. Home's current account is thus intertemporally balanced, but it has been able to consume more goods in period 0 than it would have been able to, based only on its own production capacity. In return, it has to pay goods back in period 1. Correspondingly, this results in a current account deficit for Foreign in period 1, as it can now live off means received from credit loan repayment. For Foreign, the current account is intertemporally balanced as well. This intertemporal mechanism of balances is represented in Table 3.1.

Table 3.1 Intertemporal mechanism of balances

	Home	Foreign
Period 0	Current account deficit, import of capital, indebtedness	Current account surplus, export of capital, loan
Period 1	Current account surplus, export of capital, debt repayment	Current account deficit, import of capital, debt repayment received

In Figure 3.6, the national markets for capital are shown. In autarky (point A), Home's interest rate is relatively low, whereas Foreign has a relatively high interest rate (point A*). With free movement of capital, a uniform world market for capital exists. Home exports capital (EX) and has a current account surplus. Foreign imports capital (MP) and has a current account deficit.

3.4 The relationship between national investment and national savings

The world market for capital as a peak balancing device

One approach to determining world excess demand for capital is to add up national excess demand. The volume of the excess demand for new capital can be observed from the sum of the negative current account balances. Summing up the negative current account balances of the 128 countries featured in the *World Development Report*, the total deficit for the year 1996 amounts to 347 billion US$. Putting the current account deficits into relation with the world national product yields a value of only 1.15 percent of world GNP. According to this, the peak balancing function of the world capital market, measured against the current deficits, makes up for only a small portion of the world national product. Gross savings, however, amount to 22 percent of the world domestic product. Thus, only 5 percent of gross investment in the world economy is financed through international (real) capital movements. Data of portfolio investments (gross inflows) and direct investments are reported in Table 3.2; they suggest a somewhat higher, but basically similar, dimension. In individual countries, the current account deficits regularly reach a maximum of 2–3 percent of GDP (see Bosworth 1993). In rare cases higher deficits of up to 5–6 percent are observed (see chapter 8). For example, the US (211 billion US$, 2.5 percent of GDP),

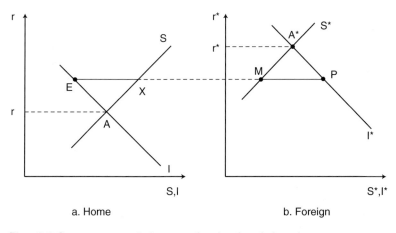

Figure 3.6 Current account balances and national capital markets

Table 3.2 Gross capital inflows (billion US$)

		1991	1993	1995	1996	1997	Annual average[a]
World	Portfolio investments	466.4	754.4	595.1	919.2	1,002.2	659.8
	Direct investments	154.4	218.6	329.2	334.0	418.1	266.2
	Other investments	104.4	438.7	775.2	831.9	1,276.9	605.7
	Total	725.2	1,411.7	1,699.5	2,085.1	2,697.1	1,531.7
Industrialized countries	Portfolio investments	418.3	620.7	538.4	785.2	847.9	559.1
	Direct investments	113.7	143.3	207.4	191.5	235.9	164.2
	Other investments	36.7	359.0	568.0	694.5	1,154.1	485.9
Developing countries	Portfolio investments	31.0	117.1	47.2	122.0	127.6	86.0
	Direct investments	40.7	75.3	121.8	142.5	182.2	102.0
	Other investments	64.1	74.8	165.3	113.3	91.0	89.3
Latin America	Portfolio investments	26.0	74.2	5.9	54.7	31.5	42.5
	Direct investments	13.1	14.3	30.7	42.4	61.5	29.3
	Other investments	4.5	−5.1	44.7	−5.3	3.7	5.1
Asia[b]	Portfolio investments	3.7	28.5	30.6	47.1	25.8	24.5
	Direct investments	20.8	46.2	64.8	73.0	80.0	52.6
	Other investments	36.9	35.3	72.6	81.9	55.5	50.3
Eastern Europe[c]	Portfolio investments	0.8	10.7	6.0	14.4	53.8	13.4
	Direct investments	2.7	5.7	17.3	16.4	22.9	10.9
	Other investments	3.7	20.7	24.5	30.1	14.7	15.5

Source: IMF, Balance of Payments Statistics Yearbook (1998)

Notes
a Annual average: for the years 1991–1997
b Asia: not included are Hong Kong and Taiwan
c Eastern Europe: including Malta, Turkey and Cyprus. Figures rounded to one digit

Canada (19 billion US$, 2.9 percent) and Australia (19 billion US$, 5.1 percent) show relatively high current account deficits for 1998.

Capital flows run mainly between the industrialized countries. About 60 percent of the world's direct investments are capital inflows into the industrialized countries. However, the share of the newly industrializing countries has risen considerably (Table 3.2). The portfolio investments (transactions in shares and bonds and also in money market instruments and derivatives) show a similar picture. Portfolio investments differ from direct investments in the way that the investor is not durably interested in the firms he or she is investing in.

The close relation between national investments and national savings

Feldstein and Horioka (1980) found out that the national capital markets are of considerable importance for the clearing between capital demand and capital supply. For a panel of 21 OECD countries and the time from 1960 to 1974, they found a high correlation between the national savings rate and the national investment rate with a regression coefficient close to 1. The rates were calculated as averages for the total period of 15 years and also for subperiods of 5 years. The simple OLS (ordinary least squares) regression $(I/Y)_i = \alpha + \beta(S/Y)_i$ for the 21 countries $(i = 1, \ldots, 21)$ and the 15-year period yields a regression coefficient β of 0.89 for gross savings and of 0.94 for net savings. Similar coefficients were found for the 5-year period. These coefficients can be interpreted as savings retention coefficients. With perfect capital mobility one would have expected no relation at all between the savings rate and the investment rate, β thus equaling zero. However, since the coefficient is closer to 1 than 0, the hypothesis $\beta = 0$ has to be rejected. The results of Feldstein and Horioka suggest that national capital markets have considerable weight and that only small excess demands and supplies are balanced on the world market for capital. Perfect capital mobility does not exist.

Recent tests show that the close relation observed by Feldstein and Horioka has become less tight in recent times. Based on annual data for 1960–1988, S. Sinn (1992a) has shown for 23 OECD countries that the long-term average of the relationship between the national rates of savings and investment has declined considerably, especially since 1973 (the coefficient of the regression equation is 0.68 for the 1980s); international capital mobility has thus increased.

In Figure 3.7, savings rates and investment rates in 1997 are shown for selected countries. As can easily be observed, the values for most countries lie close to a straight line with an angle of 45°.

Considerable capital inflows for particular countries

Even if the world market for capital in general only seems to balance peaks between savings and investments, capital inflows can gain a considerable importance for particular countries and in particular periods. The share of direct

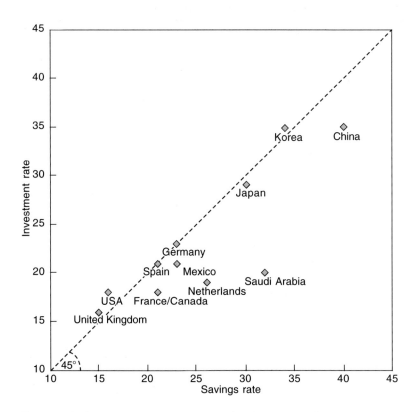

Figure 3.7 Savings rates and investment rates in selected countries, 1997
Source: World Bank, *World Development Report 1998*

investments in gross investment attains 20 percent and more in Chile and Hungary in a number of years (Table 3.3).

3.5 The debt cycle: from net debtor to net creditor

The debt cycle

In its historical development, an economy can go through a debt cycle (Siebert 1987, 1989). It begins as a 'young' debtor because capital import is worthwhile due to $F_K > r$. The marginal productivity of capital exceeds the world market interest rate, for instance when considerable investment opportunities exist in a country. By capital imports, a stock of capital is built up in the debtor country. This increases the production possibilities. From the additional production, interest payment and debt repayment can be financed so that debt decreases in the course of time. At some point in time, the country moves into a creditor position.

Table 3.3 Inflow of direct investments, as percent of gross investment

	1986–1990	1992	1994	1995	1996	1997
Czech Republic[a]	0.3	n.a.	7.4	15.4	7.7	8.0
Hungary	n.a.	20.0	13.7	53.6	20.6	n.a.
Poland	0.1	4.8	12.5	18.2	17.6	n.a.
European Union	5.9	4.9	4.8	6.9	5.1	7.1
Argentina	11.1	10.5	5.5	9.5	9.7	9.9
Brazil	1.7	2.9	2.7	3.4	7.6	12.5
Chile	20.6	9.9	21.8	19.1	27.5	27.9
Mexico	7.5	6.2	13.5	20.6	15.5	15.9
Korea	1.2	0.7	0.59	1.06	1.3	1.8
Malaysia	11.7	24.7	14.9	11.1	12.1	12.2
Thailand	6.5	4.8	2.4	2.9	3.1	5.5

Source: International Monetary Fund, IFS CD-ROM 1998; Heinrich (1996)

Note
a   Czech Republic 1986–1990: Czechoslovakia

The cases of the US and of the UK

One example for such a development is the US. Especially during the time of the railroad boom (1840–1870), the US attracted foreign capital. At some point foreign debt was more than 20 percent in relation to its gross domestic product (Figure 3.8). The debt amount was then reduced and the US became a net creditor from 1914 onwards before moving into a net debtor position again in 1985. In Figure 3.8, two different statistical sources are used for the US, but their results show similar tendencies. The United Kingdom had a net creditor position in the world economy until the beginning of the 20th century; afterwards it got into a net debtor position which was partially reversed by the oil discoveries in the North Sea.

Debt half-cycle

An economy will not always succeed in going through a full debt cycle from debtor to creditor. The expected marginal productivity of capital may be overestimated, or the foreign debt may not be used for capital formation, but to finance the government budget and, in the end, for consumption, e.g. to finance social programs or election promises. Then the commitment of the foreign debt weighs heavily on the economy. From a country's budgetary restriction $\dot{V} = I - S + rV$ (with V: debt, $\dot{V} > 0$: new indebtedness) it follows that reducing debt ($\dot{V} < 0$) at a given investment level (I) and given interest payments (rV) requires high savings if a country has accumulated high debt. This is equivalent to the statement that there has to be a high export surplus for a country to be able to pay interest and repay its foreign debt.

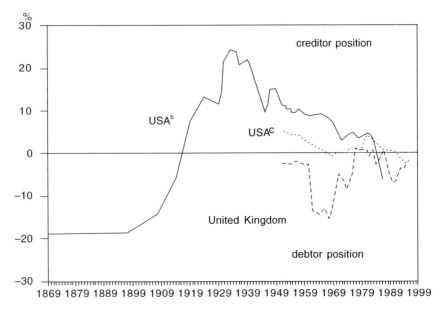

Figure 3.8 Debt cycle of the US
Note: Debt in percent of gross domestic product
Sources: [b]Holtfrerich and Schötz, 1988. [c]All other data: IMF, *International Financial Statistics* CD-ROM,
May 1997

3.6 The factor-price frontier

Due to the production function, a unique relationship exists between prices of
the different production factors. Intuitively, a factor's marginal productivity under
a given production function can increase by employing less of this factor and
more of the other factor; the marginal productivity of the increasingly employed
factor then falls. The real factor prices correspond to the marginal productivities.
Taking the price of one factor as given, determines the price of the other factor
because of the production function. The factor-price frontier describes this relationship. It is the locus of all combinations of real factor prices which are conceivable with a given production function and thus with a given technology. For a
substitutional, linear-homogeneous production function, the factor-price frontier
is shown in Figure 3.9.

Assuming a production function for the world, there is an interdependence
between the real interest rate (r^R) and the real wage (l^R) under given conditions of
production. In factor market equilibrium, one distinct combination of the conceivable combinations is realized on both factor markets (point A). Assume that
the real factor prices are just high enough for full employment of both factors in
the world. If the labor supply now rises in the world and the equilibrium wage
falls due to this rise, the real interest rate rises (from point A to point B). The
change of real factor prices already described in chapter 2 occurs. The integra-

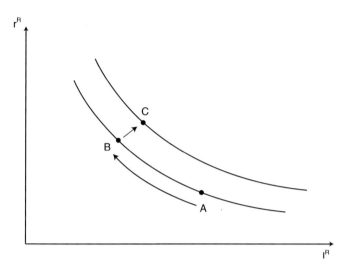

Figure 3.9 The factor-price frontier

tion of economies rich in labor, like China, thus changes both absolute and relative factor prices.

If we take into consideration that technological progress is stimulated by globalization, the factor-price frontier moves outwards. The real wage can thus rise (from point B to point C).

The factor-price frontier is also valid for single economies or regions of the world. Depending on the production technologies, the frontier may be different for different countries. With the factor-price frontier we may also show what it means for a country if capital moves out: the real interest rate rises, the real wage falls. Locational competition for the mobile capital thus has consequences for labor as a production factor.

3.7 The world market for natural resources

The previous considerations can analogously be applied to natural resources as a production factor. Taking natural resources (R) into account as an additional production factor in the production function $Q = F(L, K, R)$, the demand for resources is determined by the real resource price (nominal resource price w divided by the product price p) being equal to the marginal productivity of the resource (F_R): $w/p = F_R$. Thus, the world market for resources can be represented similarly to Figure 3.1.

A sudden resource shortage (like during the oil crisis in the 1970s) can be interpreted as a shift of the factor-price frontier (in Figure 3.9) to the left. The existing capital stock being adjusted to low oil prices becomes partly obsolete as oil prices rise. The marginal productivity of capital and also of labor falls. This means that the real factor incomes for capital and labor are reduced. In the course of time, this movement of the factor-price frontier to the left can be partly reversed if technological progress, e.g. opening up new energy resources and saving energy, moves the factor-price frontier outwards again.

A special problem with natural resources is depletion. We distinguish between non-renewable resources (oil) and renewable resources (wood, fish populations). When non-renewable resources are in finite supply and when substitution is not possible, they may eventually be exhausted. The optimal rate of resource extraction over time is therefore a decisive issue. When resources are renewable, the issue is how the rate of renewal and the rate of withdrawal have to interplay in order to secure an optimal pattern of resource use over time. Another issue is allocating the environment for competing uses (chapter 13).

3.8 Changes on factor markets and world market equilibrium

A new equilibrium in the world factor markets has to be found when conditions change. Here are some cases:

- A technological breakthrough leads to an increased demand for capital. The capital demand curve on the world market for capital moves upwards. The interest rate rises. The same effect can be observed in the case of stronger growth, e.g. due to a higher growth path or during a recovery in the business cycle.
- A shortage of natural resources (oil) reduces the marginal productivity of capital. The interest rate falls.
- Institutional changes can influence the factor markets as well. In Western Europe, a high level of unemployment has developed over the past 30 years due to the institutional setting of the labor market. Another example of the impact of institutional arrangement is the introduction of capital-funded old-age insurance systems in the world; this stimulates savings and reduces the interest rate.

Notes

1 In the figure given here, let BD be equal to DA, i.e. let the straight line have a slope of 45°. Then BC indicates how much is necessary to keep the household indifferent relative to point A and CB/DA is the preference rate (of consumption) in time. For consumption, the marginal rate of substitution in time results from totally differentiating the utility function

$$U = U(C_0) + \frac{1}{1 + \delta} U(C_1)$$ at a constant utility (so-called Euler equation):

$$\left| \frac{dC_1}{dC_0} \right| = \frac{U_0'(C_0)(1 + \delta)}{U_1'(C_1)}$$

2 From the intertemporal utility-maximizing calculus

Max $U = U_0(C_0) + (1 + \delta)^{-1}U_1(C_1)$
s.t. $C_1 = Y/p_1 - (p_0/p_1)C_0$

it follows that

$(1 + \delta)^{-1}U_1'(C_1) - U_0'(C_0)p_1/p_0 = 0$

or

$$\frac{p_0}{p_1} = (1 + \delta)U_0'(C_0)/U_1'(C_1).$$

4 Growth processes in the world economy

Previous chapters have analyzed the world markets for goods and for factors of production, this chapter continues the global economic view, looking at the way growth processes take place in the world economy. The historical record of the last two centuries shows a continuous upward movement in income per capita interrupted by two world wars and the hyper-inflation of the 1920s and the Great Depression of the 1930s (section 4.1). Growth processes overlap with cyclical movements (section 4.2). The driving force of economic growth is the augmentation of production factors, comprising capital accumulation, population growth and technological progress (section 4.3). Capital exports and imports play a decisive role in the growth processes of open economies (section 4.4). We discuss why openness is important (section 4.5). Localization factors are surveyed in section 4.6. Empirical evidence suggests the relevance of capital accumulation for growth (section 4.7). An intensely discussed topic is whether economic processes are characterized by divergence or convergence (section 4.8). Economic growth is a process with many different features (section 4.9). To conclude, some special aspects of the world economy's growth process are dealt with (section 4.10).

4.1 Economic growth – the historical record

The world economy is not static, but dynamic in character. In the course of time, various changes take place. In the last 200 years, a sizable increase in per capita income of the early industrialized countries can be observed (Figure 4.1). However, the two world wars, the European hyperinflation in the 1920s and the Great Depression halted the increase in economic welfare.

A decisive question for growth processes is whether economies are open or closed. Historically, there seems to be a relation between the openness of an economy and economic welfare. In the countries that were industrialized earliest, gross national product has risen with growing openness. The two world wars of the 20th century reduced the openness; they represent a period of decline and stagnation. This also holds for the 1920s and early 1930s of this century whereas after 1945 a continuous upward movement begins.

Figure 4.1 Development of real per capita income and export ratio in the early industrial-
ized countries, 1820–1990
Note: The countries considered are Australia, Austria, Belgium, Canada, Denmark, Finland, France,
Germany, Italy, Japan, Netherlands, Norway, Sweden, Switzerland, United Kingdom, United States
Source: Maddison (1992), own calculations

4.2 Global economic growth and cyclical movements

Cyclical fluctuations

In the world economy as well as in a national economy, long-term growth
processes are characterized by cyclical movements. In Figure 4.2, a growth trend
with cycles is shown for the industrialized nations, i.e. the OECD countries. Real
gross national product oscillates around a trend. The recessions of 1974/75,
1982/83 and 1992/93 in the industrialized countries are clearly visible.
Economic growth is thus not constant over time, but varies with the ups and
downs of economic activity.

Cyclical movements are not necessarily synchronized in the world economy.
One region of the world may be in a recession while other regions are in an
upswing. In this case, different regional factors are responsible for the cyclical
movements, such as a temporarily expansionist fiscal policy in one country. The
cyclical situation in a big country spills over to other economies (international
business-cycle interlink). If a worldwide disturbance (like the oil crisis) occurs, the
world business cycle evolves in a rather synchronous way, resulting in a uniform
world business cycle.

The processes of economic growth are accompanied by crises and other disturbances. The disintegration of the world economy in the 1930s, for example,
was accompanied by a breakdown of the world economy characterized by a significantly negative growth rate (see the Kindleberger spiral in Figure 1.3).

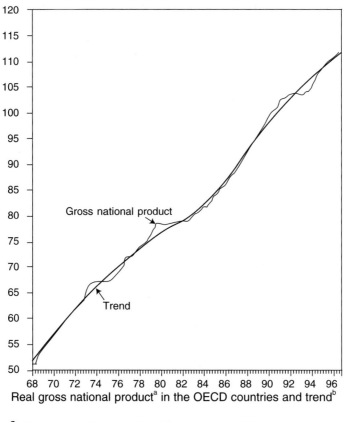

Real gross national product[a] in the OECD countries and trend[b]

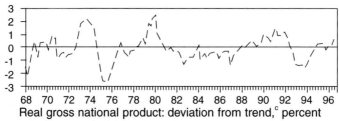

Real gross national product: deviation from trend,[c] percent

Figure 4.2 Growth and business cycle in the OECD countries
[a] Index 1990 = 100
[b] Hodrick/Prescott filter (smoothing factor 1600)
[c] Deviation from a Hodrick/Prescott filter (HP 1600)
Source of original data: OECD: *Main Economic Indicators,* current volumes

Crises

Whereas periods of growing integration in the world economy, like the two decades after the Second World War, went along with high growth rates, the oil crisis of the 1970s partially devalued the existing stock of capital that was contingent on low energy prices. This lowered the marginal productivity of capital, with the consequence that growth collapsed. At the same time, the export revenues of the OPEC countries increased. With higher purchasing power, this increase led to a redirection of trade flows, to trade balance surpluses, to the accumulation of financial assets and to a redirection of financial flows (petrodollar recycling). Other disturbances had their effects on the growth process as well, like the Korean War which led to a boom with strong price rises, and the Vietnam War, where the strong expansion of the money supply in the United States led to the inflation of the Bretton Woods system's anchor currency and, finally, to the collapse of this system. The debt crisis of the 1980s cut the Latin American countries off from real capital inflows. In real terms, a temporary transfer of capital in favor of the industrialized countries took place ('capital flowed up the hill'). The collapse of the centrally planned economies is another aspect of the subject of growth processes in the world economy.

Some impulses of growth

Technological breakthroughs like the first industrial revolution in Great Britain in the 18th century represent an impulse for world economic growth. This also holds for the settlement and the industrialization of new areas such as North America. Moreover, changes in a country's economic policy can influence growth processes worldwide through the redirection of investment flows.

4.3 The driving forces of growth

World production function

Following at first a global view, i.e. of the world economy as a whole, a possible approach to the analysis of growth processes in the world economy is a world production function

$$Y = F(L, K, T, R, \ldots)$$

where the world national product Y depends on the productions factors labor (L), capital (K), technological knowledge (T), resources (R) and other production factors. Therefrom, the growth equation

$$\hat{Y} = G(\hat{L}, \hat{K}, \hat{T}, \hat{R}, \ldots)$$

can be derived; according to this the growth rate of the world national product is a function of the growth rates of labor, capital stock, technological knowledge, natural resources and other production factors. As a rule, we refer to an increase (or decrease) of per capita output ($y = Y/L$) when analyzing world economic growth, as it is a measure for people's provision with goods and thus a rudimentary measure for welfare.

Such a formulation of a world production function is certainly interesting for historical analyses, where the importance of particular growth factors like capital accumulation, population growth, technological progress or changes of the natural resources supply can be investigated. The world production function and the growth equation represent a general framework for an economic analysis and can also be the basis for econometric studies. In the ideal case, however, a formulation like this would require us to be able to empirically measure with sufficient accuracy the inputs of a world production function, like the world's capital stock, the world's labor supply and its technological knowledge. This is impossible at the moment. We thus have to content ourselves either with applying the production factors and the growth equation to the world as a whole in a rather general interpretation, or to refer to the growth processes of particular regions of the world where outputs and inputs can be measured accurately. In both cases, it is worthwhile to further investigate the role of the particular determinants of growth.

Growth through capital accumulation

A first approach to explaining growth refers to capital accumulation in the context of neoclassical growth theory (Solow 1956).

Capital accumulation does not concern a static look at the allocation of capital in one period, i.e. a flow equilibrium (as in chapter 3), but the accumulation of capital over time. In such an intertemporal context, we distinguish between a long-term equilibrium and the time path to the equilibrium. In a long-term equilibrium (steady state) all variables grow at the same rate and the ratios between these variables remain constant. A special case is the stationary state where the equilibrium growth rates of all variables equal zero. The time path indicates how an economy moves from the initial situation to the long-run equilibrium.

Pure capital accumulation without population growth or technological progress is the simplest case of growth. The world accumulates capital and a higher capital stock means more output, i.e. growth. The process of accumulating capital continues until the marginal productivity of capital and the discount rate (of utility, δ) are equal. Using a per capita version of the production function $y = f(k)$ with k being the capital intensity we have as an optimality condition for capital accumulation $f_k = \delta$ (Figure 4.3). As long as $f_k > \delta$, capital is accumulated; when $f_k = \delta$ (point G), capital accumulation comes to a halt (stationary state).

According to this concept, the world moves downwards along the negatively sloped marginal productivity-of-capital curve. The growth rate of gross national income, however, falls with increasing capital formation (increasing k) because each additional unit of capital has a lower marginal productivity. In the long-term equilibrium (point G), the growth rate is then zero because no further capital is built up.[1]

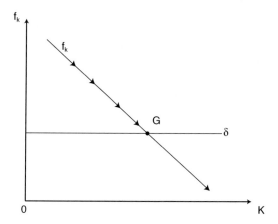

Figure 4.3 Optimal accumulation of capital

Real capital and human capital

Besides real capital (K), human capital (H) can also be regarded as a production factor of its own, comprising the skills, the capabilities and the knowledge of workers. All these characteristics are influenced by formal education or by 'learning on the job'. Furthermore, a traditional factor 'labor' (L, simple labor) is regarded as input. The production function, e.g. of the Cobb–Douglas type, then takes the form $Y = K^\alpha H^\beta L^{1-\alpha-\beta}$ instead of $Y = K^\alpha L^{1-\alpha}$. Obviously, the weight of the traditional factors, labor and capital, measured by the elasticities of production α and $(1-\alpha)$, changes. Under the assumption of perfect competition, the factors' elasticity of production corresponds to their shares of national income. With the share of labor in national income being $1-\alpha = 0.7$, the production elasticity of labor is estimated by that value in the traditional Cobb–Douglas function (and the share of capital at $\alpha = 0.3$). By taking human capital into account, the share of traditional labor is reduced, whereas the importance of capital formation (including human capital) increases. The formation of human capital in the form of education requires abstaining from consumption, i.e. saving, like the formation of real capital. Saving thus becomes increasingly important. If we correspondingly define a broad notion of capital Z: (K, H) that comprises real and human capital, this factor is attributed a weight of $\alpha + \beta$.[2] Empirical studies show that this elasticity of production $\alpha + \beta$ is higher than 0.7 and that traditional labor's elasticity of production lies at 0.3 and lower (Mankiw 1995). Income differences between economies can thus be explained not only by differences in the provision with physical capital, but also by different qualities of human capital, especially a different impact of education systems (years of schooling, universities).

Population growth

Taking population growth into account as well and assuming a discount rate near zero, a long-term equilibrium would be reached when the marginal productivity of capital (f_k) and the growth rate of the labor supply (n) are just equal, i.e. $f_k = n$ (point G in Figure 4.4). This follows from the neoclassical growth model and is called the 'golden rule of capital accumulation'. It ensures the highest per capita income possible in long-term equilibrium. This golden rule is not valid, however, if a positive discount rate is explicity assumed.[3] With a higher capital stock per worker, it would indeed be possible to achieve a higher domestic product, but due to the positive discount rate, the economy is not willing to wait for it. With a positive discount rate, less capital is accumulated (point G' in Figure 4.4). The rule for optimal allocation is $f_k = \delta + n$. Here we have an analogy to renewable resources where it would be possible to achieve a maximum extraction quantity ('maximum yield') at a discount rate of zero, but due to a positive discount rate, the resource stock that is being held is smaller. Analogously, less capital is accumulated (Blanchard and Fischer 1989, p. 45; Siebert 1983, chapter 5).

The optimum time path for consumption and capital

The position of the long-term equilibrium and the adjustment path leading to the equilibrium can be represented in a *c–k* diagram. The long-term equilibrium is defined by per capita consumption (c) and the capital stock per capita (k) not changing anymore. This means $\dot{c} = 0$ and $\dot{k} = 0$ where a dot indicates the change of a variable over time. Per capita consumption does not change anymore when the condition $f_k(k) = \delta + n$ is satisfied.[4] From this condition follows that in the *c–k* space, the $\dot{c}$ curve is a vertical line (Figure 4.5). From the system's equation of motion $\dot{k} = f(k) - c - nk$, it follows for $\dot{k} = 0$ that $c = f(k) - nk$ meaning that with k increasing, c first rises on the $\dot{k} = 0$ curve (if $f_k > n$), but then decreases again due to

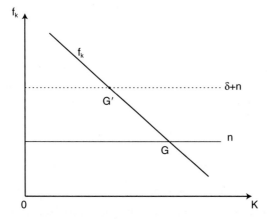

Figure 4.4 Optimum capital accumulation, time preference and population growth

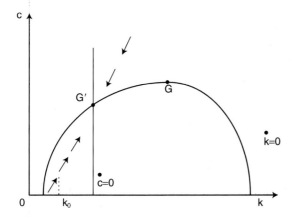

Figure 4.5 Long-term equilibrium.

falling marginal productivity ($f_k < n$). At a positive discount rate $\delta > 0$, point G' will result in the world economy in long-term equilibrium. Note that for $\delta \to 0$, point G would be reached (maximum yield). The positive discount rate implies a lower capital formation. Note that Figure 4.5 also holds for renewable resources where c is resource withdrawal from nature and $f(k)$ represents a production function of a natural resource stock k (i.e. a regeneration function of a forest or a fish population) with $f_k > 0$ below a natural equilibrium $k*$ and $f_k < 0$ above $k*$.

If technological progress is present and if labor input is measured in efficiency units $\tilde{A} = a(t)A$, a figure analogous to Figure 4.4 results in the simple Solow-type model, where n has to be replaced by the term $n + x\varepsilon \approx n + e$ (where ε: rate of technological progress and $x = -cu''/u'$). In this case as well, a positive discount rate causes the accumulation of capital to come to a stop earlier. In Figure 4.4, new technological knowledge moves the marginal productivity of capital curve upward, shifting points G and G' to the right. Technological progress thus prevents a 'walking down the marginal productivity of capital curve'.

Technological progress

As a rule, the growth rate decreases with a growing capital stock per capita, due to decreasing marginal productivity. Every additional unit of capital has a smaller output effect. If we look at an economy where only the accumulation of real capital plays a role as a growth factor, capital formation comes to a standstill in the long run; a stationary state is reached. This holds, for example, with a per capita production function $y = k^\alpha$ with $\alpha < 1$.

Endogenous growth in technological knowledge

Marginal productivity does not necessarily fall if the production function shows increasing returns to scale. This is Romer's (1986; see also Grossman and

Helpman 1991a) concept of knowledge capital ($\mathcal{Z}$). With capital formation per worker in an enterprise (k), knowledge capital $\mathcal{Z} = \mathcal{Z}(k)$ develops as well, and this capital can also be used in other enterprises, i.e. capital accumulation in one firm has positive effects in other enterprises. For the marginal productivity of capital, we then have ($f_k(k,\mathcal{Z})$); that is, the marginal productivity of capital is positively affected by knowledge capital. Assuming $\mathcal{Z}(k) = k^\gamma$, the production function takes the form $y = k^\alpha \mathcal{Z}(k) = k^{\alpha+\gamma}$. Here, the traditional production function shows constant returns to scale for labor and capital and thus a decreasing marginal productivity of capital intensity k^α ($\alpha < 1$). The production function as a whole, however, has increasing returns to scale. This is related to technological knowledge being not a private commodity with rivalry in its use, but a public commodity, e.g. software that can be used in various places without the occurrence of rivalry. If the effect discussed here is strong enough and if $\alpha + \gamma$ approaches 1, decreasing marginal productivities of capital disappear completely.

What drives the determinants of growth?

To explain growth processes, it is important to know what drives the determinants of growth. Thus, capital accumulation depends on the savings and on the expected return on investment. A country having a low time preference rate will tend to have higher savings. High rates of return are an incentive to invest and to build up a capital stock. Institutional arrangements such as a pay-as-you-go system or a capital-funded system influence the volume of savings. Technological progress depends on investments into research and development. High expected profits from research and development are an incentive to invest and to innovate. In the Romer model (1986), for example, the profit expectations in the high-technology industry drive the expenditures for research and development. The development of the growth determinants has thus to be explained endogenously.

The historical shift from physical capital to intangible capital

Historically, different growth factors were the driving force in the growth process; the importance of growth factors has shifted considerably over time. Looking at the US as an example (David 1999), working capital was the source of growth in labor productivity at the beginning of the 19th century; fixed (physical) capital took the leading role in a process of capital deepening in the later part of the 19th century. In the 20th century, intangible capital (knowledge capital) with investments in education and training became the dominant growth factor.

4.4 Capital importers and exporters

Let us now study open economies that do not have to rely on their own savings for their investments, but can import capital. Similarly, other countries may export capital. In order to determine whether a country is a capital importer or exporter, the interaction between the marginal productivity (f_k), the discount rate (δ), and the world market interest rate (r) has to be discussed.

Efficiency gains through capital movements

If the marginal productivity of capital and the discount rate in a country are higher than the world market interest rate, i.e. $f_k = \delta > r$, it is worthwhile to import capital from the world market for capital (Figure 4.6a). If, however, the discount rate is lower than the interest rate in the world market for capital, it is worthwhile to export capital (Figure 4.6b). The capital importer gets an advantage (in the case of $\delta > r$) by passing from autarky to free capital mobility: with capital from the world market, they can produce more in their home country (point G instead of point A). The importer pays interest on the imported capital amounting to the rectangle CBGD and additionally produces the area CAGD. The part of the production that additionally remains for the importer is the triangle BAG. This is the advantage from importing capital.

The capital exporter also has an advantage by passing from autarky to free capital mobility. They produce less than in autarky, but receive a higher income from interest. The exporter gains the area GFA in Figure 4.6b.

Figure 4.6 only exhibits an equilibrium in the short run. In the long run, the

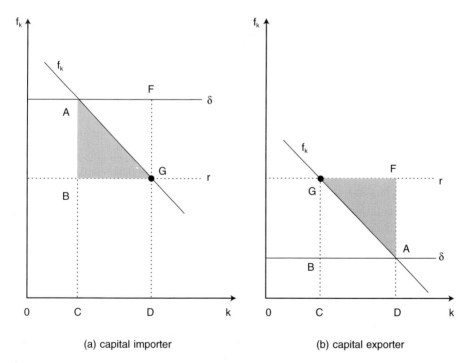

(a) capital importer   (b) capital exporter

Figure 4.6 Long-term equilibrium with capital import and capital export current account has to be balanced for the two equilibrium solutions G, so there is an intertemporal budget restriction to be respected. To balance its current account in the future, the debtor country thus has to fulfill its interest obligations by exporting goods to the creditor country. For the capital-importing country, gross domestic product exceeds gross national product which can be interpreted as gross residents' product. In long-term equilibrium, it cannot use its whole production for consumption, but has to set some part aside for paying interest and acquittance.

Capital movements and the time path of consumption

In Figure 4.7, the long-term equilibrium of a capital-importing country is represented in the c–k diagram. G characterizes the long-term equilibrium without capital import and thus in autarky. Starting from the capital endowment of the original situation k_0, this equilibrium is reached through own savings. This takes time. Compared to the autarky situation, a capital-importing country can reach the consumption level G′ faster by importing capital instead of saving on its own (G). But in the long-term equilibrium, this country has to pay GG′ for debt service and debt acquittance. Its long-term consumption level is lower; through own savings it could have reached a higher consumption level (point G), but waiting for it would have been longer, meaning a loss of utility. The mirror image is the capital-exporting country that reaches a higher consumption level (Maurer 1998).

The two-country case is represented in Figure 4.8. It is assumed that the productivity of the capital stock per capita f_k is lower in the home country, e.g. due to its lower level of technology (lower part of the diagram). At a capital stock per capita of k_0, the marginal productivity of capital in the home country is higher than in the foreign country which is assumed to have a capital stock per capita of

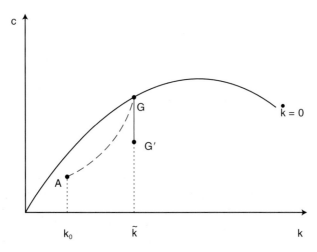

Figure 4.7 Growth path of a capital-importing country

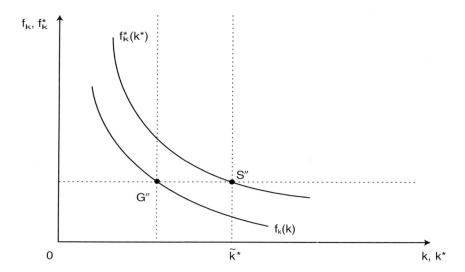

Figure 4.8 Growth path of capital importer and capital exporter

$\tilde{k}^*$. Thus, the home country imports capital. In the long-term equilibrium, the home country pays interest and acquittance (distance GG′), implying that in the long run it can consume only less than it produces. The foreign country provides capital to the home country, receiving capital income for it in the long run (distance S*S*′). For simplicity it has been assumed that in the original situation, the foreign country was in a steady state already (point S*).

Possible scenarios of capital accumulation

If all countries in the world have the same discount rate and if one country has the highest capital productivity, capital will be accumulated first in this country. The country with the highest capital productivity grows fastest at first, causing marginal capital productivity to fall gradually so that eventually capital accumulation becomes attractive for the other countries as well.

Let us now look at a situation where initially all countries have the same marginal productivity of capital, but one country has a lower discount rate. This country will be more inclined to abstain from consumption. This results in a consumption level that is lower at first, but also in faster capital accumulation due to higher savings. Because of this, it can consume more later on: its consumption increases faster in time. The other countries, on the other hand, have a high discount rate and are thus more impatient. They start with a higher consumption level, but they build less capital, and their consumption increases more slowly in time.

If all countries have different discount rates, the country with the lowest discount rate determines up to which point capital is accumulated in the world economy.[5] The country with the lowest discount rate provides capital until its discount rate and the real interest rate are equal, then its consumption stays constant. For the other countries, $\delta > r$ holds, and consumption decreases in the course of time. In a simplifying model context, the patient country finally accumulates all the capital of the world.

Taking different discount rates, different population growth rates and different rates of technological progress into consideration, the implications for the capital market become very complex. *Ceteris paribus* assumptions, the country with the low discount rate remains the world's net creditor, and this result should not change if, due to population growth, the debtor country needs more capital and has a high national discount rate. A country with strong technological progress can also indebt itself to the country with the low discount rate. The technological progress may be strong enough to finance the interest service in favor of the creditor country.

4.5 How important is the openness of economies?

Economic growth is related to the openness of economies. Figure 4.9 shows the growth rate of the early industrialized countries for the period 1870-1990 and the openness, measured as the rate of increase of the export ratio, i.e. of the share of exports in GDP. Except for the two world wars and the inter-war period, the export ratio increases, and the growth rate of the gross domestic product per capita rises. Exports are beneficial to economic growth.

There is a variety of mechanisms through which growth occurs in an open economy. The first to be mentioned here are traditional gains from foreign trade with final products, generating a higher gross domestic product. In the course of economic development, countries manage to gain comparative price advantages

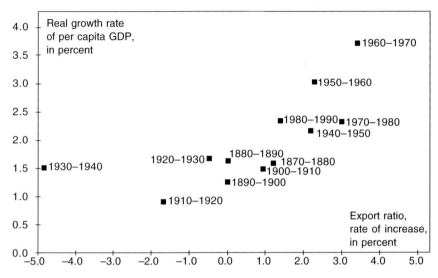

Figure 4.9 Real per capita growth and foreign trade in the early industrialized countries 1870–1990
Note: Countries are detailed in caption of Figure 4.1
Source: Maddison (1992), own calculations

through the formation of real and human capital. The advantages of endowment change; and these advantages can be influenced by policy ('acquired comparative advantage'). At the same time, some comparative advantages migrate away from industrialized nations to the developing countries, e.g. because production does not pay off anymore due to increasing factor costs (like labor costs or regulation). Gains of specialization add to the welfare gains; especially, economies of scale (learning effects) are of relevance. A wider variety of products is made possible. The hypothesis of the product cycle also explains why production moves away from industrialized countries (via a diffusion of knowledge from the innovator to the imitators) and eventually finds its locations worldwide. The intensification of competition that is related to foreign trade (with the consequence of falling costs and new technological knowledge discovered) result in higher growth as well.

If trade with capital goods is taken into account as well, additional effects result. Debt allows the import of capital goods so that the capital stock can be accumulated faster; the economy moves on a higher growth path towards the long-term equilibrium. Competition in the production of capital goods is intensified so that efficiency gains can be expected. The sectoral resource allocation between research and development on the one side and production on the other are improved through trade with capital goods, leading to a higher long-term growth path with income gains. In the long-term equilibrium, a higher per capita production is reached. Finally, the international diffusion of technological knowledge, like the trade in patents and the flow of ideas, is a channel through which the growth process can be influenced favorably in open economies.

4.6 Localization factors

Economic activities are not uniformly distributed in space (Krugman 1991). One reason is that space itself is not homogeneous, but structured by resource deposits, agricultural areas, natural highways and harbors, settlement possibilities and other factors. Beside these basic locational advantages, advantages of agglomeration play an important role as factors that constitute spatial structure. These concern positive external effects between economic activities, referring to technological as well as pecuniary external effects. This comprises spatially limited diffusion processes related to new technological knowledge (spillover, spatially bound knowledge capital), informal or formal information networks delimited in space and 'proximity advantages', e.g. between enterprises and politics. An important aspect is the size of the market. A case in point is the labor market. If a region has a qualified labor supply at its disposal (historical examples: the Swiss Jura for the watch industry, Baden-Württemberg in Germany for precision engineering), it is easier for the enterprises to rely on a pool of qualified workers. If a region is occupied by enterprises that demand similar qualifications, such a region is attractive for qualified workers simply because they do not depend on just one company. They have the option of switching to other companies, and thus their risk of becoming jobless is smaller.

Transport costs are another factor that has structuring effects on space. Once a certain structure is given, like the existence of a city with a homogeneous area around it, it can be shown that rings of economic activity develop around the city (Thünen 1826); other things equal, businesses with high transport costs will settle near the city (Alonso 1964).

Furthermore, the historical development of the spatial structure is path-dependent. The spatial structure given in a specific moment of time is the base for economic decisions that for their part have spatial effects in the future. Thus, the future spatial development is in some way shaped by the original structure. Old locations have the advantage that various investments have already been made there, comprising real capital of the companies, durable consumption goods of the households (real estate), infrastructural capital (roads, harbors, universities). The costs related to these are partly 'sunk costs'; production stays at the old location, even if these costs cannot be covered anymore.

In contrast, a new location does not have the sunk-cost advantage. It has to compete with an old location that can neglect the sunk costs in locational competition. As the capital stock of a region is, in a disaggregated view, defined by a variety of capital goods, the decision about choices of location for the individual capital good is dispersed on the time axis. As a consequence, decisions about the location of capital goods that are currently installed at an old location and need replacement have to be made again and again. If a capital good stays at an old location, chances improve for another capital good at that place to be renewed there as well.

However, sunk costs cannot justify a location permanently. At some time, the marginal productivity of investments may decline so much or the locational quality elsewhere may improve so strongly that a change of location becomes worthwhile, despite sunk costs.

During the process of economic development, self-amplifying factors may occur that lead to the development of growth poles, especially if a region can attract resources due to advantages of location and agglomeration (polarization). The growth process in the world economy is then seen as taking place in a large set of regional growth clusters. During the further development, such growth poles then radiate out to other regions and pull them along. Here, the question arises of whether a process of convergence will come about or whether economic development is finally accompanied by divergence (see below).

On a more aggregated scale of the world economy, the concept of the center (or centers) and periphery plays a role. Over the last century, the two centers of Europe and North America have been distinguished. In the 20th century, a third center or growth pole in Asia, with Japan, the four or six 'tigers' and China, has appeared beside the two centers of North America and Europe.

4.7 Empirical evidence: capital formation

The variety of the approaches to explaining economic growth presented here has produced a considerable literature striving for empirical scrutiny. Let us look at the importance of capital formation as a growth factor.

Economies with a high marginal productivity of capital should, other things being equal, be characterized by a strong capital formation. Capital is also needed if the population increases, to equip the additional workforce with machines. Moreover, strong technological progress will lead to high investment activity. We can expect a high investment activity to be linked to high growth rates because the capital stock is an important ingredient of the growth process. The higher the investment rate, the stronger is the growth rate. The thesis that the average growth rate is positively related to the investment rate is empirically corroborated (Figure 4.10). It is remarkable that the four tigers, with investment rates of significantly above 30 percent (Singapore 38 percent) have had annual growth rates of over 6 percent.

4.8 Catching-up processes in the world economy: convergence or divergence?

The convergence hypothesis

The marginal productivity of capital falls with growing capital accumulation. Consequently, the contribution of a unit of capital to growth decreases as well.

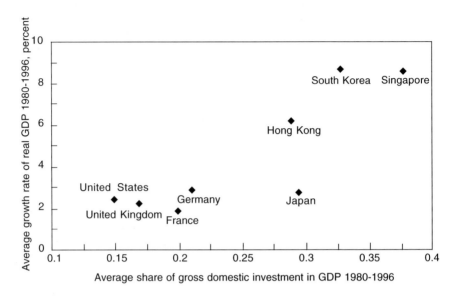

Figure 4.10 Investment shares and growth rates in selected countries, 1980–1996
Source: IMF, *International Financial Statistics* CD-ROM 1998; World Bank, *World Development Indicators* CD-ROM 1998

We thus have to expect the growth rate to fall with capital accumulation. This argument can also be pointed in another direction: as poor countries have a small capital stock, they should – all other things being equal – have a higher marginal productivity of capital and thus a higher growth rate than rich countries with better capital equipment. The hypothesis thus is: 'Poor countries grow faster'. Differences in income are then (at least partly) leveled out in the course of time.

In the extreme case, we should – with a fully integrated world market for capital and without differences in risk – expect that there cannot be any differences in the marginal product of capital. In the simplest of models with perfectly mobile capital and identical production technology everywhere, the international capital mobility would have to lead to an almost immediate equalization of growth rates. This cannot be observed empirically, however. One reason is that there is no perfect capital mobility. In reality, the international capital mobility performs a balancing function only at peaks, as the discussion of the Feldstein–Horioka (1980) result in chapter 3 has shown. In addition, there are other factors that are specific for a certain country and explain differences in economic growth; these factors particularly comprise the institutional set-up and the growth of technological knowledge.

In the very long run, differences in marginal productivity should be impossible even under imperfect capital mobility if we assume identical production technologies and institutions. In this case, there would be absolute convergence, i.e. output per worker would, in the long-run equilibrium (steady state), be equal in all countries. In the simple neoclassical model of the Solow type, though, absolute convergence is only reached if the exogenous data for the long-run equilibrium, like population growth (n) (if it is exogenously given) and the savings rate, human capital, are identical. Regarding different long-term equilibria, we have to make corrections for these differing exogenous conditions.[6] This is why we speak of conditional convergence, where the different exogenous conditions of different countries are taken into account. Then, neither do countries reach the same long-term equilibrium nor are the per capita incomes equalized between countries.

Some formulae of convergence

To get an impression of the time required for convergence, we take a look at two economies with constant growth rates g (home country) and g^* (foreign country) of per capita income. Note that this represents a simplification because on a growth path to a long-run equilibrium the rates would change. Assuming that Home has a lower initial per capita income than Foreign, i.e. $y_0 < y_0^*$, the convergence rate $\hat{a}$ satisfies $\hat{a} = \hat{y} - \hat{y}^* = g - g^*$. If Home grows at a rate of $g = 5$ percent and Foreign at $g^* = 2$ percent, the income difference is leveled out at a rate of about 3 percent per year.

The duration of the absolute convergence (t) is calculated by setting the per capita incomes of the two countries in t equal, so that

$$y_t = y_t^* \Leftrightarrow y_0 \, e^{gt} = y_0^* \, e^{g^* t}$$

with

$$t = \frac{\ln(y_0/y_0^*)}{g^* - g} = \frac{\ln(y_0) - \ln(y_0^*)}{g^* - g}.$$

With a growth difference $g - g^*$ of 3 percentage points and an income level of one third in the original situation (e.g. $y_0 = 100$ and $y_0^* = 300$), it takes nearly 37 years until both countries have the same per capita income. For the half-life of the income difference,

$$t_{\text{half}} = \frac{0.5 \ln(y_0/y_0^*)}{g^* - g}$$

holds.[7] With a growth difference of 3 percentage points and an income level of one third in the original situation, it takes 18.5 years until the income differential (more precisely: the income relation expressed in logs) is halved. For this formulation, absolute convergence and half-life depend on the original situation (Table 4.1).

Applying these considerations to East Germany, we have to expect a long-term adjustment process. In 1998, the East German region (including West Berlin) has

Table 4.1 Time required for convergence

Percentage points of lead in growth (%)	Half-life[a]: difference of per capita incomes halved in . . . years			Absolute convergence[b] in . . . years, starting from an original level of		
	30 %	40 %	50 %	30 %	40 %	50 %
1	60.2	45.8	34.7	120.4	91.6	69.3
2	30.1	22.9	17.3	60.2	45.8	34.7
3	20.1	15.3	11.6	40.1	30.5	23.1
4	15.0	11.5	8.7	30.1	22.9	17.3
5	12.0	9.2	6.9	24.1	18.3	13.9
6	10.0	7.6	5.8	20.1	15.3	11.6

[a]Calculated according to the formula: $t_{half} = \dfrac{0.5 \ln(y_0/y_0^*)}{g^* - g}$

[b]Calculated according to the formula: $t = \ln(y_0/y_0^*)/(g^* - g)$

attained 60 percent of West Germany's per capita level of production. If an adjustment to 80 percent of the West German level is set as a target and if the East German growth rate exceeded West Germany's growth rate by three percentage points, the level of 80 percent would be attained in 2008. With a growth rate differential of 2 percent one would have to wait until 2012.[8]

Convergence between regions

Up to here, the analysis has been simplified in the sense that the growth rates of two countries are assumed to be fixed. In the adjustment period of the neoclassical model, the growth rate changes, however, when approaching the steady state. Strictly speaking, convergence addresses the question whether the actual per capita income is converging against the per capita income in the long-term equilibrium $\bar{y}$. In this formulation, the average growth rate per year over a period spanning from the initial period 0 to the steady-state period T is given by the growth rate x in the long-term equilibrium and the 'distance' of the per capita income in the steady state $\bar{y}$ from the original situation y_0 (Barro and Sala-i-Martin 1995, p. 81).[9]

$$\hat{y} = \frac{1}{T} \ln\left[\frac{y(T)}{y_0}\right] = x + \frac{1}{T}(1 - e^{-\beta T})\ln\left[\frac{\bar{y}}{y_0}\right].$$

The further the per capita income in the initial situation is away from the income in the steady state, the higher is the average growth rate over the period from 0 to T. β is the rate of convergence. At a constant rate of convergence β, the expression $\frac{1}{T}(1 - e^{-\beta T})$ approaches zero if T approaches infinity. The growth rate is then dominated by the steady-state rate (x).[10]

The Barro rule

Barro and Sala-i-Martin (1992) have applied these considerations to the regions of the US for the period from 1880 until 1988. Their result was that the differences between the regions were leveled out at a rate of 2 percent per year. This is the so-called Barro rule. At a rate of convergence of 2 percent, it takes about 35 years until the difference of per capita incomes between regions is halved. As the regions of the US surveyed by Barro are relatively similar, we can assume that they approach the same long-term equilibrium (steady state) in the long run. These results suggest that catch-up processes exist, but that these processes require considerable time.

Convergence of early industrialized countries

For the period from 1870 until 1979, Maddison (1982) concludes that early industrialized countries with a high per capita income had smaller growth rates of per capita income whereas economies with a lower per capita income showed a higher growth rate. The regression[11] yields (*L*: number of workers, standard error in brackets):

$$\log\left(\frac{Y_{1979}}{L_{1979}}\right) - \log\left(\frac{Y_{1870}}{L_{1870}}\right) = 8.46 - \underset{(0.09)}{1.00} \log\left(\frac{Y_{1870}}{L_{1870}}\right), \ R^2 = 0.88.$$

The slope of -1 means that for every percent that a country's per capita income was below the average in 1870, the cumulated growth rate in the period 1870–1979 was higher by 1 percent. According to this result we thus observe a long-term convergence, in fact an absolute convergence. A critical objection to this is that the country selection is biased in the sense that all the examined countries have a high per capita income today as well. If instead countries are examined that do not have a high per capita income today, but did in 1870 (thus additionally taking into account, among others, Argentina, Portugal, Spain), and if Japan is excluded from the observation as a one-off case, we can at best speak of a convergence that is only weak.

Convergence in the OECD countries

If we take the OECD countries – and thus the industrialized countries – into account, a negative relation between the level of the growth rate and the per capita income results as well, but the differences for the period from 1870 to 1993 are leveled out at a rate of only 1 percent compared to 2 percent in the Barro estimates for regions of a country (Figure 4.11). Inside an economy, the catch-up processes are thus, as a rule, stronger than they are between countries. Since the Second World War, the European economies and Japan have grown significantly more strongly than that of the US. In 1990, the income differences per capita of 1950 had been reduced by well over a half (Obstfeld and Rogoff 1996, p. 455).

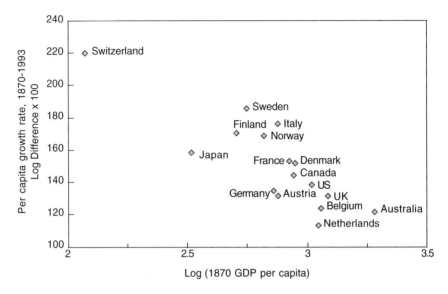

Figure 4.11 Convergence of the OECD countries, 1870–1993
Source: De Long (1988), Maddison (1982); own calculations

Convergence in the European Union

For the countries of the European Union, convergence of per capita incomes with a convergence rate of 1.4 percent for the period 1960–1995 can be observed (Figure 4.12). As countries in a regional integration like the European Union have an intermediate position between regions of an economy and the nation states like OECD countries, the catch-up processes in regional integrations (like the EU) are not as swift as between the regions of a country (2 percent), but faster than between the OECD countries (1 percent).

Divergence between industrialized countries and developing countries

Convergence does not occur anymore, however, if the number of countries is greatly increased. In a study of 98 countries, a moderately positive regression between growth rate and development level results (Barro and Sala-i-Martin 1992). Countries with a higher income level grow (moderately) stronger. Divergence prevails; accordingly, industrialized countries and developing countries grow apart. For the developing countries as a whole, again convergence cannot be found. This image presumably changes if some countries like the African countries south of the Sahara (and possibly Latin America) are excluded. A possible explanation for the fact that convergence cannot be observed in these cases is that the parameters of technology and of resource endowment are very different. Economic policy plays an important role as well, as in the misorientation of

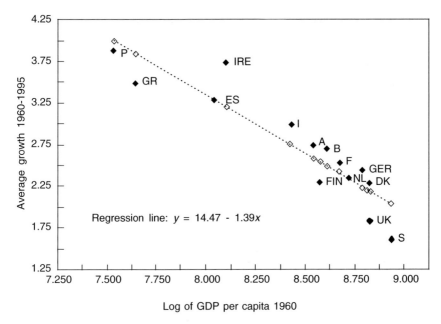

Figure 4.12 Convergence in the European Union
Key: A Austria, B Belgium, DK Denmark, ES Spain, F France, FIN Finland, GER Germany, GR Greece, I Italy, IRE Ireland, NL Netherlands, P Portugal, UK United Kingdom
Source: IMF, *International Financial Statistics* CD-ROM 1998; Gundlach (1998)

Latin America in the four decades until 1990. The countries are then characterized by different long-term equilibria.

Convergence clubs

Empirical analyses suggest that convergence can be more easily shown for a subset of countries and for a subset of regions of a country (Bode 1998). Some countries or some regions diverge; if these are excluded from the analysis of a set of countries or regions, the convergence process is stronger.

Sigma convergence

So far, the discussion about convergence has been based on the catching-up rate of the per capita income. This is called 'Beta convergence'. Sigma convergence, on the other hand, refers to the coefficient of variation of the per capita income expressed in logs. We have Sigma convergence if the per capita income coefficient of variation for a group of regions (or countries) decreases. Beta convergence and Sigma convergence are different measures. Beta convergence is geared to the growth rates of the per capita income over a period, Sigma convergence refers to the variance of the per capita incomes at two points in time. The two measures thus do not lead to identical statements about convergence processes: regions with a low per capita income can grow so strongly (high Beta convergence) that at the end of a period of comparison the variance of the per capita income is higher than at the beginning (Sigma divergence).

4.9 Growth as a process

Growth is a dynamic process where the accumulation of factors of production plays a major role, i.e. the accumulation of physical capital, of human capital and of technological knowledge. Accumulation means that there is a ratchet effect in economic growth with the process possibly occurring in a step-wise fashion. Growth is a continuous process which, if disturbed, will tend to resume. There is an immense diversity of historical experiences (David 1999), a wide diversity of outcome. Here are some aspects of the growth process.

A Schumpeterian process

Unlike in the model concept of a steady state, things do not grow in equal proportion; rather, there is some imbalance and an increase in diversity which keeps the process going. The process does not go smoothly, there is boom and bust, up and down, and there is a tremendous structural change in which existing sectors disappear and new sectors come into existence. In a Schumpeterian (1934) process of creative distruction existing capital becomes obsolete. The economy and society undergo profound changes, growth transforms society.

Growth leaders and countries that fall back

The analysis of catching-up and convergence processes says something about how fast economies close in on the countries with the highest level of wealth or the highest growth rate. But studies about catch-up processes do not answer the question how an economy manages to take the leading role in the growth process of the world economy (like the US relative to the UK in the last two centuries) and to reach a very high level of production per head. Apparently, a country has, in this case, the possibility to activate growth factors in some special manner.

The opposite image is that countries fall back, either absolutely or relatively. It is by no means a given fact that growth processes of economies go on and on. There can be stagnation and decline. Some examples are the centrally planned economies in the 1970s and 1980s until the systems finally collapsed, but also Sweden during the last 20 to 25 years, the UK after 1945, or Argentina which figured among the ten richest countries of the world at the end of the 19th century.

The new frontier

In the stagnation thesis of Alvin Hansen as illustrated by his student Higgins (Higgins 1959), the lack of a new frontier is the major reason for stagnation. In

Hansen's view, extending to the west in US history was such a new frontier opening up new investment opportunities, and his fear was the lack of such a frontier
in the future. Technological breakthroughs and the integration of the world economy with an increase in the size of the market may represent such a new frontier.

Path dependence

Initial conditions, like the capital stock per worker given in the initial situation (k_0)
which determines output per head and thus the starting point for the growth
process, can play a more important role than in the neoclassical model. Even in
the neoclassical model some aspects of endowment may not be overcome in the
growth process and economies may reach a different long-run equilibrium and,
consequently, may move on a different growth path. But the initial level may have
even greater importance. Thus, the technological knowledge available at a certain moment of time determines the direction in which the technology will
develop. Localization factors are another important example. In this sense,
growth processes are path-dependent. Added to this, the determinants of an initial constellation can interact. If a combination of factors is what matters in the
initial situation, economic policy may have to start at several points simultaneously to reach a more favorable growth path. In that sense of path dependence,
history matters.

Thresholds and the poverty trap

A different case of path dependence is that thresholds exist which must be overcome for growth to take place. Countries can find themselves in a trap of weak
growth from which they cannot find their way out. These aspects are relevant, for
instance, for growth processes in developing countries. Here, the path dependence of economic development plays a special role; a big push may be necessary
to get out of a trap (chapter 7).

Open societies

The organization of societies is an important aspect determining the growth
process. Whether societies are closed or open in the sense of Popper (1945) is of
major relevance for the growth process. An open society allows choice and individual freedom. This implies decentralization and subsidiarity. It also implies
competition as the principal element of organizing a society. Competition can be
interpreted as a discovery process (Hayek 1968) helping to find new technological, economic and institutional solutions. The alternative to competition is a cor-
porativistic approach where corporations like trade unions and employers'
associations play a decisive role in decision making. As a rule, this means that
insiders have an important weight in decision making, that the status quo is
protected and that new avenues, especially if unknown and uncertain, are not
pursued.

Self-enforcing institutional weakness

In Asia, the industrialized countries of Europe that fall back were (before the Asian crisis in 1997/98) ironically named NDCs, or newly declining countries, following the newly industrializing countries (NICs). Some of the industrialized countries, most prominently the major countries in continental Europe, France, Germany and Italy, have become rigid in their institutional structures; they seem to be unable to modernize their incentive systems, and of the conflicting aims of equity and efficiency they have chosen equity. This leads to an Olson-type inflexibility (Olson 1982). Internal institutional constraints make these countries incapable of reforming the social insurance systems or their regulatory framework of the labor market. Institutionally, they have started a silent erosion of their competitiveness.

Ageing societies

In many countries, such as in Germany, in Japan and – not to the same extent – in the US, a population has to be expected in the next decades that will be older on average. At the same time, the changing age structure is related to a decrease in population. All this causes a change in the demand structure (e.g. lower demand for housing, higher demand for leisure services and medical supply), a lower supply of labor and changed demands on the old-age insurance systems. These and other changes have feedback effects on the growth processes.

4.10 Particular topics of economic growth

Resource shortage

The stock of natural resources (Z) changes over time, satisfying

$$\overset{\circ}{Z} = -R + g(Z),$$

where $\overset{\circ}{Z}$ denotes the change of the resource stock in a period, R represents the resource extractions from nature in a period and $g(Z)$ is a natural growth function for renewable resources. In the case of non-renewable resources, this function is dropped, and the resource stock (Z) declines according to the equation

$$\overset{\circ}{Z} = -R$$

in every period.

Starting with a production function that contains natural resources as a production factor, the decisive question is whether the natural resource can be substituted. If this is not the case, nothing can be produced without natural resources, so that $Q = F(L, K, R = 0) = 0$. If substitution is possible, the non-renewable natural resource is substituted by other factors, and the production does not come to a standstill when the natural resource cannot be utilized anymore.

Sustainable development

The question of substitutability comes up in the discussion about sustainable development as well. Taking substitutability into account, the preservation of a given stock of resources is not required in a concept of sustainable development. It is then sufficient to pass a stock of production factors on to the future generation, with natural resources eventually being replaced by real (and human) capital.

Notes

1 For $\delta \to 0$, the marginal rate of capital productivity also approaches zero. Note that $\delta = 0$ violates the transversality condition; therefore $\delta > 0$ is a necessary condition for a solution to the maximization problem.
2 The production function then becomes $Y = Z^{\alpha+\beta}L^{1-\alpha-\beta}$.
3 When maximizing the present value of the utility

$$U = \int_0^\infty u(c_t)\, e^{-\delta t} dt$$

under the restrictions

$$f(k_t) = c_t + \dot{k}_t + nk_t$$

and

$$k_0 > 0 \text{ given,}$$

maximizing the Hamilton function

$$H_t = u(c_t) + \lambda_t[f(k_t) - nk_t - c_t]$$

yields

$$\frac{\partial H_t}{\partial c_t} = u'(c_t) - \lambda_t = 0,$$

$$\dot{\lambda}_t = \delta\lambda_t - \frac{\partial H_t}{\partial k_t} = \delta\lambda_t - \lambda_t f_k + \lambda_t n.$$

A dot over a variable indicates the derivative with respect to time. Differentiating the first marginal condition with respect to time and substituting the result into the second one yields, with $\lambda_t = u'(c_t)$ and $\dot{\lambda} = u''(c_t)\dot{c}$,

$$-\left[\frac{c_t u''(c_t)}{u'(c_t)}\right]\hat{c}_t = \delta + n - f_k(k_t).$$

In a growth equilibrium without technical progress, the rate of change in consumption is zero. Consequently, $f_k(k) = \delta + n$ holds. With technical progress, consumption in equilibrium grows with the progress rate ε.

4 For the equation of motion for consumption see the preceding note.

5 See Blanchard and Fischer, 1989, p. 69, in analogy to the closed economy.

6 The empirical analysis shows that factors like population growth and the investment ratios of real and human capital can make a significant contribution to the explanation of country-specific growth rates (Barro and Sala-i-Martin 1995, p. 382).

7 More precisely, the logarithm of the income relation y_0/y_0^* is halved.

8 According to the formula $t = \dfrac{\ln(y_0) - \ln(\alpha y_0^*)}{g^* - g} = \dfrac{\ln(y_0) - \ln(\alpha y_0^*) - \ln\alpha}{g^* - g}$. See Siebert (1995).

9 By rewriting this equation, $\ln(y_t) = (1 - e^{-\beta t})\ln\tilde{y} + e^{-\beta t}\ln(y_0)$ results. The half-life is defined by y_t reaching precisely a medium value between the original level y_0 and the steady-state level $\tilde{y}$. This is the case if $e^{-\beta t} = 0.5$. Solving for t, we obtain $t = -\ln(2)/\beta = 0.69/\beta$ for the half-life which is, in this formulation, independent of the original level. At a rate of convergence of 2 percent (3 percent), it takes 34 (23) years to halve the income difference. The half-life can also be calculated according to the formula $(1 - 0.02)^x = 0.5$.

10 At a constant savings rate (Solow model), $\beta = (1 - \alpha)(x + n + d)$ holds. If we insert $\alpha = 0.75$ for the elasticity of production to labor, $x = 0.02$ for the long-term growth rate, $n = 0.01$ for the population growth and $d = 0.05$ for the rate of wear and tear of capital, a value of 2 percent per year results for β.

11 The regression is taken from De Long (1988).

Part II

Monetary and financial markets

In Part II, we introduce money, different currencies and financial markets into the international division of labor. We analyze how economic processes are affected. If money were a veil it would have no impact on the real sphere of the economy. Since money is more than a veil the real economy is affected by such phenomena as inflation, exchange rate changes and fluctuations as well as currency and financial crises. An important issue is how financial crises come into existence and how they can be prevented.

5 Global money and currency markets

In national economies as well as in the world economy money plays an important role, as a unit of calculation, as a medium of exchange and as a store of value. Money reduces the costs of transaction. Its invention, i.e. the transition from an exchange economy to a money economy, must be interpreted as an important innovation to lower the costs of transaction. In the following, we start with a thought experiment assuming that there is a world money market with only one currency (section 5.1). As a result some simple conditions can be derived for an equilibrium on the global money market. But in reality this standardized money does not exist and thus the prices of currencies, the exchange rates, play an important role. The exchange rate can follow purchasing power parity (section 5.2), but it may also be determined by interest rate parity (section 5.3) and it may overshoot, at least in the short run (section 5.4). Expectations play a major role (section 5.5). Some empirical evidence on purchasing power parity is presented (section 5.6). Finally, the three major currencies of the world are discussed (section 5.7).

5.1 Global monetary equilibrium and national monetary policy

A thought experiment: world market equilibrium for a uniform currency

If there were a single currency for the world economy, an equilibrium of the world money market would require excess demand to be effectively zero for this currency, which we shall asume is the dollar:

$$E^{\$} = L^{\$}(i,Y,P,\ldots) - M^{\$}(\cdot) = 0 \qquad (5.1)$$

where E is excess demand for money, L nominal demand for money and M nominal money supply. If there were a disequilibrium, the factors influencing money demand and money supply, e.g. the interest rate (i) and world domestic product (Y), have to change until an equilibrium is reached. In principle, a monetary imbalance could also be removed if the world price level (P) were to increase if an excess money supply existed initially, so that the existing money supply is devalued. But this is not desirable: the price level has to remain stable.

The equilibrium on the global monetary market with two currencies

Of course, there is no single global currency. But we can imagine two countries that couple their currencies so firmly that the legally different currencies are perfect substitutes. During the time of the gold standard, national currencies almost came close to this scenario. To keep the argument simple, let us assume the exchange rate between two national currencies to be equal to one, so that the two countries' quantities of money $\tilde{M}$ and $\tilde{M}^*$ can be added up to the total quantity of money in the world $\tilde{M}^W$, i.e. $\tilde{M} + \tilde{M}^* = \tilde{M}^W$. The quantity of money in the world is given exogenously and is shown in Figure 5.1 by the straight line WW'. A single point of this straight line shows how the quantity of money in the world is allocated to the two countries.

The equilibrium allocation of the quantity of money in the world is determined by the demand for money in the two countries. Assume that the nominal demand for money is determined by transaction purposes only, i.e. it is governed by nominal national income ($L = kp_1 Y$ for the domestic country and $L^* = kp_2 Y^*$ for the foreign country, Ethier 1995). This is in accordance with the Cambridge equation. For simplicity let us assume that the coefficients of transaction k, k^* are equal in the two countries. Real national income in the domestic country (Y) and in the foreign country (Y^*) are considered to be exogenously given. Moreover, it is assumed that the domestic and the foreign country are both completely specialized in the production of their export goods. Then, the equilibrium of the

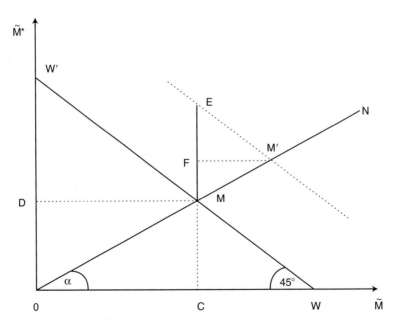

Figure 5.1 Equilibrium of the quantity of money in the world with two currencies

money market in the domestic country is given by $\tilde{M} = kp_1Y$. For the foreign country it is $\tilde{M}^* = kp_2^*Y^*$.

Dividing the conditions for the national equilibria by one another, the equilibrium allocation of both quantities of money between the two countries is given by:

$$\frac{\tilde{M}^*}{\tilde{M}} = \frac{kp_2^*Y^*}{kp_1Y} = \frac{Y^*}{pY} \tag{5.2}$$

In the monetary equilibrium, the ratio between the two quantities of money $(\tilde{M}^*/\tilde{M})$ is determined by the ratio of the national incomes and the relative price $p = p_1/p_2^*$. National income is determined on the supply side in the real sphere of the economy. The relative price is established in the equilibrium on the global product market, which is also in the real sphere. In Figure 5.1, the equilibrium ratio of the quantities of money is given by the angle α of the straight line ON, where $\tan \alpha = Y^*/pY$.

The equilibrium on the global monetary market and real economic equilibrium

In the world market equilibrium, the transaction demand for money has to be equal to the world money supply (equation 5.3). All variables in the demand-for-money equation 5.3 are determined in the real sphere of the economy, except for the domestic price level (p_1). Consequently, the domestic price level is proportional to the quantity of money in the world, $\tilde{M}^W$. When the quantity of money expands, the domestic price level has to rise as well. According to the quantity theory of money, the expansion of the quantity of money influences the price level.

$$k(p_1Y + p_2^*Y^*) = kp_1(Y + Y^*/p) = \tilde{M} + \tilde{M}^* = \tilde{M}^W \tag{5.3}$$

Under the assumption of two currencies with a fixed exchange rate, the increase in the price level is not limited to the domestic country. The price level in the foreign country increases as well. The money market equilibrium (point M in Figure 5.1) is coupled to the real economic equilibrium. If, for example, the foreign country raises its quantity of money (by the distance ME), then the world money market line is shifted outward. In point E, foreigners keep a larger quantity of money than they need for their transactions. They get rid of this excess money by demanding goods from the home country. The home country has a surplus in its balance of trade; thus its quantity of money is increased. Therefore the domestic price level has to rise. The foreign country has a balance of payments deficit; its money surplus is reduced. At the end of the adjustment process, the same real economic equilibrium (point M′) is reached for both currencies, but the price level of both countries has increased.

This simple formulation makes it clear that a national monetary policy that expands the money supply beyond the production potential, leads to an increase of the price level, i.e. to inflation. Under the conditions of the model, inflation also occurs in the country in which money supply is not changed by monetary policy.

5.2 The exchange rate and purchasing power parity

The exchange rate

What so far has been vaguely described as the ratio between two currencies, is the exchange rate. The exchange rate e is defined as the ratio of a unit of one currency per unit of another currency. Using the euro (€) and the dollar ($) as an example, the dimension is €/$. It indicates how many euros have to be given up in order to obtain one unit of US$.

From the very simple scenario of a fixed exchange rate in the previous section we can derive an obvious conclusion: whenever two national currencies have a fixed exchange rate, a stable price level in both countries can only exist, if the real money supply stays in line with real economic conditions. Under static conditions, the relative money supply is determined by the relative price of national outputs and by the ratio of national incomes. In a growing economy, the relevant point of reference for the increase of the money supply which is equivalent with price level stability is the growth of the production potential.

In the following, the exchange rate is no longer regarded as fixed but as flexible. In trade equilibrium, the law of one price is valid

$$p_1 = p_1^* e \text{ with the dimensions } €/Q_1 = (\$/Q_1) \cdot (€/\$).$$

From this there follows for the exchange rate

$$e = p_1/p_1^* \text{ as well as } \hat{e} = \hat{p}_1 - \hat{p}_1^*, \tag{5.4}$$

where ^ indicates the rate of change. Equation 5.4 is the purchasing power parity, with p_1 and p_1^* being interpreted as price levels of the two economies. A currency like the euro depreciates, which means that e rises, if the price level increases more in Europe than in the US; it appreciates, which means e decreases, if the price level increases less in Europe than in the US.

Consider now the case of complete specialization of both countries, for instance if the home country (Europe) specializes in good 1 and the foreign country (USA) specializes in good 2. Then the exchange rate can be defined as the relative price for two currencies where p_1 and p_1^* can again be interpreted as the price level in the two countries. But besides the prices for the goods 1 and 2 the relative price p also has to be taken into consideration; it is once again defined by the world market equilibrium. Hence, the exchange rate is now defined as:

$$e\left[\frac{€}{\$}\right] = \frac{p_1\left[\frac{€}{Q_1}\right]}{p_2^*\left[\frac{\$}{Q_2}\right] \cdot p\left[\frac{Q_2}{Q_1}\right]} \cdot \tag{5.5}$$

According to the concept of purchasing power parity, fluctuations of the exchange rate can be explained by the variation of the ratio of the two currencies. Equation 5.5 is shown graphically in Figure 5.2b. The tangent of α is given by $1/p$. Thus, the exchange rate is given by the purchasing power parity.

Monetary equilibrium with flexible exchange rates

Let us now look at the monetary equilibrium with flexible exchange rates. If both sides of the money market equilibrium condition of the foreign country are multiplied by the exchange rate, then we have $e\tilde{M}^* = kep_2^*Y^*$. Dividing the conditions for the national equilibria by each other, we obtain

$$e\,\frac{\tilde{M}^*}{\tilde{M}} = \frac{kep_2^*Y^*}{kp_1Y} = \frac{Y^*}{pY}. \tag{5.6}$$

Equation 5.6 describes the monetary equilibrium of the domestic and the foreign country with explicit consideration of the two currencies (i.e. of the exchange rate). With a given relative price p, with given national incomes in the domestic and the foreign country and with a given money supply in the two countries there is only one exchange rate w at which the money supply of both countries is equal to the demand for money: the product of the exchange rate and the relative money supplies is constant, Y^*/pY.

In Figure 5.2a, monetary equilibrium is shown with two currencies and a flexible exchange rate. The horizontal axis depicts the money supply of the two countries as a ratio. The distance OG denotes the exogenously given relative money supply between the foreign and the home country ($\tilde{M}^*/\tilde{M}$); the vertical line GM shows the relative supply. The curve through MM' indicates the relative money demand. Equation 5.6 can also be written as a hyperbolic equation $L^*/L = \tilde{M}^*/\tilde{M} = a/e$ with the constant $a = Y^*/pY$. The monetary equilibrium M is marked by the point of intersection of the two curves.

The equilibrium in the real economy is described in Figure 5.2b. According to equation 5.5, there is a unique relation between the exchange rate and the ratio of nominal prices p_1/p_2^* for a given relative price which is determined in the exchange equilibrium, i.e. $e = p_1/p_2^*p$. This relation is determined by $\tan \alpha = 1/p$ or line OL in Figure 5.2b. It portrays purchasing power parity.

Assume, now, that the money supply $\tilde{M}^*$ rises in the foreign country (US). Then the foreign currency (\$) is devalued and the long-term equilibrium moves from M to M'. The expansion of the money supply also results in an increase of the goods prices in the foreign country. In Figure 5.2b, the economy moves from

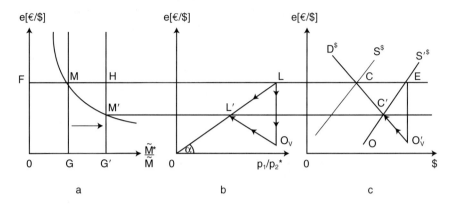

Figure 5.2 Monetary equilibrium, purchasing power parity and the foreign currency
market

point L to point L′. Thus we have two changes: the price level in the foreign
country rises and its currency depreciates. The currency of the home country
appreciates and by this the domestic (European) price level is insulated against
the expansion of the money supply in the foreign country.[1]

The foreign currency market and the balance of payments

Monetary equilibrium and purchasing power parity are also related to the foreign
currency market and to the balance-of-payments position of a country. The foreign currency market explains the demand for and the supply of the foreign currency (\$) as a function of the exchange rate (Figure 5.2c). It is assumed here that
the supply curve of foreign currency has a positive slope and does not bend back-
wards. Excess demand for the foreign currency $E^{\$}$,

$$E^{\$}(e) = D^{\$}(e) - S^{\$}(e), \tag{5.7}$$

is defined by the difference between demand for US dollars and the supply
thereof. Demand for and supply of US dollars can easily be explained if we consider commodity exchange only. Then US dollars are demanded by European
importers (IM^{EU}); and US dollars are supplied by Americans who want to import
from Europe (IM^{US}). Thus, excess demand in the foreign currency market is
equivalent to a balance-of-trade disequilibrium with

$$D^{\$}(e) - S^{\$}(e) = IM^{EU} - IM^{US} = IM^{EU} - X^{EU} \tag{5.8}$$

if it is assumed that the world consists of two countries only and that US imports
are identical to EU exports ($IM^{US} = X^{EU}$).

Assume now that the US money supply is expanded. At a given exchange rate OF, this disturbs monetary equilibrium M in Figure 5.2a. It also leads to an excess supply of foreign currency (US dollar), CE in Figure 5.2c. This is equivalent to a trade deficit for the US. Americans swap excess money (which they do not want) for European goods. This process takes time. The US dollar depreciates and the price level in the US rises until the excess money supply disappears (point M' in Figure 5.2a). The purchasing power parity reaches its new equilibrium (point L' in Figure 5.2b), the foreign exchange market clears (point C' in Figure 5.2c) and the deficit in the trade account disappears.

5.3 Interest rate parity and portfolio equilibrium

A portfolio equilibrium with respect to domestic and foreign financial assets (such as bonds) exists when the expected rate of return on assets in the home country is equal to the expected rate of return on assets in the foreign country. The rate of return on financial investment in the home country is given by the domestic interest rate, whereas the rate of return on investment in the foreign country is defined by the foreign interest rate plus the expected appreciation gains (interest rate parity),

$$1 + i = (1 + i^*)\, e^e/e_0, \tag{5.9}$$

where e^e is the expected exchange rate at some future date and e_0 is the spot rate. This is also written as

$$i = i^* + \hat{e}^e. \tag{5.10}$$

Here $\hat{e}^e$ indicates the expected rate of change of the exchange rate, i.e. the expected devaluation ($\hat{e}^e > 0$) or appreciation ($\hat{e}^e < 0$). The expected rate of change of the exchange rate is defined as ($\hat{e} - e_0)/e_0$. The interest rate refers to short-term or long-term financial assets.

If the domestic currency is expected to be devalued within the next year ($\hat{e}^e > 0$), then investing in the foreign country has the advantage that the money invested is worth more at the end of the investment period. If, for example, a devaluation by 2 percent of the domestic currency is expected, then for the portfolio equilibrium a domestic interest rate of 5 percent is compatible with a foreign interest rate of 3 percent. Therefore, in the portfolio equilibrium the foreign interest rate can be correspondingly lower than the domestic interest rate. If, on the other hand, a revaluation ($\hat{e}^e < 0$) of the domestic currency is expected to take place, then the investment in the foreign country suffers a loss in value. The foreign interest rate has to be correspondingly higher.

5.4 Exchange rate overshooting

The exchange rate has to adjust, i.e. a currency has to devalue or to appreciate, when at a given exchange rate excess supply or excess demand exists on the foreign exchange market. If the disequilibrium in the foreign currency market is due to an excessive money supply, i.e. the money supply has increased significantly more than it should relative to the growth of the productive potential, there are several ways in which the imbalance can be reduced. One is by goods arbitrage in the sense of purchasing power parity, as described above.

A disequilibrium can also be eliminated by capital flows, especially by restructuring a given portfolio (Dornbusch 1976). In this case, an overshooting of the exchange rate may occur if the prices of goods are sluggish in the short term: consider a monetary expansion in the foreign country. This implies that people hold more money than they want to. Their portfolio is not optimal. They react and adjust their portfolio. Instantaneously, they demand bonds and bond prices in the foreign country rise. The interest rate in the foreign country falls and demand shifts to the bonds of the domestic country. As a result, the demand for the domestic currency increases abruptly, there is an excess supply of foreign currency. Consequently, the foreign currency is immediately devalued as a result of the change in the money supply (point in Figure 5.2b). Note that the interest rate parity indicates the overshooting of the exchange rate. In equation 5.9, interpret e^c as the exchange rate expected in the long run equilibrium, i.e. from equation 5.6:

$$ e^c = \frac{Y^*}{pY} \bigg/ \frac{\tilde{M}^*}{\tilde{M}} . $$

Since $i^* < i$, according to the interest rate parity of equation 5.8, we must have $e_0 < e^c$ which means that we have an overshooting of the exchange rate relative to a long-run equilibrium.

Only gradually does this devaluation have an impact on the flows of goods. Devaluation improves price competitiveness of the foreign country, which then develops an export surplus. Domestic importers have to obtain foreign currency which works against the devaluation of the foreign currency. The price level in the foreign country rises. Finally, purchasing power parity is reached again (movement from point O_v to point L'). Apparently, the exchange rate can deviate from purchasing power parity in the short term. It can overshoot temporarily.

Note that the eventual long-run equilibrium of the exchange rate according to purchasing power parity is not a sufficient intertemporal fix point to prevent overshooting. Even assuming that people know that the purchasing power parity holds in the long run, the time needed to reach the long-run equilibrium allows the short-term flows to deviate from the long-run equilibrium.

5.5 The role of expectations

Exchange-rate change expectations

If the condition for the portfolio equilibrium is not fulfilled, the portfolio is adjusted, which implies capital flows. If for instance $i > i^* + \hat{e}^c$, then the rate of return on portfolio investment in the home country is higher than in the foreign country. For instance, a devaluation of the foreign currency may be anticipated, because a less favorable economic development is expected in the foreign country, or because of greater political instability or of rising public debt with the expectation of policy uncertainty. This will be an incentive for adjusting the portfolio in favor of the domestic assets. Another possible reason for the anticipation of a devaluation might be an excessive increase in the money supply of the foreign country.

The interplay between interest rate parity and purchasing power parity

Purchasing power parity and interest rate parity interact. The interest rate parity $i = i^* + \hat{e}^e$ determines the capital flows, the purchasing power parity determines the exchange rate expectations, $\hat{e}^e = \hat{p}^e - \hat{p}^{e*}$. Combining both equations, exchange rate expectations have an influence on interest rate parity, so that $i = i^* + \hat{p}^e - \hat{p}^{e*}$ holds (Figure 5.3). If people expect a stronger rise of the price level in the foreign country than in the home country, they expect a devaluation of the foreign currency. Of course, the anticipation of the exchange rate change is not determined by changes in the price level only, but also by a number of other factors, e.g. by political instability. But usually these factors also have a long-term effect on the price level.

An example for the interplay between the interest rate parity and the purchasing power parity is the European exchange rate mechanism (ERM) in the European Monetary System (EMS) before EMU started. On the one hand, the interest rate parity set in motion capital flows as soon as economic policy of a single country erred away from the stability target. The markets quickly required a risk premium on the national interest rates and eventually induced a devaluation of the national currency. Therefore, interest rate parity determined the pain of instability; it served as a control mechanism.

On the other hand, the purchasing power parity shaped the exchange rate expectations, which entered into interest rate parity. If a larger price differential between countries developed, market participants expected that the exchange rate would have to be adjusted. Governments anticipated the consequences of a stability-averse policy which were made explicit by this mechanism, and consequently they had to aim at stability. An example of this controlling force is the economic policy situation in France in 1983. The Mitterrand government had to

$$i = i^* + \hat{e}^e$$

$$\uparrow$$

$$\hat{e}^e = \hat{p}^e - \hat{p}^{e*}$$

Figure 5.3 Interest rate parity and purchasing power parity completely reverse its economic policy approach which had led to budget and balance-of-payments deficits, a rising price level and a devaluation of the French franc.

Defending an exchange rate by interest rate policy

A country that wants to defend its weak currency may have to take recourse to high interest rates in order to prevent portfolio capital from leaving the country. A case in point is the 500% interest rate that Sweden used in the days of financial crisis in September 1992 in order to prevent the outflow of short-term capital and in order to defend the Swedish krona. Another example are the high real interest rates of 30% of Brazil prior to the devaluation of the *real* in January 1999. Applying interest rate parity, a high interest-rate differential $i - i^*$ is needed to compensate negative expectations with respect to the domestic currency. Assuming a given expected depreciated exchange rate at a future date e_t, interest rate parity $i - i^* = (e_t - e_0)/e_0$ indicates how high i must be to prevent e_0 from rising. For example, if the expected exchange rate $e_t : 100$ and if the spot rate $e_0 : 5$ is to be defended and if the interest rate i^* is given as 6 percent, the domestic interest rate must be chosen as 25 percent in order to prevent a capital outflow, so that $25 - 6 = (100 - 5)/5$.

In 1997/98, the Russian rouble was devalued (the exchange rate rouble/US dollar increased). There was an attempt to prevent the devaluation of the rouble by high nominal interest rates up to more than 100 percent in the spring of 1998. Such a high interest rate, however, did not prevent the rouble from being devalued (Figure 5.4).

In the case of South Korea, it seems that a high interest rate relative to the US has (together with other measures and the IMF stand-by credit) helped to keep the Korean won from depreciating further (Figure 5.5). The reason for the different reaction of Korea can be seen in better fundamentals relative to Russia.

Defending an exchange rate by a high interest rate poses quite a burden on an economy. Private investment including construction is suppressed, and this impedes economic growth. Therefore, such a policy can only be followed temporarily in order to establish confidence. A policy of high interest rates is not sustainable in the long run. Moreover, the exchange rate must be in line with the fundamentals.

5.6 Long-term purchasing power parity versus medium-term deviations: the empirical evidence

Every day foreign currency transactions on the foreign exchange markets of the world amount to a volume of 2 trillion US$. Compared to this, the world trade volume of a complete year amounts to only 5.6 trillion US$ (1997). The world trade volume of a single year is reached on the foreign currency markets in two days. There may be a lot of double counting and counter-transactions, for instance hedging, which have to be excluded to determine the net transactions.

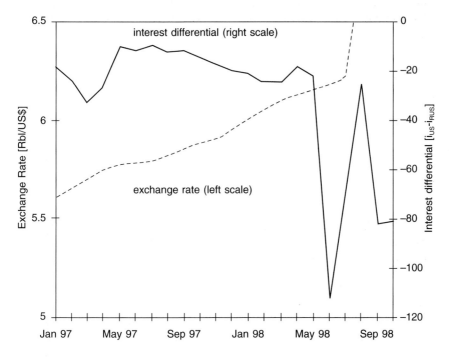

Figure 5.4 Russia: exchange rate and interest rate[a] with respect to the US, 1997–1998
[a] Russia: overnight interbank rate; United States: one month interbank rate
Source: Central Bank of the Russian Federation, *Bulletin of Banking Statistics*, various issues 1998; Datastream 1998; IMF, *International Financial Statistics*, 1998

And yet, it is undisputed that capital flows can influence the exchange rate in a way quite different from the transactions of goods. Therefore the exchange rate does not follow purchasing power parity in the short run. Empirically, we observe such divergences from purchasing power parity.

For the DM/$ exchange rate a remarkable deviation can be found for the time from 1980 to 1985 when the US dollar appreciated, but in the long run the exchange rate between the D-mark and the US dollar follows purchasing power parity (Figure 5.6). The exchange rate between the deutsche mark and the Italian lira deviated from purchasing power parity in the European Exchange Rate Mechanism (Figure 5.7). But when the discrepancy between the national developments became too large, the exchange rate had to give in. In the end, purchasing power parity came through. When the lira left the European Exchange Rate Mechanism in the summer of 1992, it strongly devalued. The Italian lira rejoined the European Exchange Rate Mechanism in the fall of 1996. The expectations that Italy would be one of the founding members of the European Monetary Union led to a revaluation of the lira.

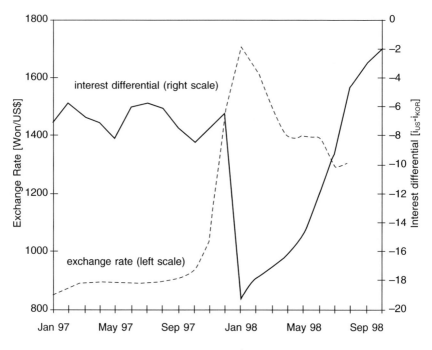

Figure 5.5 Korea: exchange rate and interest rate[a] with respect to the US, 1997–1998
[a] Korea: overnight call rate; United States: one month interbank rate
Source: Datastream 1998; IMF, *International Financial Statisitcs*, 1998

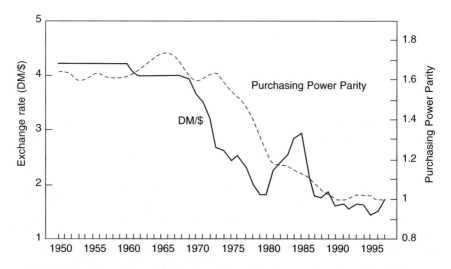

Figure 5.6 DM/$ rate and purchasing power parity[a]
[a] Consumer price index Germany to consumer price index USA, 1990 = 100, annual averages
Source: IMF, *International Financial Statistics*, July 1998

DM/1,000 Lira

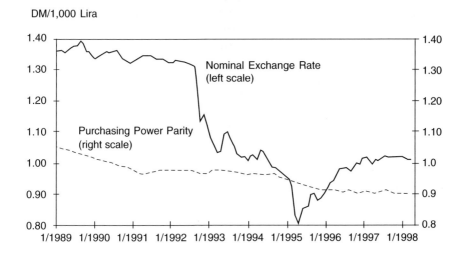

Figure 5.7 Exchange rate DM/lira and purchasing power parity[a]
[a] Purchasing power parity: consumer price index Germany over consumer price index Italy (1990 = 100)
Source: Deutsche Bundesbank, *Monthly Reports*; IMF, *International Finanical Statistics 1998*

Purchasing power parity reigns in the long run. This should be no surprise since in the long run all sorts of instability will eventually be reflected in the price level and thus in the exchange rate. Regarding changes of the price level over periods of ten to twenty years, a correlation between changes of the exchange rate and differences between inflation rates becomes visible. In Figure 5.8, there are recorded the appreciation of the D-mark (vertical axis) and the differences of the inflation rate between different countries and Germany from the second quarter 1973 to the first quarter 1998. It is obvious that purchasing power parity is valid for this time period.

Purchasing power parity holds for the exchange rates in the long run of ten or twenty years, but when a disturbance occurs the alignment to this long-term tendency takes time. Empirical studies show that divergences from a filtered trend are reduced only by a rate of 15 percent per year. The half-life, i.e. the time period in which the divergence halves on average, is 3 to 5 years (Rogoff 1996). At the same time, the short-run divergences are high and volatile.

Figure 5.9 shows monthly data for the DM-$ rate and a trend line using a Hodrick–Prescott filter for the period 1970–1998. The US dollar depreciated against the deutsche mark in the 1970s, appreciated in the first half of the 1980s and then depreciated again. The Hodrick–Prescott filter (Hodrick and Prescott 1997), basically a moving average with variable weights, uses a smoothing parameter that determines the maximum deviation of the monthly rate from the filtered trend: the higher the parameter value, the more linear is the trend and the larger are the permitted deviations. The parameter level also limits the maximum

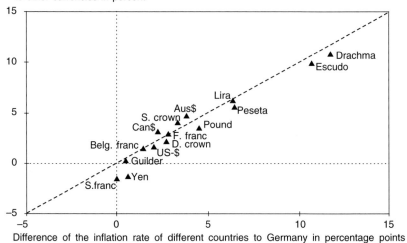

Appreciation of the D-Mark relative
to other currencies in percent

Difference of the inflation rate of different countries to Germany in percentage points

Figure 5.8 Inflation and exchange rate changes of some important currencies 1973–1998
Note: Geometrical average of the period ranging from the 2nd quarter 1973 until 1st quarter 1998
(Austral. $, Pound, Yen, Lira, Escudo, Can$, and Dan. K until 4th quarter 1997)
Source: IMF, *International Financial Statistics,* July 1998

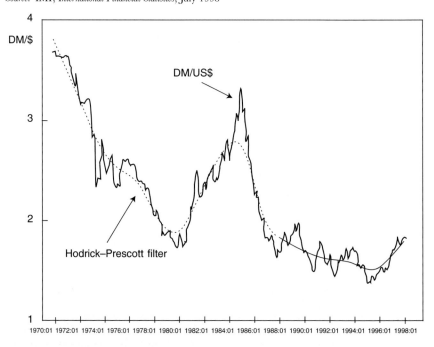

Figure 5.9 DM/$ rate[a] and a filtered trend
[a]Monthly Data: January 1970–April 1998, Hodrick–Prescott with smoothing parameter: 14400
Source: IMF, *International Financial Statistics,* July 1998, own calculations

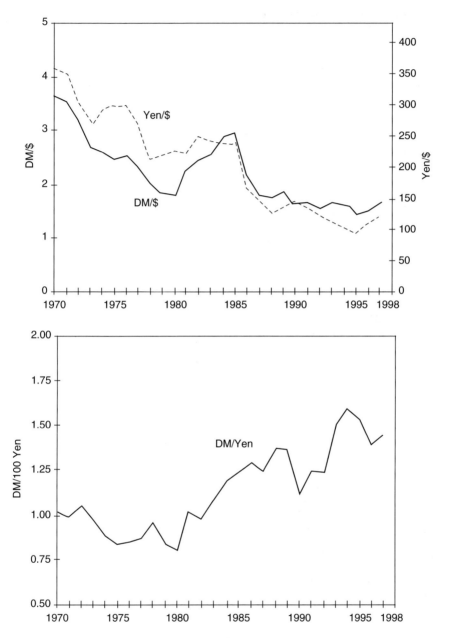

Figure 5.10 US dollar, deutsche mark and yen[a]
[a]Yearly averages
Source: IMF, *International Financial Statistics 1998*; Deutsche Bundesbank, *Monthly reports,* various issues

frequency level, or volatility, of deviations that pass through the filter; deviations above this volatility limit are evened out.

5.7 The three major currencies of the world

The values of the three major currencies of the world, the US$, the deutsche mark and the yen, reflect fundamental changes in the three major economies, including differences in the strength of economic growth, long-term shifts in comparative advantages and trade flows, and switches in capital flows, as well as other phenomena such as synchronous or asynchronous business cycles between the countries and differences in stabilization policies, i.e. in monetary, fiscal and wage policies. Moreover, institutional arrangements for the exchange rate are of relevance.

In the 1950s, 1960s and 1970s, the catching-up process of Germany and Japan and the growth of their exports worked towards appreciation of the DM and the yen. During the 1950s and 1960s, the exchange rates between the US$ and the deutsche mark and the yen were revalued at intervals, but remained relatively stable due to the Bretton Woods system. From 1970, both currencies appreciated against the US dollar (Figure 5.10). In the 1970s, Japan was exposed more intensively to the oil crisis, so that the yen had to depreciate temporarily. In the first part of the 1980s, the US dollar appreciated. After 1985, the DM and the yen gained value relative to the dollar. After 1980, the DM depreciated against the yen.

Notes

1 There is a complete insulation of the home country, if p_2^* rises proportional to $\tilde{M}^*$ and inversely proportional to e, so that $\tilde{M}$ in the home country as well as p_1 remain unchanged.

6 Financial crises versus stable currencies

Portfolio capital is highly mobile. An optimal portfolio is a delicate equilibrium (section 6.1). Expectations play an important role and if they lose touch with fundamentals a bubble develops (section 6.2). A divergence between the nominal and the real exchange rate can be a signal that a currency crisis is in the making (section 6.3). Some recent currency crises are surveyed in section 6.4. How to prevent a crisis is discussed in section 6.5. The role of the IMF is the topic of section 6.6. Controlling capital flows is proposed by some (section 6.7). Finally, approaches to stabilizing the exchange rate are described (sections 6.8 and 6.9).

6.1 An optimal portfolio

Interest rate parity is a portfolio equilibrium condition of finanical assets in different currencies. Assets may be all sorts of interest-rate-bearing financial assets such as money market funds, bonds or shares. Neglecting risk and considering a closed economy, the rate of return of holding money in interest-bearing form like money market funds, i.e. the interest rate i, should be equal to the rates of return on other financial assets in a portfolio equilibrium. For instance, the rate of return on bonds is the interest rate on bonds (i_B) plus the rate of change in the bond price, $\hat{p}_B$. Similarly, the rate of return on shares is given by the dividend, d, relative to the share price and the rate of change in the share price, $\hat{p}_{SH}$. Besides financial assets, a portfolio may also include real estate where the rate of return is the change in the real estate price, $\hat{p}_{RS}$. Finally, storable commodities like natural resources also have a rate of return, namely the rate of change in the resource price, $\hat{p}_R$. Incorporating the interest rate on bonds and dividends into the bond price (zero bonds), the condition for an optimal portfolio is

$$i = \hat{p}_B = \hat{p}_{SH} = \hat{p}_{RS} = \hat{p}_R. \tag{6.1}$$

Price changes become relevant for portfolio decisions whenever stock variables are involved. This means that commodities, factors of production or financial assets are considered that are durable and have a longer life than a single period. In that case, an intertemporal decision has to be made as to when to sell, buy, hold or use the product or resource in question.

In an open economy, currency changes have to be taken into consideration as well. The optimal portfolio requires, for instance for shares, that the rate of change of the domestic share price is equal to the rate of change of foreign shares plus the currency gain

$$\hat{p}_{SH} = \hat{p}^*_{SH} = \hat{e}^{\,e} \tag{6.2}$$

where $\hat{p}_{SH}$, $\hat{p}^*_{SH}$ denote the rate of change in the price of domestic and foreign shares.

Such a portfolio equilibrium very much depends on expectations. If people expect prices and currencies to behave according to a certain trend, their expectations will influence their market behavior and reinforce the expected trend (self-fulfilling expectations). If expectations change abruptly, economic variables will adjust quickly if possible. Thus, portfolio capital is said to have the memory of an elephant, the heart of a roe and the quick legs of an antelope. If a portfolio equilibrium is disturbed, capital flows will reverse.

6.2 Speculative bubbles

Actual product prices, real estate prices and share prices can differ from medium-term or long-term fundamental values. At the root of such a divergence are expectations of rising goods prices, of basic material prices, real estate prices and share prices. These expectations are reinforced when the prices actually do increase (self-fulfilling expectations). The exchange rate can also deviate from the mid-term or long-term value. The value of a currency can change, for example, without the central bank changing the usual expansion of the money supply. If actual prices deviate more and more from the medium- or long-term value we speak of a speculative bubble. In this situation, self-fulfilling expectations move the price of a good or a currency away from the equilibrium level, which is determined by long-term fundamental factors.

Historic examples

Historic examples are the Mississippi Bubble, the South Pacific Bubble and the Dutch Tulipomania (Garber 1989, 1990). In the tulipomania bubble, the price of tulip bulbs rose increasingly during the years 1634–1637. Some special tulip bulbs reached a value equivalent to a house. At the end, the prices collapsed.

The Japanese stock and real estate markets between 1986 and 1990 can also be mentioned as an example of a speculative bubble. Due to a strong revaluation of the yen, the strong expansion of the money supply in Japan during the 1980s did not lead to an increase of the cost of living (i.e. there was only a minor increase in the consumer price level, at least in the case of the traditional goods). The additional liquidity, however, found its way into the demand for shares and real estate, so that these prices rose. In 1990, the speculative bubble burst, the Nikkei stock index fell from almost 39,000 in December 1989 to 20,000 in January 1990 and moved further downward from then on. The prices for real estate went down dramatically as well. The banks entered a state of crisis because of reduced asset values (Figure 6.1).

Some preconditions for a bubble

There are several prerequisites for the appearance of a bubble. One is that the valuation of goods, real estate assets and other financial assets can change over time. A second is that, apart from the spot market, there has to be a futures market, even though it may be only informal. This means that expectations of future price trends have an influence on the current price. A third condition is that expectations are reinforced. For instance, in an open economy the anticipation of a revaluation of the (domestic) currency implies the import of short-term portfolio capital, so that the currency is actually revalued. Thus, the expectation is (at least temporarily) confirmed. Finally, if there were a day of settlement in the future which was already known today, such a speculative bubble could not start because the future prices would be taken into consideration by expectations. Such an intertemporal[1] fix point would control the expectations and link them to the real economy. Without such a fix point, it is advantageous for every single individual to follow the herd. For instance, assume a currency appreciates. It will keep on appreciating as long as all participants expect it to do so and keep on buying the currency.

In order to start a bubble, there must be a stimulus in the initial situation. One such stimulus can be a change in expectations, for instance that oil prices will be

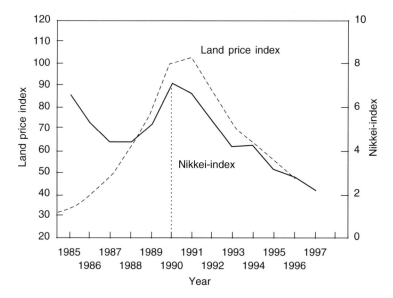

Figure 6.1 The Japanese bubble
Source: Statistics Bureau, Management and Coordination Agency, Government of Japan, *Statistical Yearbook of Japan 1993* and *1997*; Datastream

rising due to an increased actual scarcity or that additional gold will be found after the first nugget has been discovered. A specific stimulus may be an excessive expansion of the money supply. This may lead to an inflationary bubble in which the price level rises, eventually ending in a hyper-inflation. Alternatively, the excessive money supply may not affect the price index of traditional goods very much, but may show up predominately in the real estate and share prices and start a real estate and stock market bubble. Credit expansion is a usual mechanism going hand in hand with money expansion and feeding the price spiral, for instance in the real estate sector. This was the case in Mexico as well as in Thailand.

Deregulation of financial markets may make it easier for a bubble to arise. If a country's capital account is liberalized and if its banking system does not have the appropriate regulation, banks may have too easy access to foreign liquidity which then can be fed into the real estate sector. This was one reason for the financial crisis in Thailand in 1997. A similar phenomenon could be observed in Sweden (Lindbeck *et al.* 1994). Thus, there is an optimal mix of institutional reforms. A specific measure like liberalizing the current account may not be first-best if not accompanied by appropriate other institutional changes (complementarity of institutional reforms).

When the bubble bursts

At some time during the process, the speculative bubble will reach a point when people realize that the process is not sustainable. Then the expectations change. The economic agents sell their shares, real estate, natural resources, inducing prices to fall and making other market participants adjust their portfolios as well. Or banks are reluctant to renew short-term credits when expectations change. For instance, with problems in the real economy of South Korea in 1997, Japanese banks, under pressure themselves, were no longer prepared to renew credits to Korean firms.

Some reinforcing mechanisms

There are several mechanisms which reinforce the collapse of a bubble:

Balance sheet mechanics

As soon as prices are falling, the asset side of bank balance sheets is affected. Bonds and stocks lose value, and the asset side shrinks; eventually loans and advances to other banks or to customers change their risk status (Table 6.1). Banks may not have enough coverage for their credits, and they have to start restraining credits (credit crunch). An example is the magic number of 15,000 for the Nikkei index which was considered necessary to be surpassed at the end of March 1998 in order for the Japanese banking system not to get into trouble. The position of a bank is also affected if customers withdraw deposits. The balance

Table 6.1 Balance sheet

Assets	Liabilities
Cash reserves	Deposits by banks
Loans and advances to banks	Customer deposits
Loans and advances to customers	Securitized liabilities
Bonds	Equity
Stocks	

sheet mechanism is a ripple effect working its way through the banking system. It is aggravated when the majority of the banks are affected by the same phenomenon.

Balance sheet mechanics operates within a country when problems of one bank spill over to other banks. It is also relevant between countries. An example in 1998 was the credits given by Japanese banks to Korean firms. When Korean firms defaulted, the asset side of Japanese banks was affected. In addition, exchange rate changes play a major role, for instance when bonds or stocks in foreign currency lose value due to a depreciation of the foreign currency.

Running out of foreign currency reserves

As long as foreign currency reserves are sufficiently large to defend a currency, market participants will not attack the currency. As soon as reserves are exhausted, the value of the currency will fall very quickly. Moreover, when markets become aware of an increased risk that reserves will be depleted, they start to react. Losing reserves indicates that it is becoming more difficult to finance a current account deficit. Consequently, the exchange rate has to give, the currency depreciates.

Threshold values and change in expectations

For a number of reasons, expectations can change. A case in point is critical parameters in software programs for portfolio investment. Another case is when threshold values are surpassed and market participants start to ask questions about sustainability.

Contagion

A change in expectations can be contagious in a psychological interpretation. A problem showing up in one country leads to the question whether a similar problem may develop elsewhere. This triggers uncertainty and a more cautious portfolio investment and less generous credits. Once a general mood has spread and once the herd is running, other countries are affected.

The impact of the bubble

A speculative bubble may be limited to the financial sector, but in most cases it has an impact on the real sphere of the economy as well. For instance, assume the real estate sector and the construction sector are overexpanding. Too many factors of production are attracted to construction, leading to a distorted allocation of resources. When the real estate bubble bursts the construction sector collapses. In other bubbles, too many resources may have been placed into specific production sectors, for instance the oil industry. When prices fall, the resource allocation is not sustainable. The misallocations have to be corrected after the speculative bubble has burst.

The sustainability of the balance-of-payments position

A bubble will burst when it becomes apparent that it is not sustainable. An important restraint is the balance of payments, more specifically the current account. A bubble in a country will normally be associated with an inflow of short-term capital. This means that a current account deficit is financed by capital imports. The nominal exchange rate is supported by capital imports. Apparently, it is difficult to separate the bubble from a healthy environment in which a capital inflow finances capital accumulation. Then, a current account deficit is sustainable because capital accumulation will be the basis for repaying debt and serving the interest payments in the future. What are potential clues that a situation is not sustainable?

- A negative current account balance may be a warning signal if capital imports are used for consumption purposes or for non-investive government spending (such as social policies).
- A negative current account is a warning signal if it is associated with a large budget deficit of the government.
- A negative current account is a warning signal if it is associated with an excessive increase in the domestic money supply.
- A negative current account is a warning signal if it is associated with a diverging development of the nominal and the real exchange rate where the currency experiences a real appreciation but remains relatively stable in nominal terms.

6.3 The nominal and the real exchange rate

Nominal and real exchange rates

If the nominal exchange rate develops differently from the real exchange rate, this can be an indication that a fundamental disequilibrium in the balance of payments is developing even if the foreign currency market is temporarily cleared. The nominal exchange rate is defined as the relative price of two

monies, for instance the euro and the US dollar, $e = €/\$$; the nominal exchange
rate clears the foreign currency market.

The real exchange rate corrects the nominal rate by the foreign and the
domestic price levels. The real exchange rate is defined as

$$e_R = eP^*/P \tag{6.3}$$

where P^*, P are the respective national price levels being used as correction factors of the nominal exchange rate. The real exchange rate indicates the real price
of products of the foreign country, i.e. of its export goods in terms of products of
the home country, i.e. its import substitutes. The real exchange rate has the

dimension $\dfrac{Q}{Q^*} = \dfrac{€}{\$} \dfrac{\$}{Q^*} \Big/ \dfrac{€}{Q}$; therefore, it depicts the relation between the

quantities of the domestic good (Q) and the quantities of the foreign good (Q^*),
i.e. the ratio at which domestic goods can be exchanged for foreign goods. It tells
something about the purchasing power of the domestic good. Thus, the real
exchange rate is a relative price. In the simple two-goods model it has the inverse
dimension of the terms of trade (Q^*/Q), i.e. we have

$$e_R = 1/p \tag{6.4}$$

The real exchange rate brings the current account into equilibrium; it must also
be consistent with the internal (macroeconomic) equilibrium in the real economy.
For allocation decisions, for instance when a real distortion of the economy exists
because not enough exports are produced and too many imports are consumed,
it is the real exchange rate that has to do the job of bringing about a new equilibrium. Countries that want to remove a trade deficit have to carry out a real
devaluation. Putting a higher real value on exports, domestic demand for exports
is reduced; domestic supply of exports is stimulated.

A nominal devaluation of a currency may be neutralized in its effects on trade
flows, when the price level in the country that devalues rises correspondingly.
Therefore, a country devaluing its currency in nominal terms has to make sure
that a nominal devaluation is not contradicted by a strong rise of its price level.
This implies that monetary policy has to restrain a potential price increase.

What does a real appreciation mean?

A real appreciation ($\hat{e}_R < 0$) can mean two different things. i) It can signal that an
economy has gained a higher competitiveness in the exchange of goods. Due to
an improved supply in the home country or due to a higher demand of the foreign country, the price at home increases less than that abroad when the
exchange rate is given. Then the real appreciation has its root in the greater competitiveness of a country. The real revaluation is an instrument that reduces an

export surplus.[2] ii) An appreciation can also occur if the price level in the domestic country increases more than that in the foreign country because of rising labor costs or because of a failure of stabilization policy. Then, the currency is overvalued in real terms (like sometimes happens in developing countries). As a result, the real appreciation does not indicate an improved competitiveness in this case, but it indicates a need for structural adjustments. Therefore, one has to look very closely at which of the two different things is meant when we talk about a real appreciation.

A real appreciation can also take place if capital flows in. Again, it can mean two different things. i) A currency is revalued in nominal terms which implies a real appreciation if goods prices do not change. Then the real appreciation can indicate a strengthened competitiveness (attractiveness of a location) for real capital. With the additional investment, the competitiveness for goods can be improved in the future. ii) However, the inflow of capital can also be used to finance private consumption or governmental expenditure for consumption; it can go along with a bubble. Then the resulting real appreciation means an overvaluation of the currency. As in the case of commodity exchange, the real revaluation can again imply two different things. As for any real price, the real exchange rate has to be judged against the background of an equilibrium or a disequilibrium in the economy, both with respect to an internal macroeconomic equilibrium and with respect to a balance or an imbalance in the current account.

If the real exchange rate appreciates and if the nominal exchange rate remains more or less stable and if at the same time a current account deficit develops, the risk arises that the nominal exchange rate will have to give.

Figure 6.2 exhibits the real exchange rate between the US dollar and the deutsche mark. The real exchange rate of the US dollar decreased in the first half of the 1980s, i.e. the US dollar appreciated in real terms. Between 1985 and 1995 the US dollar depreciated. From 1995 on, the US dollar has been appreciating. The real exchange rate of the deutsche mark increased in the period from 1973 till the mid-1980s; this means a real devaluation of the deutsche mark. Afterwards, the real exchange rate of the deutsche mark fell again, which corresponds to a real revaluation. Since 1995, the deutsche mark has been rising.

An alternative definition of the real exchange rate

Note that the real exchange is alternatively defined as

$$e_R = eP_T^* / P_{NT} \qquad (6.5)$$

where P_T^* is the price of tradables denominated in foreign currency and P_{NT} is the price of non-tradables in terms of the domestic currency, so that the dimension is.

$$\frac{Q_{NT}}{Q_T} = \frac{\text{€}}{\text{\$}} \cdot \frac{\text{\$}}{Q_T} \left/ \frac{\text{€}}{Q_{NT}} \right. .$$

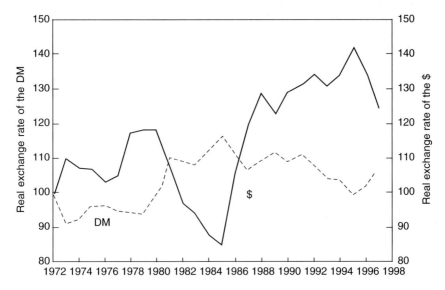

Figure 6.2   Real exchange rate[a] of the D-mark[b] and the US dollar[c]
[a]1972 = 100. [b]In comparison with 18 industrial countries (measured in consumer prices). [c]In comparison with 18 industrial countries, including Germany (measured in consumer prices)
Source: Deutsche Bundesbank, *Monthly Report*, April 1998; own calculations

A real appreciation ($e_R < 0$) means that the price of non-tradables increases more than that of tradables. The economy will have an incentive to produce more non-tradables and a balance-of-payment surplus will be reduced.

The concept of an equilibrium exchange rate

Since the real exchange rate is a relative price that brings exports and imports or tradables and non-tradables in line with a macroeconomic equilibrium, the concept of the equilibrium real exchange rate has some prominence in economics. From equation 6.4 we have

$$\hat{e}_R = -\hat{p} \tag{6.6}$$

The real exchange rate has to move in the opposite direction from the relative commodity price. If preferences shift or if relative supply conditions change, the real exchange rate must adjust so that a new macroeconomic equilibrium is reached. In Figure 5.2b this means that tan α of ray OL changes.

This long-run relationship between the real exchange rate and the fundamentals overlaps with temporary phenomena such as overshooting or bubbles. As a very simple relationship we have, from equations 5.6 and 6.3:

$$\hat{e}_R = \hat{e} + \hat{\tilde{M}}^* - \hat{\tilde{M}} + \hat{Y} - \hat{Y}^*. \tag{6.7}$$

Consider the case where the nominal exchange rate is fixed ($\hat{e} = 0$) and where the money supply in the home country ($\hat{M}$) expands much more than production potential ($\hat{Y}$), with the foreign country expanding its money supply according to its production potential ($\hat{M}* = \hat{Y}*$). Then the price level of the home country will rise, and the home country will experience a real appreciation which will hurt its competitiveness. Such a development would not be consistent with an equilibrium. Instead, the nominal exchange rate would have to adjust and, with $\hat{e} = \hat{M} + \hat{Y}$, there would be no impact on the real exchange rate.

In theory, it is possible to precisely define the equilibrium real exchange rate (as the one establishing equilibrium in the balance of payments and in the (macro)economy). For policy purposes, it is extremely difficult to determine the real exchange rate. This is especially so because this would have to be done *ex ante*. That is why concepts for exchange rate policy based on the idea of an equilibrium exchange rate (Williamson 1983) are not very promising (see below). However, if the nominal and the real exchange rate diverge for a longer period of time, it is very likely that some adjustment has to take place.

6.4 Some recent currency crises

The Czech devaluation

A divergence between the nominal and the real exchange rate developed in the case of the Czech crown (koruna). Czechoslovakia and (since 1993) the Czech Republic *de facto* pegged the crown to a basket of currencies (65 percent DM, 35 percent US$ since May 1993). Until 1997, the Czech National Bank was able to defend the nominal exchange rate. In real terms, the currency appreciated and the external value rose (Figure 6.3). This went along with an increasing current account deficit which was financed by capital inflows. The real appreciation hurt the competitiveness of the Czech economy. Eventually, a situation developed in which the nominal exchange rate could no longer be defended. The crown had to devalue.

The Mexican crisis

The Mexican peso more or less followed a crawling peg to the US dollar in the early 1990s. The rate of devaluation of the peso was lower than the inflation difference between the two countries, i.e. $\hat{e} < \hat{p}* - \hat{p}$. With prices and nominal wages rising at a higher speed than in the US, Mexico did not succeed in effectively using the exchange rate as a nominal anchor. The Pacto agreement between the government, employers' associations and trade unions to limit wage and price increases did not work out. The slow nominal depreciation and the higher inflation differential implied a real appreciation of the peso which began in the late 1980s (Figure 6.4). Monetary policy was expansionary (see chapter 8). Together with a real appreciation of the peso, a current account deficit developed which was financed by short-term capital inflow attracted by high real interest rates and a booming stock market. Eventually, investors lost confidence, capital

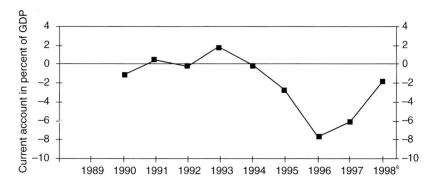

Figure 6.3 Czech Republic[a]: nominal[b] and real[c] exchange rate and current account[d]
[a]1990: Czechoslovakia. [b]Koruna/US$. [c]1990 = 100. [d]In percent of GDP. [e]Estimate
Source: IMF, *International Financial Statistics 1998*; own calculations according to EBRD, *Transition Report 1997*; from 1993: OECD, *Economic Outlook* 1998

flows reversed, and Mexico lost 122 billion US$ in foreign currency reserves in 1994. The peso had to devalue and the current account deficit was almost eliminated afterwards. Meanwhile, the nominal and real rate diverge again.

The Asian 'tigers' in financial crisis

In 1997, the Asian financial crisis broke out. Some of the Asian tigers, in the past greeted with the enthusiasm of international investors because of their high real

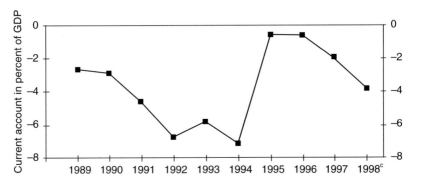

Figure 6.4 Mexico: real[a] and nominal exchange rate and current account[b]
[a]1990 = 100. [b]In percent of GDP. [c]Estimate
Source: IMF, *International Financial Statistics 1998*; OECD, *Economic Outlook 1998*

growth rates, got into trouble in spite of sound macroeconomic fundamentals in
the traditional interpretation: growth rates, savings and investment ratios were
high, inflation was low, budget deficits did not give rise to concern, and export
performance was strong. Large current-account deficits were excused because of
the booming economies.

With hindsight, the countries were vulnerable to some extent for different reasons. In Thailand, where the crisis started, the relatively high capital inflows, i.e.
the current account deficit, went hand in hand with a construction boom. Once
the construction boom was no longer sustainable or was expected not to be sus-

tainable, capital flows were reversed. The liberalization of the domestic financial sector implied that prudential standards were not being implemented. This meant that a bubble could develop due to credit expansion. Pegging the national currency to the US dollar contributed to an appreciation of the real exchange rate relative to the nominal exchange rate, which made it more difficult to reach a sustainable equilibrium even if the divergence was not too large. Finally, the Asian crisis showed that it is not sufficient to look just at budget deficits and public debt. A high indebtedness of the private sector, as in the case of South Korea, increased vulnerability.

South Korea

When the Asian crisis erupted, people did not expect South Korea – number 11 in the world economy in terms of GDP prior to the financial crisis – to become part of the problem. The real exchange rate had only slightly moved away from the nominal exchange rate (Figure 6.5). The large current-account deficit of 5 percent of GDP could be explained by the liberalization of current and capital account transactions in anticipation of South Korea's accession to the OECD. However, the deficit in the current account had increased in 1996, albeit not to high levels in comparison to Latin American countries. Moreover, the private sector had accumulated high debt, including foreign debt in foreign currencies. This represented a liability for the country as a whole. The crisis erupted when it was reported that large conglomerates (chaebols) faced insolvency.

Thailand and Indonesia

The Asian crisis started when the peg of the Thai baht to the US dollar was abandoned on 2 July 1997. Within two weeks the baht lost 15 percent of its external value. On 12 July the intervention band for the Philippine peso was widened. On 14 July Malaysia could no longer defend the exchange rate of the ringgit; the Indonesian rupiah lost about 10 percent of its value in the second half of July. By the end of October, these currencies had lost between 25 percent (Malaysia, Philippines) and 35 percent (Indonesia, Thailand) of their values. At the peak of the currency crisis, the currencies had devalued to one fourth or one third of their pre-crisis values (Figure 6.6).

The Brazilian crisis

In January 1999, Brazil had to widen its exchange rate band in the crawling peg and then to float the *real* which was devalued until March by about 40 percent. There was quite a divergence between the nominal and the real exchange rate (Figure 6.7). Brazil used a high real interest rate of 30 percent to defend the nominal exchange rate; this, however, proved not to be sustainable. The current account became more and more negative in the 1990s; at the same time, the

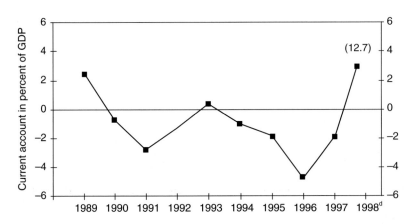

Figure 6.5 South Korea: real[a] and nominal[b] exchange rate and current account[c]
[a]1990 = 100. [b]Won per US$. [c]In percent of GDP. [d]Estimate
Source: IMF, *International Financial Statistics 1998;* OECD, *Economic Outlook 1998*

budget deficit was 8 percent of GDP. The Brazilian crisis is thus more in line with the typical Latin American pattern of a currency crisis.

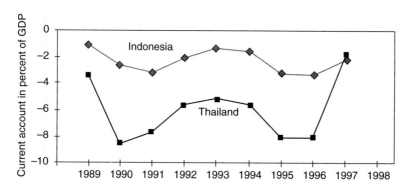

Figure 6.6 Thailand and Indonesia: nominal exchange rates of baht and rupiah and current account[a]

[a]In percent of GDP

Source: IMF, *International Financial Statistics 1998*

6.5 How to prevent a financial crisis

There are several approaches to preventing a financial crisis from arising.

Bank regulation

The financial system of a country has to be constrained such that a crisis is unlikely to start or to be reinforced. This involves setting standards for banks and other financial institutions, for instance, implementing the standards of the Basle

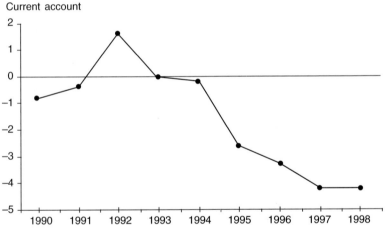

Figure 6.7 Brazil: real[a] and nominal exchange rate[b] and current account[c]
[a]First week 1990 = 100. [b]Weekly data. [c]In percent of GDP
Source: Exchange rate: IMF, *International Financial Statistics*, CD-ROM; *The Economist.* Current account: World Bank, *World Development Indicators;* Economist Intelligence Unit, *Country Report Brazil, 1999;* own calculations

Core Principles for Effective Banking Supervision, including the capital adequacy requirements (Basle Capital Accord of the Bank for International Settlement). Norms should not only apply to commercial banks but also to investment banks. Credits given to hedge funds and derivatives should be adequately reflected in the risk evaluation of banks.

Some standards should also be applied to hedge funds. One approach is to require them to register in a country; if they then go offshore, this may signal to the customer that a higher risk is involved and that these funds are less likely to be bailed out.

Exchange rate policy

Countries can only use the exchange rate as a nominal anchor if their governments are strong enough to stick to a strict stabilization policy or, to put it differently, if they succeed in controlling their budget situation and if trade unions effectively subscribe to price-level stability. If these conditions are not satisfied (as for instance in the Pacto agreement in Mexico prior to 1994), pegging the exchange rate will fail. Even a crawling peg cannot help if the inflation difference is larger than the rate of depreciation in the peg. Note that pegging exchange rates was one reason for the Asian crisis.

Sound fundamentals

The central prerequisite is that a country has sound fundamentals. This relates to solidity in public finances, i.e. aiming at the government having a sustainable budget position. It also means that the balance-of-payments situation is sustainable. More generally, economic policy should be oriented towards stability. If structural issues are not solved, if short-termism dominates, then the fundamentals are not in order. Constitutional constraints for policy makers should ensure that long-run opportunity costs of budget deficits are not disregarded. Thus, a country needs rules by which excessive public deficits are prevented. A basic rule, of course, is that public budget deficits should not be financed by printing money. Therefore, the independence of the central bank is a safeguard against deteriorating public finances. In industrial countries, the interrelations between politics and the central bank are more intricate. The central bank must be strong enough to resist political pressure for an easy money policy if such a policy is in conflict with price-level stability. It may also be wise for a country to make sure that it is not vulnerable and that it has enough strength to withstand a blow from the outside and a less friendly environment including reduced credit access to the international capital market.

6.6 The role of the IMF

The purpose of the IMF, as specified in Article I of the IMF statutes is 'to shorten the duration and lessen the degree of disequilibrium in the balances of payments' (section iv), to 'facilitate the expansion and balanced growth of international trade' (section ii) and to 'promote exchange stability' (section iii). Solving disequilibria in the balances of payments is a short-term task; promoting exchange rate stability is a more long-term objective.

Short-term and long-term tasks

To define the short-term role of restoring a balance-of-payments equilibrium and the long-term role of exchange rate stability was relatively easy during the time of Bretton Woods when the main objective of the IMF was to bridge foreign currency shortages in a world of relatively stable exchange rates and when trade in goods and services was predominant as the major driving force of balance-of-payments situations. With flexible exchange rates and with portfolio capital being the main determinant of short-term exchange rate movements, the task of defining the role of the IMF becomes more and more complex. The short-term and long-term roles are more intertwined. In a world with high portfolio capital mobility, currency runs can be a problem. Unfortunately, currency runs which are a short-run phenomenon when they take place, have long-run causes.

The two roles of the IMF are potentially conflicting. The short-run approach requires us to bridge a liquidity gap by providing liquidity. In this interpretation, the IMF is a fire brigade stopping a potential currency run from arising from a (short-run) liquidity problem. The more long-run approach is to prevent a currency run from developing; in this interpretation, the IMF undertakes a precautionary policy. But the short-run objective of bridging liquidity gaps is dominant, even when the IMF defines the long-run conditions for a sustainable situation by lending with conditionality and when it thus turns into a taskmaster of national economic policy defining a set of conditions when a credit is given.

The IMF facilities

Countries with balance-of-payments problems can use the IMF-reserve tranche which does not constitute a credit. In addition to this support, the IMF has several credit facilities. The initially created Stand-by Arrangements serve to alleviate temporary balance-of-payments disequilibria and allow members to draw up to 100 percent of their quota during a prescribed period (usually 12–18 months). The credit has to be repaid within $3\frac{1}{4}$ to 5 years. The Extended Fund Facility, created in 1974, was aimed at structural deficits, i.e. at balance-of-payments difficulties requiring a longer period of adjustment. It envolves larger amounts of financing than under Stand-by Arrangements. Repayment is within $4\frac{1}{2}$ and 10 years. More recently, the IMF has increased its lending to deal with structural disequilibria with the concessional Enhanced Structural Adjustment Facility (since 1987) targeted at low-income countries and the Systemic Transformation Facility (from 1993 to 1995) targeted at transformation countries. In 1997, a new facility, the Supplemental Reserve Facility, was established, aiming at short-run problems and extending to a period of up to one year. This is in response to 'a sudden and disruptive loss of market confidence reflected in pressure on the capital account and the members' reserves'. Repayment is expected within $1–1\frac{1}{2}$ years; the interest rate starts three percentage points above the IMF lending rates; the rate increases over time. A new facility, Contingent Credit Line, is supposed to shield member countries with solid economic policy against contagion.

More information

The Asian crisis has shown that more information on the financial status of countries is needed, including more accurate data on foreign exchange reserves (are they swapped?). In addition to macroeconomic data, more information on short-term private debt is required, especially on short-term debt of the private enterprise sector. Data must include the maturity structure of debt and its composition in terms of different currencies. Information should also cover the financial sector, for instance in the form of the consolidated balance sheet of the financial sector as a whole and of the major financial institutions (x percent of the market volume). Moreover, a measure of reserves' adequacy for the banking sector should be developed, indicating the necessary reserves in relation to total short-term debt. The problem with the approach of defining capital adequacy is, of course, that in a crisis assets melt away. An important aspect of transparency is to what extent international banking rules including prudent standards have been adopted.

Data should be provided in a standardized form; they should get a stamp of approval from the IMF or other specialized international organizations like the Bank for International Settlement. This secures comparability of the data, and it enhances credibility of the data. If countries are reluctant to provide the necessary data, there should be definite costs of non-compliance, for instance by making non-compliance public or by requiring compliance as a precondition for IMF support in case of a crisis.

An improved early warning system

The IMF should improve its early warning system. More and better information should be provided to the markets so that markets will require higher risk premiums from countries with a poor economic performance. The IMF should not be a silent supervisor who deliberates behind closed doors with the country where a problem is developing. This involves the risk that not enough is done to prevent the crisis. It is better to blow the whistle before the train crashes. It is better to allow a small crisis if, in this way, you can prevent a large one. Of course, signaling more actively to the markets that a problem is developing is a very delicate task, and the IMF should not start the hurricane or strengthen it, but it also should not hold back information so that people are misdirected from searching for shelter.

The moral hazard problem

The sums that the IMF has used in order to prevent financial crises have increased considerably over time. In the 1960s and the 1970s credits amounted to roughly 1 billion US$. In the early 1980s, the credit level reached 3.5 billion US$ (Table 6.2). In the 1990s, the amount of credits was at 20 billion US$ (Table 6.3).

The size of operation of the IMF has come under critique. The larger the size of operation, the more money the IMF takes in hand, the weaker will be the willingness of private creditors (banks) to take over credit risk in the case of a crisis and the weaker is the incentive for governments to prevent the problems that create a severe moral hazard problem.

Table 6.2 IMF credits in the 1950s, 1960s and 1980s (billion US$)

1958	United Kingdom	0.74
1960	Venezuela	0.10
1962	United Kingdom	1.00
	Japan	0.31
1965	India	0.20
1967	United Kingdom	1.40
1969	France	0.99
1974	Italy	1.20
1977	United Kingdom	3.92
1978	Egypt	0.75
1980	Pakistan	1.65
	Bangladesh	1.04
1981	Yugoslavia	1.96
	Romania	1.30
	India	5.90
1983	Brazil	4.53
	Mexico	3.65

Source: IMF, *Annual Report*, various issues

Table 6.3 IMF and other credits to countries in crisis (billion US$)

		IMF	World Bank	Regional development banks	Bilateral credits	Total
Mexico	1995	17.8	1.5	1.3	31.0	51.6
Indonesia	1997	11.2	5.5	4.5	21.1	42.3
South Korea	1997	20.9	10.0	4.0	23.3	58.2
Thailand	1997	4.0	1.5	1.2	10.5	17.2
Brazil	1998	18.0	4.5	4.5	14.5	41.5
Russia	1998	15.1	6.0	–	1.5	22.6

Source: Sachverständigenrat (1998), Table 3

Letting private lenders take the risk

The larger the scale of operation, the lower the losses that the private lenders have to take. If private lenders like banks and bondholders can expect to be bailed out, they will not have a strong incentive to be cautious in giving credits. In order to solve this problem, an arrangement is needed on how to handle private credits when private debtors and sovereign countries get into trouble. An international rule system is required analogous to national bankruptcy rules such as described in chapter 11, specifying how illiquidity of private agents whose debt can cause a currency run has to be handled. The IMF should credibly pre-announce conditions for its interventions. It should establish rules on the involvement of private lenders which the IMF wants to be respected if it is supposed to intervene. It can specify such rules as a precondition for lending support in the case of a crisis. Thus, the IMF could trigger standards written into an international agreement which have to be respected by sovereign states and private lenders when a liquidity crisis develops.

Credible rules for sovereign debtors

Since financial crises will be different with respect to size, structure and cause, only broad rules can be developed. If a crisis erupts, the IMF has to act like a bankruptcy court judge (Sachs 1994, 1997b; Minton-Beddoes 1995): a moratorium has to be declared, existing debt has to be restructured and working capital has to be arranged. Fresh working capital must have priority over obligations to previous creditors. Note that the bankruptcy rule system is only credible if in the event of a crisis the IMF sticks to its role as a bankruptcy court judge.

In this interpretation, the IMF takes over an *ex post* role, but this *ex post* role has an *ex ante* impact by forming expectations and influencing credit and debt behavior. The announcement effect of a clear *ex post* rule will be to reduce systemic risk *ex ante*. This announcement effect should be reinforced by more transparency and by an improved early warning system. Countries should experience the costs of their unsound economic policy and of lingering problems early on. The costs of unsound economic policy should not jump upward in a discontinuous way (or to infinity) if a problem develops. The IMF should apply a sliding scale of the costs of a credit, for instance in terms of interest rates rising over time or with the size of the credit. In this way, the abrupt reversal of short-term capital flows can be reduced.

Lender of last resort?

Even in the IMF role of bridging a liquidity gap, a complex moral hazard and incentive problem arises because the IMF cannot credibly play the role of a lender of last resort. There is a severe asymmetry to the national lender of last resort, in addition to the lack of a rule system for bankruptcies of sovereign states. The national lender of last resort can print money and can thus stop a crisis. For the IMF, this is not possible. On the contrary, the IMF has a limited amount of capital. A currency problem can be accentuated, if the IMF runs out of funds. The capital of the IMF of about 200 billion US$ is just a trickle if an extended crisis develops.[3]

If a systemic crisis for the world economy develops, the central banks will have to play the role of a lender of last resort. The institutional arrangement for such a scenario, however, cannot be put in writing. It has to be left open, whether and under what conditions central banks will step in. If the conditions were specified *ex ante* and if they became known, an uncontrollable moral hazard problem would develop where market participants and governments would play strategically against the central banks.

6.7 Controlling capital flows

Since exchange rate volatility and financial crises are linked to the mobility of portfolio capital, it has been proposed that the free movement of portfolio capital be limited in order to prevent financial crisis. This discussion runs counter to the view prevailing until the Asian crisis broke out, namely that the gains from the international division of labor are seriously reduced if countries restrict the convertibility of currencies. This impedes both the exchange of goods and the efficient allocation of capital. Therefore, the condition of the convertibility of currencies seemed to be generally accepted. Especially due to the experience during the Great Depression, there has been much effort to establish convertibility and to liberalize capital flows since the Second World War.

In the new discussion, different approaches have been discussed.

The level of intervention

An international Tobin tax

On an international level, a tax on the movement of portfolio capital has been proposed (Tobin tax, Tobin 1978). The intention is to raise the costs of short-term capital movements; a tax on portfolio capital moved becomes less noticeable when portfolio capital remains in a country for a longer time. Thus, a tax is supposed to reduce the amount of (short-run) capital flows. An open question relates to finding a consensus on a uniform tax rate for all countries. It is also open whether the tax is applied to outflowing or inflowing capital and which country receives the tax revenue.

National approaches to control capital flows

On the national level, a set of different instruments are being discussed, including foreign exchange controls, different types of convertibility, different exchange rates for capital flows relative to commodity trade and the taxation of capital flows.

Instruments available

Foreign exchange controls

There is a broad spectrum of controls, for instance requiring a license to obtain foreign currency, restraining convertibility or using other administrative controls. This includes making capital exports illegal.

Auctioning off the currency reserves

One way of introducing capital controls is to auction off the total supply of foreign currency reserves that a country receives in a year. However, a perfect

auction system would only mimic the market so there would be no use in introducing it. A state-run auction system would intervene in defining privileged
access or other aspects.

Multiple exchange rates

Another case in point is the privileged access to favorable exchange rates, for
instance by splitting the exchange rates between different transactions, e.g.
between goods considered to be important and less important or between trade
of goods and capital movements as practiced in the system of import licenses and
the exchange rate protectionism that was pursued in Latin America until the
mid-1980s. Such an approach *de facto* implies multiple exchange rates.

Non-residents' and residents' convertibility

Restraints on the convertibility is another way of reducing the international
mobility of portfolio capital. This relates to restricting a currency's convertibility
for foreigners (non-residents' convertibility) and for residents (residents' convertibility). In order to attract capital, countries usually first introduce the convertibility of their currency for foreigners. This implies that foreign investors have the
right to repatriate their profits and also their investment. Without this right, they
will not provide capital. Convertibility for residents is often introduced at a later
stage in the process of liberalization.

Limiting capital flight

Countries are very interested in attracting capital, but at the same they want to
reduce capital outflows, more specifically to prevent capital flight. It is difficult to
define policy instruments that apply to one aspect of capital flows only. Policy
instruments that may limit the outflow of capital such as capital export restraints
simultaneously reduce the incentive to invest in a country. Capital outflow
restraints define the expectations of potential foreign investors. Limiting exit
always reduces the incentives for entry.

Reserve requirements for portfolio capital

In order to make incoming capital less volatile, a non-remunerated reserve
requirement has been proposed for incoming capital so that no interest is paid
during a certain time period, for instance a year. Chile has used this approach in
the 1990s, requiring initially a non-interest-bearing 30 percent deposit for the
first year. This approach was given up in 1998 when Chile had problems attracting foreign capital. Such a deposit limits the inflow of capital (including short-run
capital) but it does not prevent capital that at a given moment has been invested
in a country from leaving quickly.

The cons against capital controls

Sequencing of liberalization

It has now been accepted that there is a sequencing problem in liberalizing the banking sector and the capital account. If the capital account is liberalized and if, at the same time, the banking sector is not adequately regulated, an overexpansion of credit may result. Sweden and Thailand are two examples. Due to the complementarity in institutional reforms, the liberalization of the capital account should be accompanied by an appropriate regulation of the banking sector.

Preventing the loss of credibility

It is one thing to liberalize the capital account, it is another thing to undo a liberalization that has already been introduced. In that case, reputation is lost. Liberalization should be undertaken only when a country is strong enough to live with it. Once liberalization has been introduced, care must be taken that it is not reversed.

Delineating capital flows from commodity exchange

A major issue is that all measures discussed here presuppose that capital flows can be clearly delineated from the exchange of goods and services. Experience shows that administrative capital controls can be circumvented in many ways, for instance by over- or underinvoicing.

The opportunity costs of capital controls

Another major issue in controlling portfolio capital is that controls are likely to limit the attractiveness for real capital that countries need for their development. Therefore, the countries applying these controls hurt themselves by introducing capital controls.

Assigning the correct risk premia

A promising approach is to assign the correct risk premia. This includes an effective banking regulation and an efficient supervision of the financial sector.

Stability-oriented policy

If a country wants to have the long-term benefit of capital inflows it must establish a reputation so that capital is attracted and so that capital has no incentive to leave the country. This requires that a stability policy be followed that is convincing for the international financial markets.

6.8 Stabilizing exchange rates: approaches for individual countries

The wish for stable exchange rates

Regarding money as an important innovation, which diminishes transaction costs, the volatility of exchange rates reduces the intended reduction of the transaction costs. Volatility of the exchange rate can mean two things: first, exchange rate movements can deviate in the short term (up to one year) from a long-term trend or a somehow defined frame of reference. Second, the exchange rate can follow a trend for some years and then follow a different trend, changing from appreciation to depreciation. Both types of volatility cause transaction costs. Unexpected short-term deviations from a longer trend may be hedged to some extent. A trend reversal has the consequence that trade flows and direct investment flows have to adapt to the new currency relations. This means that product specialization, factor allocation and the sectoral structure have to adjust. The transaction costs arising from volatility are the reason why there are always efforts aiming at stable exchange rates.

We distinguish between approaches that individual countries can follow, and institutional arrangements that several countries or, in the extreme, the world economy can strive for.

Price-level stability as an anchor

Usually, monetary policy is oriented towards a stable price level. It can directly aim at influencing the price level (inflation targeting), or it can follow a money supply target by keeping the increase of the money supply in line with an economy's growth of the production potential. For both kinds of monetary policy strategies, the price level is the nominal anchor. In accordance with purchasing power parity, the change of the exchange rate is simply determined by the inflation difference to the foreign country. Thus, an appreciation of the domestic currency takes place when the price level of the domestic country rises less than that of the foreign country. This way, a country is able to uncouple itself from the inflation of the foreign country.

Exchange-rate-oriented monetary policy

Individual countries can also pursue an exchange-rate-oriented monetary policy, which means they choose the exchange rate as a nominal anchor. They tie their domestic currency to another currency. That means that monetary policy has to influence the domestic price level in such a way that the exchange rate remains stable. Following the equation of purchasing power parity, $\hat{e} = \hat{p} - \hat{p}^*$, an exchange rate change $\hat{e} = 0$ is aimed at. If the currency of the foreign country is used as an anchor, then the rate of change of the foreign country's price level is regarded as the point of reference, i.e. $\hat{p} = \hat{p}^*$. The domestic price level follows the foreign price level. In the pre-euro era, Austria, Belgium and the Netherlands are examples of an exchange-rate-oriented monetary policy holding their currencies in a constant ratio to the deutsche mark.

Such an exchange-rate-oriented monetary policy is normally only carried out by smaller countries. Larger economies want to determine their price levels themselves. Larger economies could also pursue an exchange-rate-oriented monetary policy, but at least one country has to provide a stable currency as a nominal anchor (anchor currency).

The credibility of a nominal anchor

Especially the experience of developing countries shows that very often an exchange rate taken as the nominal anchor cannot be sustained, because a credible stabilization policy is given up after a couple of years. This gives rise to the issue of how credible nominal anchors are (see chapters 7 and 8).

Currency board

The currency board is a special form of an exchange-rate-oriented monetary policy. In such an approach, the domestic currency has to be covered completely by foreign currency reserves. The central bank binds itself in the way that it only provides domestic money to the extent that foreign monetary reserves are available. To give credibility to such a policy, the foreign currency can be authorized as legal tender. Then, the domestic currency has to be as stable as the foreign currency, or it is driven out of the market. Argentina has been carrying out such a policy of a currency board since 1991; Estonia also has pursued such an approach since 1992.

The approach of the currency board can only be chosen by some countries, usually small ones. These economies follow another country in their monetary policy. They use the other currency as an anchor, because they cannot provide an anchor themselves. Thus they import the stability of the anchor currency. An important condition is that the markets of the country, including the labor market, are very flexible. The country must be able to digest external shocks by price adjustments. This condition is especially relevant if the country is very sensitive to external shocks. For instance, a currency is difficult to sustain if a country is a resource exporter and if resource prices are volatile.

Crawling peg

Another approach is the crawling peg. This approach is followed when over a longer period of time it is expected that the inflation rate in the domestic country will be higher than that in the foreign country. Through the crawling peg, the exchange rate is brought in line with the inflation rate, normally with a pre-announced rate of change of the exchange rate. A crawling peg has to be chosen if it is expected that a stringent stabilization policy which would be necessary for a constant exchange rate cannot be kept up.

6.9 Stabilizing exchange rates: multilateral approaches

Anchor currency

In the case of an exchange-rate-oriented policy a (theoretical) problem is that not all of the n countries can choose the exchange rate as a nominal anchor. Formally, this can also be described as the problem of the $n - 1$ exchange rates. For n countries with n currencies, every single country has $n - 1$ exchange rates. At least one of the currencies (of the nth country) must take the role of the 'numéraire'. As a result, one currency has to be the anchor in a system of fixed exchange rates. In the system of Bretton Woods, the dollar used to be the anchor; in the European Exchange Rate System it was the deutsche mark. Normally, a currency of a large country which has proved to be stable in the long run develops as the anchor currency. Which currency is finally accepted by other countries remains to be determined on the markets.

Reference zones

With the introduction of reference zones or target zones, the exchange rate is allowed to fluctuate within a band. The exchange rate should only deviate from the (real) equilibrium exchange rate within a limited range. Coordination of monetary and stabilization policies has to ensure that the limits of the range of fluctuations are not surpassed. As long as monetary policy and the other fields of economic policy of the countries involved do not contradict the credibility of the band, the exchange rate can be kept in the target zone. But as soon as the markets doubt the credibility of the band, such a system has a destabilizing effect.

If in such a system the limit of the band is reached, the central banks have to intervene. Such a situation is shown in Figure 6.8, in which the supply of the

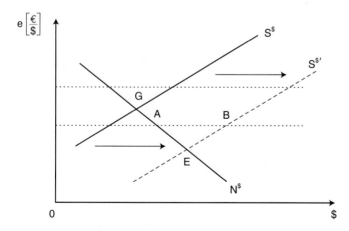

Figure 6.8 Exchange rate within a range of fluctuations

foreign currency ($) increases, for example because of an excessively rising money supply in the foreign country. The supply curve of the foreign currency shifts to the right. This means that without an intervention, the foreign currency will be devalued and the € will be revalued (point E). Such a devaluation of the foreign currency can be avoided if the central banks intervene by demanding additional foreign money to the extent of line AB in exchange for domestic money.

Two problems arise with such an approach of reference zones:

1.　Who has to intervene at the limits? If the European Central Bank supplies euros and has to buy foreign currencies, this means that the money supply of the European Central Bank is *de facto* steered by a foreign central bank. If the foreign central bank expands its money supply and the foreign currency is threatened with devaluation, then the European Central Bank would have to supply euros accordingly. But, in the end, this would imply that the European Central Bank would be heteronomous in its monetary policy. The way out of this dilemma is that the intervention has to be undertaken by the central bank whose currency is under pressure.
2.　How to determine the reference standard of the real equilibrium exchange rate? On the one hand, an equilibrium exchange rate has in theory to be established *ex ante*. In this respect, a model has to be available that includes all relevant definitions of the equilibrium exchange rate and also identifies the factors that could change the expectations of market participants. On the other hand, a political agreement of the sovereign states has to be achieved to determine the equilibrium exchange rate.

The European Exchange Rate Mechanism

The European Exchange Rate Mechanism can be interpreted as a system of reference zones. It was a distinct combination of interest rate parity, which determined the capital flows, and of purchasing power parity, which defined the expectation of the exchange rate. In their monetary policies, but also in their fiscal policies, all participating countries were eager to keep their currencies stable and to prevent devaluations. The additional risk premium for a less stable price level represented a burden for the country. National policy attempted to minimize that risk. This system managed to keep the exchange rates stable during 1987–1992 (Figure 6.9). In this case, the intervention mechanism was very helpful.

But it proved that real economic changes have to lead to an adjustment of the exchange rates when they do not influence all countries in the same way and when changes are adequately strong. These changes are called 'asymmetric shocks'. German reunification was such a shock. Real interest rates in Germany rose because of investment opportunities in Eastern Germany and because of a higher national debt. For that reason, the exchange rates had to be adjusted. In due course, Italy and the UK left the European Exchange Rate Mechanism in 1992. For the UK, too high an entry rate had been chosen in 1990, so that the British currency was overvalued. For the remaining currencies, the band of

Figure 6.9 Exchange rates in the EMS[a]
[a]January 1990 = 100
Source: Deutsche Bundesbank, monthly reports; own calculations

±2.25 percent was raised to ±15 percent in 1992. The lira and the peseta stayed at their devalued level.

Exchange rate zones can induce speculation by making it less costly. The costs of speculation are relatively low as soon as the limit of the band is reached. If a speculator can expect realignments, i.e. an adjustment of the central rates, then this implies a high expected return on investment. If the realignment does not take place possible losses are limited. If, for example, a devaluation is imminent (by a shift of the supply curve for the foreign currency to the right in Figure 6.7), the investor can speculate on an adjustment of the exchange rate. Accordingly he or she will buy deutsche marks and finance this by a credit in foreign currency, which is to be repaid later in a weaker currency. Or they will sell foreign currency now at a future date which they themselves will buy in the future at a lower price (selling short). Once the realignment has taken place, they will make a profit. If there were no realignment, the investor would not have any losses (except for the interest costs). As demand for deutsche marks is increased by speculation, any intervention of the central bank to defend the old rate is made more difficult.

The Bretton Woods system

In 1944, 44 countries met in Bretton Woods, New Hampshire (US), to reach an agreement on the post-war international monetary system. Like the GATT, which was established in 1948, the exchange rate system of Bretton Woods was created in order to establish a stable environment during the period of reconstruction. While the GATT aimed for a rule-based system for trade, Bretton Woods aimed for stable exchange rates. The system came into force in 1946. The anchor currency was the US dollar. The central banks (not the private banks) could change their dollar reserves into gold at the US central bank. The exchange rates were fixed. In order to join the International Monetary Fund each country had to establish a parity to the US dollar (or to gold). The governments had to keep the exchange rates of their currencies within a margin of ±1 percent. Only in the event of fundamental imbalances were exchange rate adjustments allowed to leave that fixed margin: international agreement was required for this. Temporary deficits in the balance of payments were to be balanced by loans from the International Monetary Fund.

The system collapsed in 1971 when the United States unilaterally discontinued the gold parity. As a result of the Vietnam war, the United States was no longer willing to maintain the necessary price-level stability of the anchor currency. Because of its economic policy problems, the US carried out an excessive short-term monetary expansion, implying a devaluation of the US dollar. Consequently, the Bretton Woods system lost its nominal anchor and was replaced by floating exchange rates in 1973.

The gold standard

The gold standard was established in the 19th century. In 1821, the obligation was established for the Bank of England to redeem bank notes into gold coins. In the Bank Charter Act of 1844, the obligation of redeeming was guaranteed by cover clauses. Later on, other countries joined the gold standard, like Germany (1871), Japan (1897) and the US (1879).

The redeemability of the bank notes into gold meant that the central banks had to exchange the money in circulation for gold at any time at a legally fixed ratio. As a result, gold became a means of international payments and constant exchange rates existed. Because of the fixed ratios mark/Q_G and \$/Q_G, the ratio mark/\$ was also fixed (Q_G units of gold). The decisive task for the central banks was to keep the official parity between gold and the domestic currency. Therefore it was important to keep sufficient gold reserves. This was guaranteed if the balance of payments was in equilibrium.

Figure 6.8, which has already been discussed above, also explains the effects of a gold currency. Suppose, for instance, that the US dollar had a lower value, e.g. because of a rising supply of US dollars shifting the supply curve to the right. Starting from an equilibrium point G with flexible exchange rates, a new equilibrium E would be reached by a devaluation of the US dollar.

But this is different in the case of a gold currency. If the dollar is sufficiently devalued, the market participant will be able to buy more US dollars, because for one mark they get a relatively larger amount of US dollars. With this amount of dollars they buy gold in the US, transport it to Germany and change it into marks. By this, the exchange rate *e* cannot sink under the so-called 'lower gold point'. Then it would be worth exporting gold from the US, i.e. dollars would be supplied. In Figure 6.8, the gold export from the US is marked by AB (this means capital export of the foreign country). The lower gold point, which depends on the costs of transportation, insurance and interest payments, indicates the lowest possible exchange rate. The upper gold point has a corresponding effect: if the exchange rate increases, i.e. if the mark is devalued, from a certain threshold onwards it is worth changing dollars into marks; it is now worth buying gold with the marks purchased in Germany and transferring it to the US (upper gold point).

If the appropriate institutional rules for a gold currency are chosen, the exchange rate will find its equilibrium between the upper and the lower gold point. Thus, the exchange rate is stable.

Coordination of national monetary policies

According to a proposition of McKinnon (1982), the exchange rates could be stabilized by a coordination of national monetary policies. The world quantity of money should increase according to the quantity rule of money. If a currency gets under pressure to depreciate, then monetary expansion of this country has to be reduced, whereas a currency with a tendency for a revaluation would need a more generous monetary expansion. It has to be kept in mind that such a system would first of all stabilize the exchange rates but there would be the risk of fluctuating national price levels. Further on, it would be necessary that the sovereign states agree on a reasonable monetary expansion. But it would be insufficient to exclusively coordinate monetary policies since expectations on interest rate and exchange rates play a role. Stabilization policy, including fiscal policy, is of great importance as well, if monetary stability is to be established.

How to prevent volatility of exchange rates?

After the Second World War countries attempted to liberalize their capital account in order to reap the benefits of capital mobility. Recently, the pendulum has threatened to swing in the opposite direction due to the volatility of nominal exchange rates. Again and again, currency turbulences have led to calls for more stability in the international monetary system. There is no doubt that nominal exchange rates are considerably influenced by capital flows, that they can overshoot and thus distort trade flows. It is also true that speculative bubbles can occur. But it has to be taken into account that it is not nominal but real exchange rates that have an influence on trade flows. Very often, changes of the exchange rate are the result of a mixture of political and economic-policy changes, especially in stabilization policy and in monetary policy. Then exchange rate changes are a barometer of fundamental trends. Also real economic changes can cause a different exchange rate: in the long run, there is no way to counteract fundamentals by using exchange rate measures.

Economic policy proposals aimed at limiting the volatility of exchange rates have to be judged skeptically:

- Reference zones (Williamson 1983) will not be feasible, unless the conditions for stability are fulfilled in all individual countries.
- To return to a system similar to the one of Bretton Woods does not take into account the globalization of financial markets.
- To throw sand in the wheels of the international financial markets, i.e. to impose a tax (Tobin tax; Tobin 1978) on short-term portfolio-movements, works against the objective of reducing the costs of transactions for the allocation of real capital.

Stable exchange rates can be obtained by a commitment of all countries to establish a credible currency system and to pursue a policy dominated by the stability of the price level. One possible solution could be that all countries accept a stability-guaranteeing system. From the historic point of view, the gold standard was such a system. The countries gave up their national stabilization policies. They accepted fluctuations in the output of production and in employment to realize exchange rate stability. Today, such an approach is not practicable worldwide. On the one hand, there is no anchor; gold can hardly serve as an anchor, since the gold-producing countries would gain enormous rents. On the other hand, the willingness to submit to such an international system is not given. Small countries can solve the problem of too high a volatility by an exchange-rate-oriented monetary policy or by a currency board. For bigger countries this option is politically not acceptable. Furthermore, one strong country would have to provide the anchor.

National stabilization policy as a contribution to the currency stabilization in the world

Too often – if not always – the triggers for exchange rate volatility are political ones reflecting economic policy conditions, above all failed stabilization policy, fiscal disorder and misguided monetary policy. Exchange rate movements thus represent a barometer of fundamental disturbances.

In the face of the difficulties of the possible systems shown above, it is a realistic assessment of the possibilities for the stabilization of exchange rates to emphasize national responsibility. The scenario is as follows. Each country aims at monetary stability at home. It basically expands its money supply according to the growth of the national production potential. Then, the price level remains stable in each country. Consequently, the exchange rates do not change as far as monetary policy is affected. However, stability orientation of monetary policy alone is insufficient to keep exchange rates stable. Fiscal policy and the whole economic policy, including wage setting, also have to be oriented towards stability.

Thus, a solution can only consist in each individual country's keeping its own house in order and maintaining a stable domestic price level. Then exchange rates will generally remain stable. This approach should be complemented by some minimum agreement on prudential rules for the financial sector in order to shield the overall system against instability and contagion.

Notes

1 In intertemporal models a transversality condition prevents the emergence of speculative bubbles.
2 Appreciation also shows a better competitiveness, if (with unchanged productivity in the foreign country) productivity in tradable goods of the home country increases more than in non-tradables (for this definition of the real exchange rate see below).
3 Total external debt of low- and middle-income countries is at 2.1 trillion US$ (World Bank, *World Development Report* 1997), international claims by reporting banks outside the reporting region is at 1.1 trillion US$ (BIS 1998).

Part III

Regional dimensions of the world economy

Apart from a global view of world economic structures and processes, economic phenomena within regions of the global economy are of interest. This is especially true for the integration of developing countries into the international division of labor. Quite a few of these newly industrialized countries have successfully managed to adapt to the global economy, but some countries still remain in poverty (chapter 7). The transformation of the formerly centrally planned economies and their integration into the international division of labor is another important world economic theme (chapter 8). Regional integrations in the world economy are an interesting trend (chapter 9) with the European Union being the most advanced form of integration (chapter 10).

7   Developing countries

Developing countries are commonly considered to be caught in a poverty trap from which they cannot escape (sections 7.1 and 7.2). A closer look can lead to a more differentiated view. For example, we have to distinguish between underdeveloped countries, newly industrializing countries and newly industrialized countries (section 7.3). Import substitution and export diversification are discussed as the main development strategies (section 7.4). An important condition for a successful development is an institutional infrastructure (section 7.5). Its lack is one of the reasons for the debt crisis of the 1980s (section 7.6). Macroeconomic instability is a severe economic problem of most developing countries (section 7.7). Finally, the approaches of expenditure reduction and expenditure switching are discussed (section 7.8).

7.1 Characteristics of developing countries

An economy is regarded as underdeveloped when it is characterized by a very low income level or high poverty. Characteristics are malnutrition, diseases, high infant mortality, low life expectancy, and an inefficient supply of public goods in, for example, the public health sector, schools and universities. Further characteristics are illiteracy, few opportunities to earn a sufficient income, and insufficient living and housing conditions. In comparison to other countries in the world, the developing countries only reach a low income level (Table 7.1).

On the production side of gross national product, a developing country is characterized by a primary sector (agriculture, exploitation of natural resources) contributing a relatively high proportion of total national income and of employment. Agriculture has a relatively low productivity and is often economically discriminated against in favor of other sectors like manufacturing. Very often, agricultural production is concentrated on just a few products (single-crop farming). Far too often, the natural resource sector represents an export enclave, i.e. it is not intensively linked with the rest of the economy, and therefore does not exert noticeable economic spillover effects. The manufacturing sector accounts for only a small share of national income and of employment. The tertiary sector, especially domestic commerce, binds many employees.

In developing countries, real income, which is on average lower than in other countries, is unevenly distributed. This means that the Lorenz curve of income distribution strongly deviates from the 45-degree line. Most of the population is

Table 7.1 The ten poorest countries in the world (gross national product per capita in
US$, 1997)

Countries	Gross national product per capita	
	At current nominal exchange rates	At purchasing power parity
Mozambique	90	520[b]
Ethiopia	110	510[a]
Congo, Dem. Rep. (Kinshasa)	110	790[b]
Burundi	180	590[a]
Sierra Leone	200	510[a]
Niger	200	920[b]
Tanzania	210	n.a.
Rwanda	210	630[a]
Nepal	210	1,090[a]
Malawi	220	700[a]
For comparison:		
Portugal	10,450	13,840[a]
Germany	28,260	21,300[a]
United States of America	28,740	28,740[a]
Japan	37,850	23,400[a]
Switzerland	44,320	26,320[a]
World	5,130	6,330

[a]Extrapolated [b]Regression
Source: World Bank, *World Development Report 1998*, Table 1

characterized by a low income per head. There is no middle class, so that there is
a big gap between rich and poor. This implies that an important condition for
political stability is missing. However, the relationship between the level of development and an uneven income distribution is not altogether clear. Based on the
same development level, there is more dissimilarity in Africa (south of the
Sahara) and in Latin America than in Asia. Any analysis is also made difficult by
statistical problems, since measuring the distribution of the personal income is
one of the most unreliable fields in development economics. There is also hidden
unemployment, which is marked by many employees' having a marginal productivity close to zero. Their work could be abandoned without a noticeable reduction of production.

The expenditures of the majority of the population are directed towards the
necessities of life. Because of low incomes, savings are nearly impossible.
Savings that do exist flow into durable consumer goods without productive
capacity. Groups with a high income often have a traditionally high propensity
to consume, so their savings are quite small. Very often the desire to be an
entrepreneur is missing. If there are savings at all, they frequently flow into
capital exports.

All in all, the underdeveloped countries are characterized by a dual economy:
on the one hand, there are export enclaves of the raw material sector and, on the
other hand, a few industrial products are produced which have quite good profit

potential but cannot stimulate the rest of the economy sufficiently. Too often the underdeveloped country remains a subsistence economy.

7.2 Reasons for underdevelopment

Several factors have to be considered as possible reasons for underdevelopment.

Excessive population increases

Even if the gross national product rises strongly, the growth of income per capita can be quite low or even negative, if the population grows fast. This is shown in Figure 7.1 (Nelson 1956). Assume that the growth rate of gross national product ($\hat{Y}$) is higher than the rate of increase of income per capita ($\hat{y}$), because, above all, a higher income per capita allows more savings, i.e. a higher capital formation. At some time of the development process, the growth rates of gross national product will diminish (cf. chapter 4 concerning catching-up processes). First of all, the expansion rate of the population ($\hat{B}$) increases with a rising income per head, but then it stays constant (or even decreases in 'old' economies). Above all, this development of the population is explained by a reduction of the mortality rate in the case of an increasing prosperity at a given birth rate. Above an income level y_0, the mortality rate falls very quickly, thus the population rises strongly, because of a higher life expectancy and especially a far lower infant mortality as a result of better medical conditions. Eventually, with a higher income per head the birth rate falls, inducing the population to be stable (or even to shrink). Below an income per capita y_0, the population decreases.

From the definition of income per capita, $y = Y/B$, it follows for the rate of

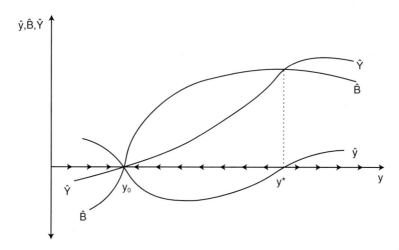

Figure 7.1 The development trap

change of income per capita that $\hat{y} = \hat{Y} - \hat{B}$. As long as the population is growing faster than national product, income per head decreases ($\hat{Y} < \hat{B}$, i.e. $\hat{y} < 0$). But when gross national product increases more strongly than the population ($\hat{Y} > \hat{B}$, i.e. $\hat{y} > 0$, i.e.), income per capita rises. Income per capita y_0 is a steady-state equilibrium on a low level. Below y_0, there is a tendency of a rising income per capita, because the population rises less fast than national product. The economy moves to the point y_0. Above y_0, at first the population rises more strongly than national product. This is the reason why the economy tends to go back to the point y_0. Only when the level y^* is exceeded does income per capita rise, because then national product rises more strongly than the population. Between y_0 and y^* the economy always moves back to y_0. The country persists on a low level and is captured in a trap of underdevelopment. It requires a push, normally a positive external shock, to get out of the situation.

Missing institutions

In many developing countries, there are no institutions that make sure that necessary long-term concerns, i.e. long-term opportunity costs, are taken into consideration. As a result, politicians are very often satisfied with short-term and populistic solutions, which lead to long-term costs for the country. As an example, there are no adequate rules to prevent a budget deficit of the state.

Because of the lack of efficient tax systems and because of too small a tax base – above all the trade of international goods is taxed by a system of export and import duties – the state finances itself partly by the central bank and monetizes the public debt. As a consequence, inflation appears, occasionally turning into a hyper-inflation. This means that the state is actually levying an inflation tax. The domestic currency loses its value, and due to the anticipation of a devaluation capital flight occurs. One of the reasons why the government cannot be forced to balance its budget deficit is that the central bank is not independent.

Lack of capital formation

Low savings result in a small capital stock which implies that production is quite low. Usually, new physical capital embodies new technological knowledge. Thus, weak capital formation means that hardly any new technological knowledge can be realized. Little capital formation, i.e. only little abstinence from consumption, also means that human capital is not built up sufficiently, for example by training on the job. Impediments to capital formation are also due to a low income per head. If a government tries to finance its expenses by an inflation tax, the high inflation will work against savings, because people flee into unproductive inflation-proof uses of their income.

No entrepreneurship

Developing countries often lack entrepreneurship. This can have several reasons. One reason is that the role of the entrepreneur is not highly valued in a society and that value orientation does not assign a special importance to achievement. Another reason is that the country has no entrepreneurial tradition, for instance because of its educational system.

National debt

Some developing countries, especially in Latin America, have accumulated a high foreign debt (V) on the international financial markets for several reasons, mainly because of high budget deficits of the state. This requires high interest payments (rV) and leads to a negative balance of services. Ignoring other positions of the balance of services and transfer payments, the financing restriction for an open economy is given by $S - I + (T - G) = Z^H - rV$ (where Z^H is the trade balance). For highly indebted countries, the trade balance minus the interest payments is negative, with low domestic savings and an often prevalent budget deficit of the government. This means that indebtedness rises ($\dot{V} > 0$). It is hard for such an economy to reduce consumption in order to balance the public budget, to achieve positive net financial investment and a positive trade balance in the end.

Vicious circle

A multitude of factors can keep developing countries on a basic level. Strong growth of the population, a low savings rate, a small stock of real capital (including infrastructure capital) and of human capital lead to a small output, which itself does not allow a sufficient formation of capital (Figure 7.2). High

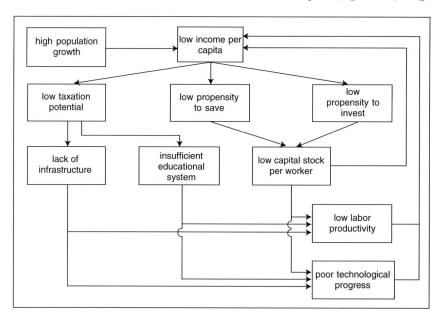

Figure 7.2 Vicious circle of underdevelopment

inflation rates and high foreign debt accelerate this vicious circle, which has to be broken for economic development to take off. Instead of 'vicious circle' or 'cumulating effects' this phenomenon is also called a 'low-level equilibrium'. Such a low-level equilibrium can be characterized as hysteresis. It is path-dependent in the sense that once such a situation is reached it is extremely difficult to get out of it. Similar considerations define the so-called economics of thresholds (*'économie des seuils'*) which has to be overcome before economic development can take place.

Different endowment conditions

Yet another aspect is that the countries of the world are characterized by different conditions for economic growth. Some of these conditions are determined by nature, like access to the oceans (coastal country versus inland, tropical conditions, etc.), others are man-made (acquired comparative advantage). This can lead to different growth rates.

7.3 Developing countries – newly industrializing countries – new industrialized countries: a broad spectrum

The picture described above has been related to those countries where the developing process has not yet started ('underdeveloped' countries). A number of African economies south of the Sahara and a few South Asian countries (including e.g. Bangladesh) belong to this category. But it would be wrong to put all countries which are normally called 'underdeveloped countries' in this category. In the industrializing countries, sufficient growth processes have already started, e.g. in most Latin American countries and in South East Asia. For some economies the term 'newly industrialized countries' is becoming more accepted – such as for example Argentina, Brazil, Chile, Mexico, Korea, Hong Kong, Singapore and Taiwan. In the statistics of the World Bank these countries are ranked in the middle-, upper- or even high-income groups (Table 7.2). Meanwhile some of them (e.g. Mexico, South Korea) have been admitted to the OECD. These countries have succeeded in a broad increase of their industrial exports and manufactured goods constitute a considerable part of their exports. The industrializing countries and the newly industrialized countries are on the way to another stage of economic development. Some of the economic policy problems to be discussed below have already been solved by these countries.

7.4 Development strategies

Concerning strategies of economic development we have to distinguish between import substitution and export diversification.

Table 7.2 The newly industrialized countries, 1997

	Gross national product per capita in US dollars		Share of industry-exports in total exports (in percent)[a]
	At current nominal exchange rates	At purchasing power parity	
Countries in the upper level of the middle-income group			
Mexico	3,680	8,120	78
Brazil	4,720	6,240	54
Chile	5,020	12,080	15
Argentina	8,570	9,950	30
Countries with a high income			
South Korea	10,550	13,500	92
Hong Kong	25,280	24,540	92
Singapore	32,940	29,000	84
World	5,130	6,330	78

[a]The shares of industrial production in the exports refer to the year 1996
Source: World Bank, *World Development Report 1998*, Tables 1 and 20

Import substitution

During the four decades from 1950 to 1990 the development policy of Latin America was characterized by a lack of confidence in the international division of labor as an important source of economic growth. Latin American development policy followed the strategy of import substitution. The starting point of this strategy was the thesis of decreasing terms-of-trade, which was developed by Prebisch (1950) and Singer (1950). This policy was directed at replacing imports by domestic goods. The domestic sectors were supported in their development and shielded against foreign suppliers. A basis for the industry was supposed to be built up by the protection of young industries (infant industry argument). In this respect it is significant that traditional trade relations had been interrupted by the Second World War. Unlike the European countries, Latin America did not place its hope on a closer integration of the world economy.

Typical instruments of such a policy were protectionist instruments like import licenses or import duties, which increased with the vertical level of processing and thus protected the domestic producers of finished goods. This development strategy, which was predominant in the 1950s and 1960s, at first seemed to be successful in Latin America, but from the mid-1960s onwards the problems became visible. Above all, the industrial sector developed very poorly. One reason was that the policy of import substitution was associated with considerable distortions. Intermediate goods became more expensive because of import protection, and this reduced the competitiveness of the export sector. Import protection had the same effects as taxation. The price structure was distorted in favor of the domestic import-substitutes so that this sector expanded too much and attracted too many resources. Because of the protection from international competition, the domestic producers did not feel the necessary pressure to cut costs and to innovate. The system of import licenses opened the doors for corruption. In the end, the strategy of import substitution caused serious misallocation and created more market failure – and also political failure – than had existed initially.

Export diversification

While the strategy of import substitution is rather inward-oriented, the strategy of export diversification, which was pursued by some Asian countries, can be seen as an outward-oriented development strategy. The objective was and still is to expose the export sectors to international competition and not to distort the allocation between the export sector and the sector of the import substitutes. Detrimental effects of import protection for exports were at first compensated by special export promotions. Due to high domestic savings this was not harmful to a balanced budget for the state. In short, it tried to enhance domestic production by intensive competition and by this to develop a sustainable economic basis. The predominant philosophy was that the world markets would offer interesting opportunities to the domestic producers. The exchange rate policy could prevent massive overvaluations. There is no proof for undervalued currencies over a longer period of time; the real exchange rate was mainly left to the markets. There have been almost no bureaucratic restrictions for currency-related questions in the commercial area.

Particularly the Asian economies followed the policy of export diversification, which has proved to be very successful. The exports were an enormous stimulus for the process of industrialization and economic development. They provided the countries with high gains from trade and made considerable real growth rates possible.

7.5 Institutional infrastructure

An essential requirement for a positive economic development is a reliable institutional framework, providing a good basis for decisions in the private sector. Many economic decisions have a long-term impact. This is valid for real capital investments, for the tapping of natural resources, for the decisions to start up businesses, and also for human capital investments. This requires stability of the institutional set-up. One important institutional condition is the right of ownership, i.e. the acceptance of private property rights. Another crucial prerequisite is a stable tax system, preventing taxes from being changed frequently and irregularly thus creating uncertainty for private investors.

Above all, it has to be guaranteed that the state must not balance the budget by printing money, i.e. by making the central bank increase monetary expansion and widen the supply of money. Monetization of the budget deficit is only possible because in many countries the central bank is not independent from political influence. For that reason, another important aspect is the independence of the central bank and the explicitly formulated prohibition of financing budget deficits by monetary policy. The institutional framework of the monetary system has to be credible. In the extreme case of a currency board (e.g. in Argentina), this credibility is in fact imported, since the domestic currency has to be completely covered by foreign currencies (US$).

7.6 The debt crisis

Especially for the countries of Latin America, the 1980s were marked by the debt crisis. For example, the volume of foreign debt in Argentina reached 93 percent of its gross domestic product (Figure 7.3). Net foreign debt in relation to exports of the 17 most indebted countries was at 384 percent, in comparison to the 200 percent which is considered to be acceptable by some (Cline 1995). Interest payments have been one important reason for a negative current account. New credits had to be borrowed so that countries were able to pay interest. The newly raised debts were rather used to finance the budget deficits of the state rather than to create a new capital stock.

When the financial markets realize that a country is not able to fulfill its interest and repayment commitments, then the markets lose the willingness to provide the country with credits, i.e. capital. As usually happens when a devaluation is expected, capital flight takes place. The prices of bonds of highly indebted countries fall. Normally, bank syndicates and international organizations have to provide a fresh starting position for new capital. Creditors lose a considerable amount of their claims by accepting a write-off on their debt (Brady Plan).

The debt crisis of the 1980s has now been overcome, if it is interpreted as a crisis of insolvency of the middle-income countries. But it is still relevant for the

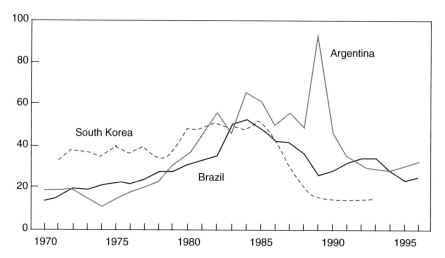

Figure 7.3 Debt of Argentina, Brazil and South Korea, 1971–1996 (in percent of gross national product)
Source: For 1977–1992: World Bank, *World Development Indicators* CD-ROM, 1997; for 1993–1996: World Bank, *Global Development Finance* (Country Tables), 1998

indebted countries. Argentina and Brazil, for example, still have to use more than 40 percent of their export revenues to pay the interest on their net foreign debts, foreign debt reaching roughly 300 percent of the export revenues (see Table 7.3).

Some Asian countries like Korea and some transformation countries like the Czech Republic are in a far better position. However, other Asian countries like Thailand and Indonesia have now reached similar magnitudes of debt relative to GDP to those of some Latin American countries (Figure 7.4).

Table 7.3 Foreign debt of selected countries, 1996

	Foreign debt in percent of gross national product	of exports	Debt service in percent of exports
Argentina	31	323	44.2
Bolivia	57	270	30.9
Brazil	26	292	41.1
Chile	48	166	32.3
Mexico	44	154	35.4
Indonesia	64	236	36.8
Thailand	56	131	11.5
Czech Republic	42	70	8.3
Hungary	62	158	41.0
Poland	31	102	6.4

Source: World Bank, *World Development Indicators*, CD-Rom 1998; World Bank *World Development Report 1996*

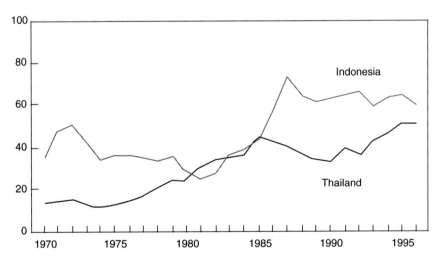

Figure 7.4 Debt of Thailand and Indonesia, 1970–1996 (in percent of gross national product)
Source: For 1970–1992: World Bank, *Word Development Indicators* CD-ROM, 1997; for 1993–1996: World Bank, *Global Development Finance* (Country Tables), 1998

7.7 Macroeconomic instability and Latin American countries

Macroeconomic instability is a special problem for the newly industrializing countries in Latin America, for example with exorbitantly high inflation rates of 2,314 percent in 1990 for Argentina or 2,938 percent in the same year for Brazil. The inflation rate is correlated with an unusually high expansion of the money supply (Table 7.4). Besides inflation another major problem is the volatility of the inflation rate. Most of the time, high public deficits and current account deficits occur simultaneously. This can be explained by insufficient institutional conditions for macroeconomic stability.

Money expansion and inflation

The correlation between the expansion of the money supply and inflation can clearly be seen for Argentina and Brazil (Figures 7.5 and 7.6). Argentina managed to get the expansion of the money supply under control and to keep the price level stable by economic policy reforms and not least by the transition to a currency board.

Usually, inflation has an effect on the exchange rate, although the impact might be delayed temporarily. This results from the purchasing power parity $\hat{e} = \hat{P} - \hat{P}*$. For instance, the peak of the inflation rate in Argentina in 1989 and 1990 is related to a visible devaluation of the peso (Figure 7.5).

Brazil seems to be a somewhat different story. At the beginning of the 1980s a strong devaluation took place, but the money supply and the price level did not change significantly. This is the effect of the beginning of the debt crisis. At relatively constant product prices, a nominal devaluation induces a real revaluation, which is necessary to improve the current account. The other phases of

Table 7.4 Macroeconomic instability, 1985–1997

	Expansion of the money supply[a]	Inflation rate[a]	Budget deficit[b]	Current account balance[b]
Argentina				
1985–1990	525.7	597.8	−2.1	−2.9
1991–1997	33.3	22.2	−0.7[c]	−1.9[c]
Brazil				
1985–1990	590.7	569.4	−12.7	−0.1
1991–1997	375.9	370.2	−10.9[d]	0.1[e]
Mexico				
1985–1990	62.0	57.5	−8.7	−0.7
1991–1997	13.7	16.9	0.1[e]	−3.9

[a]Expansion of the money supply and inflation rate in percent. [b]Budget deficit and the current account balance in percent of GDP. [c]1991–1996. [d]1991–1994. [e]1991–1995
Source: IMF, *International Financial Statistics 1998*; OECD, *Economic Outlook 1998* (Current Account of Mexico)

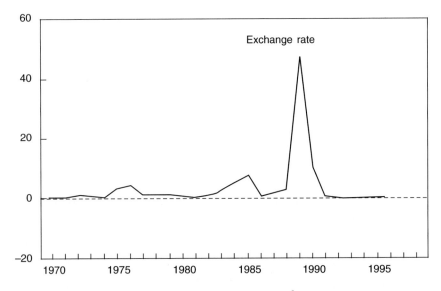

Figure 7.5 Money expansion, inflation and the exchange rate[a], Argentina 1970–1997
[a]Change in percent
Source: IMF, *International Financial Statistics 1998*

devaluation were marked by monetary reforms. In the mid-1980s the cruzeiro was replaced by the cruzado. Its exchange rate was regularly devalued in the framework of a crawling peg. The cause of the monetary reform was an internal imbalance with a budget deficit of 11 percent. At the beginning of the 1990s the

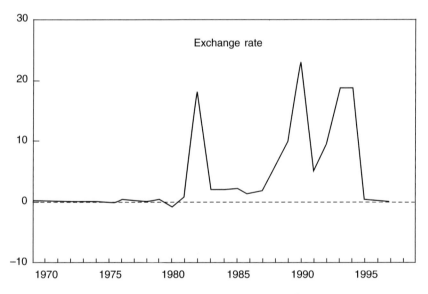

Figure 7.6 Money expansion, inflation and the exchange rate[a], Brazil 1970–1997
[a]Change in percent
Source: IMF, *International Financial Statistics 1998*

cruzeiro was introduced once again and was devalued by floating. Now, the cause was an external imbalance accompanied by a drop of foreign capital inflows. Finally, with a new monetary reform in 1993 the *real* was introduced.

In Mexico (Figure 7.7) there is also a connection between the expansion of the

Figure 7.7 Money expansion, inflation and the exchange rate[a], Mexico 1970–1997
[a]Change in percent
Source: IMF, *International Financial Statistics 1998*

money supply and the inflation rate but it is not as visible as in the case of Brazil. Thus, during the debt crisis in the beginning of the 1980s, the increase in the inflation rate was stronger, while at the same time – like in Brazil – a strong devaluation took place. A drop in the inflow of foreign capital was visible in the mid-1980s and in connection with the peso crisis at the end of 1994. The strong expansion of the money supply in the early 1990s surprisingly had at first neither an effect on the price level nor on the exchange rate. This might be the temporary result of the policy of an active crawling peg, attempting to stabilize the expectations on the foreign exchange markets. But if for a period of time the rate of change of the price index is higher than in the reference country like in 1983 and 1984 and in the period from 1988 to 1994, there has to be a realignment of the nominal exchange rate (compare also Figure 6.4). In 1994, the peso crisis occurred and the peso was strongly devalued.

Chile pursued different exchange rate policies. During 1980–1981, a policy of fixed exchange rates was pursued. This was combined with a real revaluation. This approach could no longer be carried out after the outbreak of the debt crisis. After a period of flexible exchange rates, Chile moved on to a passive crawling peg, in which since 1989 real economic realignments are regarded as more important than the fight against inflation. The parity of the peso is regularly adjusted to a basket of currencies. Relative to a constant real exchange rate, a crawling peg has the advantage of preventing abrupt adjustments later on if it is applied correctly.

Budget deficits and the exchange rate

Changes of the exchange rate are a reaction to internal as well as external imbalances. For instance, there was a remarkable public budget deficit in Mexico in the 1980s (Figure 7.8). Combined with an expansion of the money supply, this was the cause for the rise of the price level and the devaluation of the peso. Although the budget deficit had been reduced until the beginning of the 1990s, the current account deficit increased after huge short-term inflows of portfolio investment. The collapse occurred in December of 1994, when the capital flow turned around and the peso had to be devalued. At the same time, an international support program became necessary. During the 1980s, Brazil also had a significant budget deficit with up to 20 percent of its GDP. An increase of the budget deficit became visible in Argentina particularly in the first half of the 1980s. These budget deficits signal that credible stabilization policies were not carried out.

The experience of the Latin American countries shows that a stabilization policy with the exchange rate as a nominal anchor could rarely be kept up, for example if public budget deficits could not be avoided. Then the confidence in the stability of a currency gets lost. Something similar can be seen when economic policy is dominated by income distribution considerations (or policies). A lack of flexibility of the labor market as well as of wages that do not correspond to labor productivity, make a stabilization policy far more difficult in the long run.

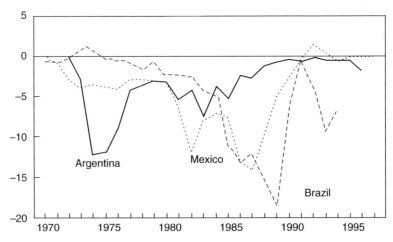

Figure 7.8 Budget deficits of Argentina, Brazil and Mexico, in percent of GDP
Source: IMF, *International Financial Statistics 1998*

Instability and the real exchange rate

Fixing the nominal exchange rate does not imply a constant real exchange rate. Very often the domestic inflation rate is higher than the foreign one. Then, a real revaluation takes place. P rises stronger than P^*. The real exchange rate $e_R = eP^*/P$ falls. This is also valid for the crawling peg if the devaluation rate does not fully compensate the difference between the two inflation rates. A real appreciation can turn out to be even stronger if high net capital inflows occur. The real appreciation has allocative effects. Furthermore it is linked to deficits in the current account. If the currency is overvalued in real terms an adjustment is unavoidable. Then, a real depreciation has to take place. Normally this means a nominal devaluation; the fixed exchange rate is given up. As an alternative, the price for imports or for non-tradables has to rise.

Although the newly industrialized countries of Latin America have been successful in establishing macroeconomic stability for some time, the question is whether this stability will last or whether a new crisis will occur thus making necessary new stabilization efforts. Because of political constraints, too often there are deviations from the stabilization programs. This happens because institutional changes are insufficient to keep the expansion of the money supply at a low level in order to assure a constant money value. The volatility will remain the Damocles sword of Latin America.

7.8 The real exchange rate once more: expenditure reduction and expenditure switching

A crucial role for development processes is played by the real exchange rate (e_R). As we know from chapter 6, the real exchange rate differs from the nominal exchange rate in that the nominal exchange rate is weighted by a ratio of goods prices. If the ratio refers to the prices of foreign and domestic goods, the real exchange rate, i.e. $e_R = eP*/P$, provides information on the production incentives for domestic goods relative to foreign goods. If the ratio refers to the prices of tradables and of non-tradables, i.e. $e_R = eP_T^*/P_{NT}$, the information signal is on incentives for the production of tradables relative to non-tradables.

The real exchange rate is an important variable that influences both the equilibrium of the balance of payments and the internal equilibrium of the goods market. The real exchange rate is a determinant of absorption and of production.

Developing countries, which all too often have a current account deficit, have to reduce this deficit. Such a situation can be seen in Figure 7.9. The real relative price eP_T^*/P_{NT}, i.e. the real exchange rate (Q_{NH}/Q_H), is given by the tangent of the angle α. The country's production point is D and the consumption point is F. The country absorbs more than it would be feasible according to its production conditions. There is a trade deficit between demand and supply of the tradable DF. If the deficit is to be reduced, there are two possible ways. First, absorption can be reduced (expenditure reduction, movement from F to D). For instance, government demand can be reduced. Higher taxation can cut down private consumption (then, with given relative prices and a homothetic utility function the point of consumption is on a line OF). Second, the country could carry out a real devaluation, i.e. the real exchange rate has to increase in order to reduce the deficit of the current account (expenditure switching, movement from D to G

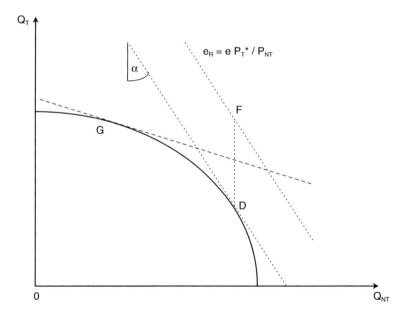

Figure 7.9 The real exchange rate

along the transformation curve). This implies that the price of the tradable good denominated in national currency rises relative to the non-tradable good. This implies that the sectoral structure has to change. After a real depreciation, it is more profitable to expand the production of the tradable good and the production of the non-tradable good decreases. Due to the change of relative prices there is a reallocation of resources towards the tradable good (export and import substitutes). The trade account is balanced in point G. The production of the non-tradable good has decreased and the production of the tradable good has risen.

A real devaluation can be brought about by a nominal devaluation; but it can also take place when the price for the non-tradable goods falls in the home country while prices for tradables remain constant.

8 The transformation countries

At the end of the 1980s and the beginning of the 1990s a radical change took place in the world economy. The countries of Central and Eastern Europe gave up central planning and switched over to a market economy approach. They had to – and to some extent they still have to – rebuild their economic systems and adapt their economies to the new conditions. Together with the new economic concept, the political decision structures and the institutional set-up changed (section 8.1). Initially, a collapse of output occurred (section 8.2). Especially the sequence of reform steps was the subject of intense discussions (sections 8.3 and 8.4). A lot of economic problems such as privatization, tightening budget constraints and inflation had to be solved (section 8.5). The international economic aspects of transformation are of particular interest (section 8.6). More than thirty formerly centrally planned economies are in a process of reform at the moment. East Germany is a special case of the transformation process (section 8.7). Already at the end of the 1970s, China had begun to decentralize and to reorganize its economic system, though without changing its political structures (section 8.8). The Soviet Union dissolved into a number of countries, among them Russia, Ukraine, Belarus, Uzbekistan and other nations (section 8.9).

8.1 Rebuilding a centrally planned economy

In the process of rebuilding a centrally planned economy into a market economy, there are three main areas of reform which can be distinguished: the creation of a new institutional framework, macroeconomic stabilization and the real adjustment of the firms and sectors on the microeconomic level (Figure 8.1).

The institutional framework

The rules and incentives of the centrally planned economies have to be replaced by institutional arrangements that allow market transactions, that let firms decide on their production and their investments autonomously and that let households determine their consumption, savings and labor supply on their own. A legal framework is imperative, particularly the law of contract and the law of enterprises. A decentralization of economic decisions is not possible without reliable property rights. Property rights are responsible for long-term effects being taken into account in economic calculations. But property rights are also a crucial

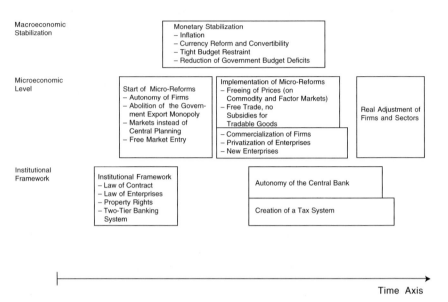

Figure 8.1 Areas and sequence of reforms
Source: World Bank, *World Development Report 1995*

incentive for individuals to do business. Above all, property rights establish an area of decisions in which the individuals can move without being influenced by government. After all, one essential element of the framework of a market economy is from which responsibilities the government withdraws, that is, which responsibilities the government leaves to the private sector. Finally, a two-tier banking system, in which the responsibilities of monetary policy and intermediation are separated, can be regarded as an important aspect of the institutional framework.

Macroeconomic stabilization

During the transition from a centrally planned economy to a market economy, macroeconomic instabilities arise. The existing excess supply of money causes inflation, which is hard to keep under control. As a result, there are negative effects on the real sphere of the economy during the transformation process. Therefore one objective has to be a stable money. Usually, this can only be achieved by a currency reform, when a new currency with a new name is introduced or when a massive currency cut is carried out. Moreover, the newly independent successor states of the Soviet Union and Yugoslavia have had to introduce their own new currencies.

But a currency reform remains unsuccessful unless the necessary institutional design for the monetary sector is introduced. One important step is to guarantee the independence of the central bank. It must be prohibited, in particular, that the central bank finances government budget deficits with its monetary policy. Finally, macroeconomic stabilization cannot succeed and an increase in efficiency for the whole economy cannot be obtained unless the state budget deficit is reduced and a tight budget restriction for the government is introduced. Exchange rate policy must take the purchasing power parity into account. For that reason the nominal rates must move in line with the inflation differences. A higher domestic inflation rate than abroad means a real appreciation, possibly causing a deficit in the balance of payment.

Real adjustment of firms

The institutional framework and macroeconomic stability are necessary requirements for the transformation process, but, at the core, the transformation must take place on the microeconomic level inside the enterprises. Micro-reforms include the introduction of markets with price liberalization, the conversion of state enterprises into separate legal entities (commercialization) and their privatization. The real adjustment process must then take place inside the privatized firms. The transition to a market economy means a 'shock' for the firms: some of their products cannot be sold any more, prices of the production factors are now based on scarcity, factor allocation does not correspond to the new market prices, the capital stock of the enterprises is largely obsolete. The existing firms have to find new products, change the factor allocation and build new capital. Even more important for the real adjustment process on the microeconomic level is the setting up of new firms.

8.2 The J-curve of transformation

The transformation of a centrally planned economy involves a collapse of national output. A crucial reason for this breakdown is that the capital stock of the transformation country that was adapted to the old conditions of a centrally planned economy became obsolete to a large extent due to the new scarcity relations. Therefore the reform countries have to rebuild their capital stock. This process takes time and, moreover, involves adjustment costs. Additionally, the existing human capital has to be integrated into the new factor allocation. Another aspect of the economic breakdown is the institutional vacuum at the beginning of the transformation process, which implies uncertainty over the rules that will hold in the future.

The Visegrad countries (Poland, Hungary and the then still united Czech and Slovak Republics), where the reforms started about 1989, had to face a breakdown of roughly 20 percent of their gross domestic products (Figure 8.2). While the breakdown took place at a similar pace, the Czech Republic, Hungary and the Slovak Republic have needed more time to recover than Poland.

In Russia, where the reforms started about 1991 rather than 1989, the gross domestic product halved (Figure 8.3); the decrease in Lithuania was even stronger. There was also a massive breakdown in East Germany, where the industrial production fell to one third of the former level (section 8.7).

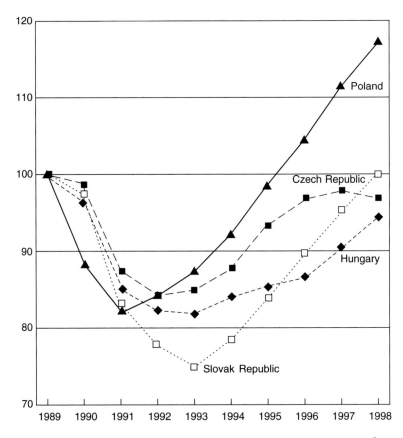

Figure 8.2 The J-curves in Central Europe (gross domestic product in real terms)[a]
[a]1989 = 100
Source: EBRD, *Transition Report*, various issues; 1997: preliminary estimates; 1998: EBRD projection

8.3 The sequence of reform steps

There are different opinions on strategies of transformation. It is fair to point out that American economists emphasized the importance of macroeconomic stabilization, taking the experience with stabilization policy in Latin America as a frame of reference. German economists, on the other hand, put more emphasis on the development of the institutional framework. For them, the process is characterized by the Erhard reforms of West Germany in 1948.

A time pattern of the most important reform steps in the three main areas of institutional framework, macroeconomic stabilization and real adaptation is shown in Figure 8.1.

At the beginning of reforms, the creation of an institutional framework is required. This is a prerequisite for the reforms on the microeconomic level and the real adjustment. The reforms on the microeconomic level can start a little bit

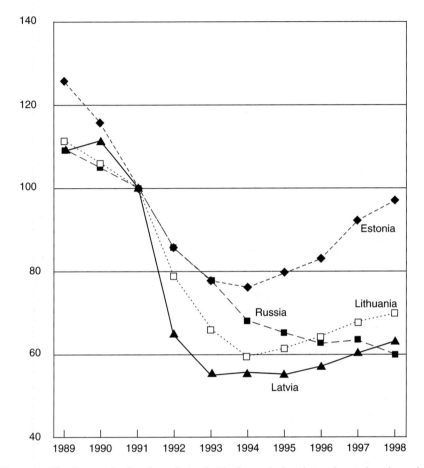

Figure 8.3 The J-curve in Russia and the Baltic States (gross domestic product in real terms)[a]
[a]1991 = 100
Source: EBRD *Transition Report*, various issues; 1997: preliminary estimates; 1998: EBRD projection

later. Central planning is replaced by market allocation. The export monopoly of the state is abolished, firms decide autonomously.

In a second step these micro-reforms are implemented. The prices on the commodity markets are liberalized. Additionally, scarcity prices on the factor markets are established. The wage structure has to be adapted to the new situation. After commercialization of enterprises, privatization has to start.

Approximately at the beginning of the micro-reforms, monetary stabilization must be tackled. This includes a currency reform and an (at least partial) independence of the central bank with the appropriate institutional arrangement. In this phase, it is important to tighten the budget constraint. Centrally planned economies were characterized by 'soft budget constraints' for state enterprises and for the state itself (Kornai 1980). Enterprises received cheap credits and direct subsidies from the national budget. This practice has to be given up. The newly developing banking system cannot support the old enterprises by favoring them with special rates of interest any longer, because this implies a higher interest burden for the new firms, and this in turn means an international competitive disadvantage for the economy as a whole. As the government should not be allowed to cover its deficits with the help of the central bank any longer, a tax system must be developed that allows government expenditures to be financed by taxes. In this context, the question arises to what extent the state is able to cushion the social problems (old age insurance, health care, unemployment) that are partly caused by transformation.

Finally, the economy has to adjust in real terms. This means that the factor allocation within the firms must be changed (see above). The set of goods that is produced and the sectoral structure have to adjust.

In principle, it is reasonable to carry out as many reform steps as possible in a short period of time. There is a bundle of essentials which has to be introduced at once. For example, there is good reason to believe that after the creation of an institutional framework, the decontrol of prices, the opening of commodity markets to foreign countries, the privatization of enterprises and monetary stabilization must be put into effect more or less simultaneously. This must be quickly followed by the autonomy of the central bank. With regard to the tax system, one will have to start with a rudimentary tax system (customs duties, sales taxes) that will gradually be rebuilt towards a value-added tax and income tax system. It can also be discussed whether some steps can be postponed, for example the residents' convertibility of the domestic currency. But the problem is that thereby the reform loses credibility.

8.4 Big bang or gradual adjustment?

The different elements of the reform can be realized in one big step ('big bang') or gradually (Figure 8.4). It has been intensively discussed in the literature whether the 'big bang' or rather the gradual approach promises to be more successful. Psychological aspects and political economy arguments speak well in favor of the 'big bang' approach. After the collapse of a centrally planned economy, people are prepared to try a new approach and to make sacrifices for it. For example, real wages (we use producer wages for lack of data on consumer wages) in Poland (1990) and in the Czech Republic (1991) fell by more than 30 percent within one year (Table 8.1). The quicker the necessary and painful steps of adjustment are carried out, the quicker the country will get out of the 'vale of tears'. The Poles have expressed this philosophy with the motto: 'You cannot cross a gorge with two leaps'. When the countries of Central Europe introduced the new economic system, they simultaneously changed their political system and introduced democracy. This is another important argument in favor of the 'big bang' approach: there is a narrow window for reform. If the fundamental social consensus for reform loses momentum, the government can be replaced; then, the consistency of the reform approach can be lost.

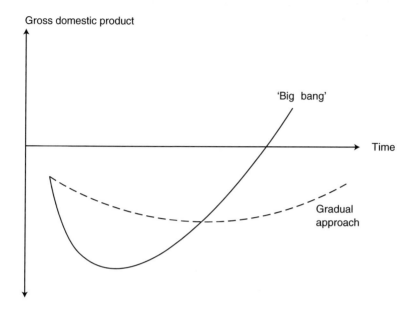

Gross domestic product

'Big bang'

Time

Gradual
approach

Figure 8.4 'Big bang' versus gradual adjustment

As an alternative, a gradual approach was discussed in the early literature on the transformation. The argument in favor of the gradual approach was that the transformation process would turn out to be less hard if the steps of reform were stretched over a longer period of time. But this requires a deep breath for the transformation, particularly a prolonged willingness of people to stand the necessary reform steps. If the willingness to reform is lost in the course of time, the transformation process can come to a halt. The growth rates of Poland (more than 5 percent after 1993) and the comparatively lower budget deficits in Poland of around 3 percent after 1992, compared to Hungary (deficits of more than 5 percent in the period 1993–1995), seem to confirm the advantages of the 'big bang' (Table 8.1, Figure 8.2). This is all the more valid in comparison with the many successor states of the Soviet Union, like Russia, where the reforms were tackled only hesitantly and where the collapse of production was nevertheless sizable. The experience of the Czech Republic with the financial crisis in 1997 suggests that a big bang may lose the support of the voter.

8.5 Some central issues of economic policy

Privatization

An important step in the transformation process is the privatization of the state-run enterprises. In this context, different procedures were used. In the Czech Republic, the problem was solved by means of coupon privatization: citizens

Table 8.1 Important economic variables in the transformation process

	1990	1991	1992	1993	1994	1995	1996	1997[a]	1998[b]
Real GDP growth (percent)									
Czech Republic	−1.2	−11.5	−3.3	0.6	3.2	6.4	3.9	1.0	−1.0
Hungary	−3.5	−11.9	−3.1	−0.6	2.9	1.5	1.3	4.4	4.6
Poland	−11.6	−7.0	2.6	3.8	5.2	7.0	6.1	6.9	5.2
Slovak Republic	−2.5	−14.6	−6.5	−3.7	4.9	6.9	6.6	6.5	5.0
Russia	−4.0	−5.0	−14.5	−8.7	−12.7	−4.1	−3.5	0.8	−5.0
Consumer price inflation (percent)									
Czech Republic	10.8	56.6	11.1	20.8	10.0	9.1	8.8	8.5	11.0
Hungary	28.9	35.0	23.0	22.5	18.8	28.2	23.6	18.3	15.0
Poland	585.6	70.3	43.0	35.3	32.2	27.8	19.9	14.9	11.0
Slovak Republic	10.8	61.2	10.1	23.2	13.4	9.9	5.8	6.1	7.5
Russia	5.6	92.7	1526	875	311.4	197.7	47.78	14.7	40.0
Change of real producer wages in the manufacturing industry (percent)									
Czech Republic[c]	0.1[c]	−31.5	8.7	13.4	9.9	9.8	12.3	8.2	na
Hungary	0.7	−5.3	12.1	12.5	11.0	−5.9	−0.2	1.4	na
Poland	−34.8	15.8	3.1	2.7	9.1	5.8	12.9	8.3	na
Slovak Republic	−1.2	−31.1	10.5	4.4	7.5	6.3	10.2	7.1	na
Russia[d]	na	na	−41.4	−6.1	−14.8	−33.6	13.3	0.0	na
Budget deficit (in percent of GDP)									
Czech Republic	0.1	−1.9	−3.1	0.5	−1.2	−1.8	−1.2	−2.1	−2.4
Hungary	0.4	−2.9	−6.8	−5.5	−8.4	−6.1	−3.1	−4.9	−4.9
Poland	3.1	−6.7	−6.7	−3.1	−3.1	−2.8	−3.3	−3.1	−3.1
Slovak Republic	0.1	−2.0	−11.9	−7.0	−1.3	0.2	−1.9	−3.8	−4.0
Russia	na	na	−4.1	−7.4	−9.0	−5.7	−8.3	−7.4	−8.0
Current account deficit (in percent of GDP)									
Czech Republic	−1.1	1.2	1.0	0.3	0.1	−2.7	−7.6	−6.1	−3.1
Hungary	0.3	0.8	0.9	−9.0	−9.4	−5.6	−3.7	−2.2	−3.4
Poland	1.0	−2.6	1.1	−0.7	2.5	4.6	−1.0	−3.1	−4.5
Slovak Republic	na	na	na	−5.0	4.8	2.3	−11.2	−6.9	−9.6
Russia	na	na	na	1.1	3.2	2.2	2.8	0.7	1.4

[a]Preliminary. [b]Projections. [c]1990: former Czechoslovakia. [d] large- and medium-sized companies
na = not available
Source: EBRD *Transition Report*, various issues; own calculations from EBRD-data.

received coupons which allowed them to buy company shares at an auction. The relative price between shares and coupons was found on the market, i.e. at the auctions. In Russia, coupons were used as well, but insiders of the enterprises got preferential treatment. Employees were entitled to keep up to 51 percent of the shares of their enterprise out of the coupon auctions that were otherwise open to the public. In addition, they could acquire shares under preferential conditions. The consequence was predominantly an insider privatization. In fact, the managers appropriated the right of disposal for the enterprises. Meanwhile, external investors increasingly succeeded in acquiring larger share packages in connection with capital increases, via stock markets or directly from the employees. Coupons were also used in most other transformation countries. In East Germany, the trustee approach was applied: the enterprises were sold to investors by a government agency (Treuhandanstalt). The same holds for Hungary and Estonia.

Privatization has probably reached the most advanced level in the Czech Republic, where 75 percent of the gross domestic product originates from the private enterprise sector. Poland (65 percent) and Hungary (80 percent) are at a similar level. For Russia, the privatization ratio is also given as 70 percent; for China the figure is 72 percent if the municipal enterprises are considered as private enterprises (Table 8.2). The level of privatization, measured by the production share of the private sector, does not correspond to the high share of government spending in GDP, as the state draws resources from the private sector by means of taxes.

The tightening of the budget restraint

Transformation countries are often characterized by high budget deficits. After 1993, the deficits amounted to significantly more than 5 percent of the GDP in Hungary and to 9 percent in Russia (Figure 8.5). Changing present expenditure structures is difficult. The government cannot give the remaining state-run enterprises cheap credits through the banks any longer, or only to a limited extent. The state does not succeed in tightening the budget restriction for state enterprises. The social cushioning of the transformation process requires additional expenditures, especially if the reorganization process is delayed and the new tax system has not yet been developed. The budget deficits increase government borrowing and restrict the maneuvering space of the state due to interest payments. Moreover, budget deficits force the interest rates up and in this way crowd out private investment. Besides, high budget deficits reduce the credibility of monetary policy. People prepare themselves for higher inflation and a

Table 8.2 Privatization of production and government expenditure of the state in distribution in percent of GDP

	Private production[a]	Government expenditure[b]
China	32 (72)[c]	na
Czech Republic	75	41.6
Hungary	80	52.9
Poland	65	48.1
Russia	70	40.7
Slovak Republic	75	51.0
Ukraine	55	40.4 (1996)

[a]Percentage share in GDP mid-1998 (estimates). [b]1997 (estimates). [c]In brackets: including local and collective enterprises. na = not available
Source: EBRD *Transition Report 1998*; State Statistical Bureau, People's Republic of China, *China Statistical Yearbook 1997*

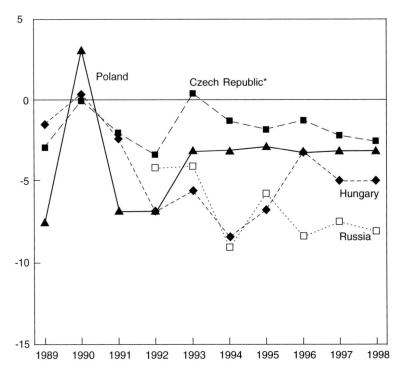

Figure 8.5 Budget deficits of selected transformation countries (in percent of GDP)
*1989–92: Czechoslovakia. 1998: projection
Source: EBRD *Transition Report,* various issues

devaluation of the domestic currency. High budget deficits must therefore be interpreted as a warning signal of vulnerability.

The tightening of the budget restrictions for enterprises can turn out to be difficult if, *inter alia,* the enterprises give credits to each other – as in Russia – and fall into arrears with their payments. In 1998, the payments in arrears were estimated at 300 percent of the money supply M_2 or at 37 percent of GDP.

Current account deficits

In Hungary, the budget deficit coincides with the current account deficit (twin deficits). The current account deficits of Hungary after 1993 in relation to its gross domestic product were large (Figure 8.6). In the Czech Republic and the Slovak Republic large current account deficits have been recorded since 1996 (Table 8.1). A profligate financial policy seems to be the reason for the high current-account deficit in Hungary, whereas in the Czech Republic the situation has probably been caused by relatively high real wage increases in connection with rather low productivity gains and a constant nominal exchange rate. The Czech

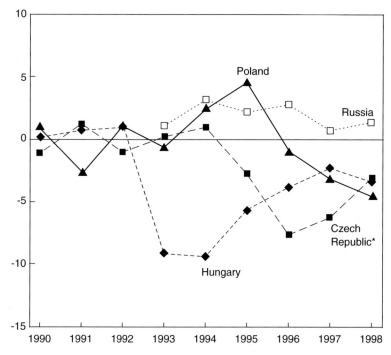

Figure 8.6 Current account deficits of selected transformation countries (in percent of GDP)
*1990–92: Czechoslovakia
Source: EBRD *Transition Report*, various issues

Republic turned to a flexible exchange rate in 1997 and took measures to dampen the domestic demand.

Inflation

The transformation process is often linked to a high rate of inflation, not least due to the lack of an institutional framework for the monetary system and a loose monetary policy (Russia 1992–1994). Monetary stability proves to be a necessary condition for the transformation process. Empirical studies of the transformation countries come to the conclusion that the annual rate of inflation must be lower than 50 percent if a growth process is to begin (Fischer et al. 1996). In Central Europe and in the Baltic States, the gross national product decreased up to the year when the stabilization was started. Two years later the growth rates became positive.

8.6 Foreign trade aspects of transformation

Opening up to foreign trade

The opening up to foreign trade is of great importance for the reform countries because trade signals the world prices to those countries. This reduces distortions and sets the right incentives to allocate resources for the production of goods efficiently.

Efficiency gains from foreign trade

The opening up to foreign trade involves efficiency gains from international exchange. The domestic enterprises are exposed to international competition. Relative prices of the reform countries are brought into line with those of the world economy. Inefficient enterprises get under pressure from imports. We can see a dramatic new orientation of the foreign trade of the reform countries. For example, the reform countries that are currently negotiating to become new members of the European Union exported roughly 60 percent of their exports into the EU in 1997 (compare Table 10.4). The reform countries resemble the EU members not only in trade volume, but also in the product structure of trade. With the gains from trade, higher growth rates become possible.

Capital inflow

The opening up to foreign trade improves the prospects for attracting foreign capital that can give significant new growth momentum. Thanks to their liberal foreign trade policies, Poland, the Czech Republic and Hungary have attracted considerable foreign direct investment, comparable to that of Latin America and Asia. The share of foreign direct investments in total gross investment, for example, amounted to 20 percent in Hungary and more than 10 percent in Poland in 1992–1996 (Table 3.3). China has also been successful in attracting foreign direct investment. Without the special economic zones in the south of the country that were vested with foreign trade privileges and without the considerable sums of foreign investment capital that were attracted by those zones, China's economic rise during the last twenty years would have been completely unthinkable. For years, China has by far been the most important location for new foreign direct investments in developing countries and was the number two worldwide from 1992 until 1997, after the US.

Exchange rate policy

In the sense of the purchasing power parity ($\hat{e} = \hat{P} - \hat{P}*$), the nominal exchange rates must reflect the differences in the inflation rates. For example, Russia had to strongly devalue the rouble; at first, the devaluation of the rouble approximately followed, though with a certain delay, the rate of inflation. Then the rate of devaluation exceeded the rate of inflation, i.e. a real devaluation took place (Figure 8.7). Poland (Figure 8.8) and the Czech Republic (Figure 6.3) also underwent massive nominal devaluations early in the transformation process. The excessive money supply in Poland was significantly larger than in the Czech Republic, therefore the devaluation had to be stronger as well. In the Czech Republic, the macroeconomic imbalance and foreign debt were relatively low at the start of the transformation process and the country pursued a consistently restrictive fiscal policy after its independence in 1993. Moreover, a wage restraint was prevalent at first, and capital inflow from abroad increased quickly. Thus, the nominal exchange rate could be kept stable in relation to a basket of currencies for a long time. Due to a growing current account deficit, however, the Czech crown had to be devalued in 1997; the fixed currency anchor was abandoned.

In Poland, the nominal exchange rate was further adjusted even after the initial devaluation. Since the autumn of 1991, an active crawling peg linked to a basket of currencies has existed, meaning that the domestic currency is devalued by a pre-announced margin each month. After an initial quick stabilization success, the rate of inflation was maintained at a high level, compared to the Czech Republic. Hungary devalued at the beginning of the reforms and in discretionary steps afterwards.

In Russia, several early attempts to stabilize the exchange rate failed. The high rates of inflation in 1991 and 1992, which were due to a budget deficit that got out of control and to an expansionary monetary policy, led to massive devaluations of the rouble. In the middle of 1995, an exchange rate corridor, though

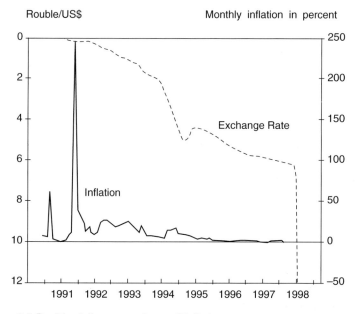

Figure 8.7 Rouble–dollar rate and rate of inflation
Source: Russian Economic Trends (1998); IMF, *International Financial Statistics 1998*

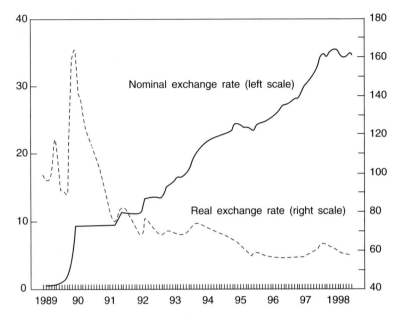

Figure 8.8 Polish zloty: nominal[a] and real[b] exchange rate *vis-à-vis* the US$
[a]Zloty/0.1 US$. [b]January 1989 = 100
Source: IMF, *International Financial Statistics*, CD-ROM; own calculations

with significant ranges of fluctuation, was introduced. In 1996, the government went on to a gradual, pre-announced adjustment of the corridor. As the range of fluctuation was decreased by a certain percentage at the same time, the exchange rate policy increasingly resembles an active crawling peg. In August 1998, this policy was more or less abandoned.

The reform states practice a crawling peg, with the continuous devaluation falling short of the current inflation rate by a predetermined percentage. The currencies are thus nominally overvalued. In this way, price increases are dampened. As the domestic currency usually undergoes a drastic nominal devaluation at the beginning of a stabilization program, it is undervalued in real terms at first. In the course of time, this undervaluation changes into an overvaluation.

Real exchange rate

A possible option for an exchange rate policy is to choose the nominal exchange rate as an anchor. Following this strategy, the leeway for price divergence is narrowed and the inflation expectations are stabilized. These goals can – partly – be achieved by means of a crawling peg as well. But if the inflation difference relative to the anchor currency decreases only slowly under a crawling peg, the consequence is a real revaluation. The real exchange rate $e_R = eP*/P$ falls due to a strongly increasing domestic price level; this means a real appreciation. The less monetary policy is oriented towards stabilization, the higher will be the real revaluation. This also holds for fiscal policy. The inflow of capital also involves a (nominal and) real revaluation. This is completely harmless if the international competitiveness improves and if thereby the equilibrium exchange rate rises.

The strong nominal devaluations in Poland (1990) and Czechoslovakia (1991) first went hand in hand with a real devaluation that was also necessary to restructure expenditures in favor of tradable goods (expenditure switching). But later on, a real revaluation can be noticed (Figures 8.8 and 6.3). In Poland, the devaluation within the framework of the crawling peg was not sufficiently large to counteract the real revaluation; the rate of inflation was not compensated by nominal devaluation. The Czech Republic, on the other hand, had a lower real revaluation, with a nearly constant nominal exchange rate for quite some time. This was not sustainable. We have to take into account that a real revaluation counteracts positive net exports. It dampens price increases and therefore partly keeps inflationary tendencies under control.

Eventually, the nominal exchange rate policy cannot be judged from the point of view of monetary stability alone. In addition, it must be guaranteed that the resulting real exchange rate allows a current account that can be maintained in the long term and that is compatible with a national economic equilibrium between absorption and production. If an imbalance occurs here, the real exchange rate must be corrected. In this context, a nominal devaluation is a possible lever to achieve a real devaluation.

8.7 The transformation of East Germany

East Germany is a special case in the transformation process. Two of the three big reform steps in the transformation process – the creation of an institutional infrastructure, macroeconomic stabilization and the economic adjustment in real terms – were realized practically overnight: by joining the Federal Republic, the constitution and all other legal arrangements of West Germany were taken over. At the same time, the currency union guaranteed monetary stability. The real economic adaptation is therefore at the core of the transformation process in East Germany.

But East Germany is also a special case because transformation overlaps with integration, i.e. German reunification. Due to this, the exchange rate was not available as a buffer in the transformation process, and the enterprises did not only have to cope with the inefficiency of the centrally planned economy, but also had to accept a strong revaluation of the East German mark (by approximately 400 percent). The population pressed for similar living conditions and a quick wage alignment. In this way, a wide gap opened up between wages and productivity. This involved high unemployment and, moreover, hampered investment. East Germany is also a special case in the sense that, quite differently from the usual transformation process, significant transfers were made. They amounted to 5 percent of the gross domestic product of Germany as a whole, per year ('big bang with a big brother').

East Germany experienced a dramatic collapse of production. Gross industrial production, with all reservations regarding the comparability of data, fell to less than one third of its former level. The low level of industrial production after 1990 as drawn in Figure 8.9 is partly due to a lack of comparable data. After 1990, net production is shown; prior to 1990, gross production (including inter-mediate inputs and depreciation) is shown. Moreover, East German 'industrial production' included huge amounts of additional contributions such as fringe benefits, which are not counted anymore. Starting with 1992, an increase in net industrial production can be observed. Gross domestic product fell to approxi-mately two thirds. Employment decreased from 10 million by almost 5 million if the political measures concerning the labor market (for example, up to 2 million short-time workers at times) are not considered (Siebert 1995).

East Germany reached approximately 60 percent of the West German labor productivity level and also of the production capacity per head in 1997, after approximately 30 percent in 1991. The gross wage and salary sum per employee reached approximately 75 percent. The process of replacing and building up the capital stock is under way. An export basis is still being built up. If the results con-cerning catching-up processes are analogously applied, we have to conclude that a complete alignment will still take some time (see chapter 4).

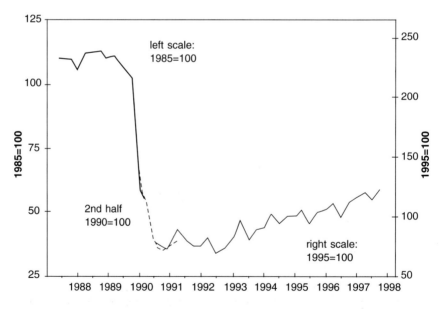

Figure 8.9 The J-curve in East Germany, industrial production, 1988–1998[a]
[a]Quarterly data
Source: Statistisches Bundesamt, *Produzierendes Gewerbe,* various issues; Statistisches Amt der DDR, *Statistisches Jahrbuch der Industrie* (1990); Statistisches Amt der DDR, *Wirtschaftsbereich Industrie, Produktion und Auftragsbestand* (June 1990); own calculations

8.8 The experience in China

In contrast to the reform countries of Central Europe and Russia, China does not show a J-curve of transformation (Figure 8.10). Gross domestic product has continuously risen with real growth rates of approximately 10 percent per year since the beginning of the reforms at the end of the 1970s. Some reasons have been given for this development: on the one hand, property rights for land were introduced in the rural areas. These rights, even though only valid for 50 years, but including transfer and bequest permissions, constituted strong production incentives. The free economic zones guaranteed sufficient leeway for the private sector; but, apart from that, the private sector (including the enterprises that were put under the control of the local authorities) could also expand strongly. The private sector generated approximately 55 percent of gross domestic product in 1996. In this way, the public sector is losing relative importance. Moreover, the economic policy approach is characterized by a certain pragmatism, expressed by the motto: 'You have to touch the stones if you cross a river'.

Another reason for the fact that China did not have to go through a transformation crisis is that China, still being a developing country at the beginning of the reforms, only had a relatively small capital stock and a weakly developed industrial sector at its disposal. Therefore it was possible to realize substantial efficiency gains by liberalizing economic activity only in the countryside and without a reform of the state-run industrial enterprises in the cities.

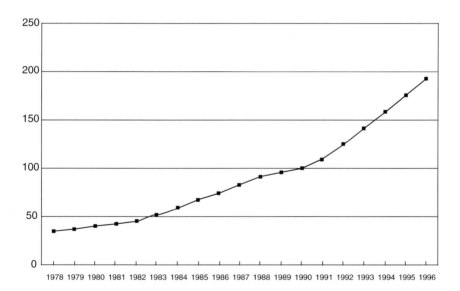

Figure 8.10 Growth of real GDP in China[a]
[a]1990 = 100
Source: IMF, *International Financial Statistics 1998*; State Statistical Bureau, People's Republic of China, *China Statistical Yearbook 1997*; own calculations

8.9 The disintegration of the Soviet Union

The transformation crisis becomes particularly apparent in most of the successor states of the Soviet Union. The former Soviet Union, a union of 15 'republics', dissolved at the end of 1991 (Gros and Steinherr 1995). It dissolved into a number of now autonomous states, as the communist party lost its power. The political center was not accepted any longer; it disappeared. The individual states declared themselves independent and pushed through their own laws instead of the rules of the Soviet Union that were in place at that time. But this presupposes that each country creates its own new institutional set-up. This held especially true for tax revenue and public spending, but new social security systems and a separate currency also had to be created. The rouble zone dissolved in 1992 when the countries began to introduce their own currencies, starting with the Estonian crown. The collapse of the Soviet Union and of the rouble zone also involved an almost total collapse of the system of payments between the successor states, and thus the trade relations suffered significantly. As the successor states showed particular patterns of specialization within the former Soviet Union but maintained only minor trade relations with the rest of the world, they were severely hit by the breakdown of trade flows among themselves. The necessity to adapt their production structure to the changed scarcity conditions and to divert their trade to the world markets is therefore even bigger for the successor states of the Soviet Union than for other transformation countries.

Up to now, many successor states have not succeeded in coping with these problems. They have not yet passed the bottom of the transformation crisis. But the example of Estonia proves that the problems are not insoluble. Due to a policy that was consistently oriented to free-enterprise principles, Estonia managed to limit the initial fall in output as well as to stabilize the economy quickly and to follow a growth path.

9 Regional integration in the world economy

With regional integration countries aim at intensifying the international division of labor, albeit within regional borders. We first report the experience with different forms of regional integration (section 9.1). An important aspect is the impact of regional integration on regional and world welfare, i.e. whether regional integration is trade-creating or trade-diverting (section 9.2). A fundamental question is whether regional integration facilitates or impedes the development of a multilateral order (section 9.3).

9.1 Regional integration

Types of regional integration

Regional integration is characterized by a lowering of transaction costs between member states relative to non-members. In fact, it is a mutual preferential treatment between countries in international trade. Thus, regional integration deviates from the principle of non-discrimination because of different rules being in force with regard to non-members. The WTO rule of non-discrimination has a waiver for regional integrations (see chapter 14). Depending on the extent of economic integration, different types of regional integration have to be distinguished.

Preferential trade agreements (PTA) are the least strict form of regional integration. For certain goods tariffs are reduced among the members of a preferential area (sometimes even unilaterally). There is no equal treatment of non-members according to the most-favored-nation clause. Within preferential areas there is neither a general reduction of internal tariffs nor a common external tariff. Examples of this type of economic integration are the ACP treaty (70 participating countries in Africa, the Caribbean and the Pacific areas – also known as the Lomé Convention) with the European Union as well as the preferential system of the Commonwealth.

Free-trade areas (FTA) abolish internal tariffs, but there is no common external tariff. Each member maintains its own external tariff against non-FTA members. To prevent opportunities of arbitrage in conflict with the FTA agreements, rules of origin and strict controls of the origin of goods are of great importance. Examples are EFTA (European Free Trade Association, founded in 1960 by Austria, Denmark, Norway, Portugal, Sweden, Switzerland and the United Kingdom, with Finland becoming a member in 1961), NAFTA (North American Free Trade Agreement) and CEFTA (Central European Free Trade Area).

Customs unions abolish internal tariffs like free-trade areas, but additionally there is a common external tariff as well as a common external trade policy with respect to third countries. Examples are the European Economic Community, founded in 1957, which changed into the European Community (EC, from 1967) and then the European Union (EU, from 1993).

Common economic areas, as established by the EU of twelve and by five EFTA countries (Austria, Finland, Iceland, Norway and Sweden) in 1994, are characterized by the use of common rules and common technical standards. The European Economic Area now consists of all 15 member countries of the EU as well as three of the four current EFTA countries (Iceland, Norway and Liechtenstein); in 1992, Switzerland, the fourth remaining EFTA country, decided by plebiscite not to participate in the European Economic Area.

A *common market* is characterized by the complete abolition of all barriers, not only with respect to the free trade of goods, but also the free exchange of services and the free movement of capital and labor. Additionally, it is aimed at a common competition (or antitrust) policy and common rules for procurement as well as a subsidy code.

A *monetary union* performs a common monetary policy, and an *economic union* strives for harmonization of other elements of economic policy including the institutional framework of the market economies, for instance in common competition policy and subsidy control.

Finally, in a *political union* common institutional mechanisms (constitution) are created in the area of political decision-making (i.e. the right to vote, a common parliament) with some political power being allocated to a central level, especially the power to tax.

Existing groups of regional integration

Since the establishment of the GATT in 1948, nearly 150 regional trade agreements have been notified by GATT/WTO. Of these agreements, around 80 are currently in force.

Europe

The European Union (EU) with its now 15 member states has developed from the European Economic Community, which was founded in 1957 by Belgium, France, Germany, Italy, Luxembourg and the Netherlands. With the northern enlargement, Denmark, Ireland and the United Kingdom joined in 1973. With the southern enlargement in the 1980s, Greece (1981) and Portugal and Spain (1986) became members. With another enlargement the neutral states Austria, Sweden and Finland joined in 1995. The realization of the four freedoms allows the free movement of goods and services, of capital and labor. The European Monetary Union has started in 1999, and within the next few years an eastern enlargement by the new market economies of Central and Eastern Europe is expected to take place (see chapter 10).

The European Free Trade Association (EFTA) was founded in 1960 by Austria, Denmark, Norway, Portugal, Sweden, Switzerland and the United Kingdom in order to secure free trade in industrial goods. Since then Denmark and the United Kingdom (1973), Portugal (1986), and Austria, Finland and Sweden (1995) have left the EFTA, which now consists of Iceland, Liechtenstein, Norway and Switzerland.

The Central European Free Trade Area (CEFTA) between the Czech and Slovak Republics, Hungary and Poland, the so-called Visegrad states, came into force in 1993. They were joined by Slovenia in 1996 and by Romania in 1997. The aim is to reduce tariffs and barriers to trade and to increase intra-regional trade which collapsed with the breakdown of the COMECON in 1990. At the same time, CEFTA is a waiting room for EU membership. By the end of 1998 all members of CEFTA had applied for EU membership.

The Americas

The North American Free Trade Agreement (NAFTA) between the US, Canada and Mexico started in 1994. Its aim is to remove tariffs and substantially reduce non-tariff barriers over a period of 10–15 years. By liberalizing the trade of goods and services, facilitating foreign investment and establishing an effective dispute settlement mechanism, NAFTA is expected to become an important area of regional integration in the world. Additional agreements have been concluded upon environmental standards, intellectual property and labor standards.

In contrast to the European Union, NAFTA is not a customs union with a common external tariff; it is a free trade area. NAFTA does not intend to introduce a common market with the free movement of people. Moreover, NAFTA does not have an executive arm, the NAFTA commission only plays a mediating role in resolving conflicts. Finally, there is no transfer of resources.

At the moment there is discussion about widening NAFTA by the accession of new members in Central and South America (e.g. Chile) as well as plans for further free-trade agreements with African and Asian countries. The NAFTA countries are members of APEC (see below).

A Trans-Atlantic Free Trade Area (TAFTA) is proposed to integrate the European Union and NAFTA. But instead of a free-trade area it may be attempted to first create a common economic area, in which production standards creating non-tariff barriers would lose their significance, e.g. by mutual recognition of standards. In a Trans-Atlantic Free Trade Area, the development of basic elements of a common competition policy seems to be necessary; moreover, the agricultural sector should be included.

In 1960, Mexico and most of the South American countries formed a free-trade area called the Latin American Free Trade Association (LAFTA). As a result of the reduction of tariffs and non-tariff barriers, intra-trade between the LAFTA countries was growing until the end of the 1970s. But, as the barriers to trade with the outside world remained in place, the competitiveness of their economies diminished. In 1980, eleven of its members changed the LAFTA into the Latin American Integration Association (LAIA), which has not so far been successful in liberalizing trade. In 1991 Argentina, Brazil, Paraguay and Uruguay created the MERCOSUR (Mercádo Común del Sur), which is a customs union, additionally linked with Chile and Bolivia by a free-trade agreement. Within this free-trade area, internal tariffs have been abolished, but Chile has a lower external tariff with respect to third countries than do the members of MERCOSUR.

The Caribbean Community (CARICOM, comprising Antigua and Barbuda, Bahamas, Barbados, Belize, Dominica, Grenada, Guyana, Jamaica, Montserrat, St. Christopher and Nevis, St. Lucia, St. Vincent and the Grenadines, and Trinidad and Tobago) is a free-trade area and has mostly succeeded in eliminating all barriers to intra-regional trade.

In the long run, the creation of a so-called Free Trade Area of the Americas (FTAA), which would require an integration of both NAFTA and MERCOSUR and other Latin American countries, is aimed at reducing barriers to trade in the Western hemisphere. Negotiations for an FTAA are scheduled to be concluded by 2005.

Asia

There are two reasons why regional integration is not particularly important in Asia: one is that some countries are large, the other is that economies have been open to the world market anyhow.

The Association for South-East Asian Nations (ASEAN), consisting of the seven countries Brunei, Indonesia, Malaysia, the Philippines, Singapore, Thailand and Vietnam, was founded in 1967. ASEAN is mostly oriented towards economic cooperation. Recently, plans have been discussed to establish an Asian Free Trade Area (AFTA).

In 1989, the Asia–Pacific Economic Cooperation (APEC) was founded in order to encourage free trade among its member states, now comprising Japan, China, Australia, New Zealand, South Korea and Taiwan as well as some other fast-growing economies of South-East Asia, the NAFTA members and Chile. In accordance with the WTO principles, APEC wants to reduce barriers to the trade of goods and services, but there is no desire to establish a common external tariff (open regionalism).

Between Australia and New Zealand, the Australia New Zealand Closer Economic Relations Trade Agreement (ANZCERTA or CER for short) came into force in 1983, and induced the unrestricted free trade of goods. Additionally, both states strive for a liberalization of the trade in services as well as a harmonization of regulations and business law.

9.2 Elementary theory of integration

Usually, static and dynamic effects of regional integration are distinguished. In a static (or comparative-static) framework, it is analyzed how the allocation of resources, of production, of sectoral structure and of welfare change when some countries form a customs union and others remain outside. Dynamic effects arise when the impact of integration on economic growth is considered.

Trade-creating and trade-diverting effects

According to Viner (1950), the static effects can be trade creation and trade diversion. Assume country A forms a customs union with country B, excluding country C. We analyze both effects first from the point of view of country A (the home country), then from the point of view of countries A and B together, and finally from the point of view of all countries (the world). We will use the partial analysis of a market diagram rather than a general equilibrium analysis.

When analyzing trade creation (and trade diversion), we have to specify for which country trade is created (and for which it is diverted). From the point of view of the home country, a simple case of trade creation is realized when despite import tariffs the home country A had obtained imports from country B before the customs union came into being. By abolishing internal tariffs trade is created. This is shown in Figure 9.1a, depicting the curves of demand (DD) and supply (SS) of the home country. Before the customs union was established, the home country had imported quantity MQ, afterwards it imports $M'Q'$. Supposing that the total revenue (c) generated by tariffs before the trade union was transferred to the households, the households of the home country will have a net gain from the customs union equal to the amount of the triangles a and b.

The case is different when a third country with a horizontal supply curve C is more favorable for the home country than that of country B, i.e. $B > C$. Prior to the customs union, country C is competitive even though the home country imposes a tariff, whereas country B is not competitive when a tariff (T) is introduced. $B + T$ lies above $C + T$. It should be noticed that the initial import tariff

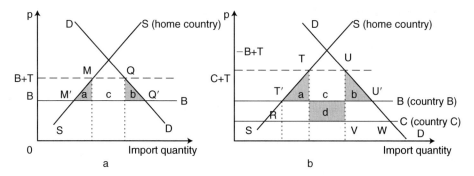

Figure 9.1 Trade-creating and trade-diverting effects of a customs union

in Figure 9.1b is supposed to be higher than in Figure 9.1a. In the initial situation, the home country imports TU from country C. After the formation of the customs union country C still has to pay the tariff (in this case the initial tariff), but for country B the tariff has been abolished. As a result of the customs union country B now supplies the imports T'U', whereas country C loses its price competitiveness.

What is the effect on the welfare of the home country? On the one hand, there is additional trade with country B which induces a gain in consumer surplus of $a + b$. The previous revenue from tariffs c has become a consumer surplus for the households. On the other hand, the country now loses revenue from tariffs d of the previous imports that have been transferred – as assumed above – by the government to the households. If the area d exceeds $a + b$, the net welfare effect for the home country is negative. The negative effect of trade diversion exceeds the positive effect of trade creation. Then the home country loses. Consequently, in a partial analysis, the result of integration can be a loss of welfare for a member country of a customs union. It is important to notice that in this partial analysis the home country would experience even stronger gains from introducing free trade globally instead of joining a regionally restricted customs union. In comparison with a customs union, the additional gain from global free trade would consist of additional consumer surplus as indicated by the area RT'U'W.

In order to find out whether the total effects of a customs union are positive for the union members as a whole, it would be necessary to calculate the trade-creating and trade-diverting effects for all member states and net them out.

A third country loses when the revenues generated by its exports, induced by a shrinking demand in the members of the customs union, are smaller after the formation of the customs union. Its terms of trade deteriorate and the consumer surplus shrinks. Remember that welfare is measured in terms of consumer surplus, which means that other criteria, e.g. the change in unemployment, are not relevant in this respect.

Finally, it is necessary to consider whether the welfare of the world as a whole – all the member states of the customs union and the third country – has been increased by the formation of the customs union. To assess the total effect for the world as a whole, the trade-creating and trade-diverting effects for the customs union as well as for the third country have to be calculated and netted out.

Dynamic effects

Apart from a comparative-static change of trade flows of a customs union in the partial equilibrium models there are additional effects in a richer analysis. These impacts are in fact equal to the advantages of foreign trade (see chapter 11). These effects are, *inter alia*, the exploitation of economies of scale and increased specialization, intensified intra-industry trade, and – in a more general sense – a higher mobility of both capital and labor. In addition there are dynamic effects stemming from an improved competitiveness of firms, from innovation, from the accumulation of capital and from higher growth. These gains in efficiency also have positive effects on third countries because a higher GDP implies an increased import demand. For regional integrations of developing countries enhancing industrialization has been given as an argument (Hiemenz *et al.* 1994; Langhammer and Hiemenz 1990). Empirical studies have emphasized the relative importance of dynamic effects in comparison with comparative-static effects.

9.3 Block formation as a step towards a multilateral order?

Regional integrations may eventually lead to a multilateral order and may thus be a way to reach a maximum of welfare in the world economy in the long run. Or they may lead to separation and thus reduce the chances of increasing welfare. This is a central issue for trade policy. Clearly, regional integrations violate the WTO rule of non-discrimination (and the most-favored-nation principle); this is a kind of discrimination against non-members. Nevertheless, there is a waiver for regional integrations.

Consider the three largest trading blocks in the world, the European Union, NAFTA and Japan, which had a combined share in world trade of about 64 percent in 1997 (Table 9.1). In Europe, an internal market is clearly established; eastern enlargement is in the making. In America, politicians aim at strengthening NAFTA by integrating the countries of Latin America. In Asia, it remains to be seen whether the Pacific area with Japan (and China?) might develop into a region similar to an internal market, with low barriers to trade.

Figure 9.2 illustrates some possible time paths depicting the development of welfare in respect of multilateral trade liberalization and regional integration (Bhagwati 1992). In the initial position, a utility level U^0 is given. Different paths are portrayed.

Path I characterizes the development of welfare in a scenario of multilateral rounds of liberalization. At the end of this process, a situation of free trade providing a utility level U^* is realized. Paths II and III show the effect of regional

Table 9.1 EU, NAFTA and Japan, 1997

	EU	NAFTA	Japan
Population (mil.)	371.5	393	126
GDP (bil. US$)	8,088	8,684	4,202
GDP per head (US$)	21,772	22,096	33,346
Exports in percent of world exports (1996)	38.9[a]	17.8[b]	7.0
Exports in percent of GDP (1996)	11.1	7.9	9.9

[a] 62.8 percent of total EU trade is intra-EU trade. [b] 45.1 percent of total NAFTA trade is intra-NAFTA trade

Sources: IMF, *International Financial Statistics 1998*; World Bank, *World Development Report 1998*; OECD, *National Accounts 1998*; US Department of Commerce, *International Trade Administration 1998*; EUROSTAT, *Internal and External Trade of the EU 1997*; National Institute of Statistics, Geography and Informatics, *Mexican Bulletin of Statistical Information*, various issues; Statistics Canada 1998; own calculations

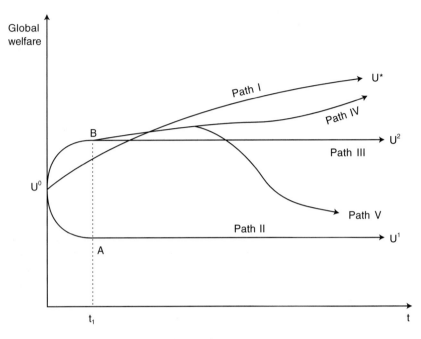

Figure 9.2 Regional integration and free trade

integration having both a trade-diverting and a trade-creating effect. When the trade-diverting effect prevails, then utility is falling to a level U^1 (point A) and remains at this level (path II). When the trade-creating effect is stronger, then welfare is rising to U^2 (point B). If only short-term effects had to be taken into account, then the world economy would stay on this level (path III). But there are also dynamic effects which raise welfare. Especially when regional blocks open up to new members and expand liberalization according to the most-favored-nation principle to third countries, and, vice versa, when third countries themselves grant such 'concessions', then regional integration is moving towards the utility level of free trade (path IV).

Does a multilateral approach to liberalization represent a faster and more secure track towards free trade than a regional approach (Bhagwati 1992; Frankel 1997)? The advantage of the regional approach is that barriers to trade are more or less totally abolished within a partial area of the world. In addition, the member states are enabled to conclude an agreement much more easily. For that reason, regional integration might be realized faster. Further barriers can be dismantled in the long run, when the regional integration opens itself to additional members. This is especially the case when regional integration can be extended multilaterally by the use of the most-favored-nation rule.

The advantage of the multilateral approach consists in creating a set of rules that are legally binding nearly all over the world. GATT article XXIV, which

Table 9.2 Share of intra-regional trade (exports plus imports) as percentage of each region's total trade 1948–1996

	1948	*1958*	*1968*	*1979*	*1993*	*1996*
Western Europe[a]	42	53	63	66	70	68
North America[b]	27	32	37	30	33	36
Asia	39	41	37	41	50	52
World[c]	33	41	47	46	50	52

[a]Share of intra-European trade in total Western European trade. [b]Canada and the USA. [c]Weighted average
Source: WTO Annual Report (1995, 1997)

departs from the most-favored-nation principle by explicitly allowing free-trade areas and customs unions, in principle gives rise to the risk of destroying the multilateral order by the formation of regional trading blocks. Regionalism might be combined with protectionism which would impede utility from rising to U^*, the level of free trade. Then the path could lead away from U^*; and even U^2 might not be reached in the case of retaliation against third countries (path V). Thus, the risk of disintegration of the world economy exists. For instance, the world economy could be subdivided into the triad Europe, North America and Japan. Up to now, however, regional integration has not led to important forms of separation. In Latin America, attempts towards regional integration have not proved to be powerful, with the exception of MERCOSUR. In East Asia, APEC has the goal of market integration with no tendency towards protectionism. European integration has proved to be open to new members, and despite some protectionist measures trade-diverting effects unfavorable to the rest of the world have been, judging with a grain of salt, over-compensated by its growth. The European Union has been open to the accession of new members in the northern, southern and neutral enlargements. The importance of intra-regional trade has been rising steadily during the last forty years (Table 9.2). The internal coherence of NAFTA is different from that of the European Union. Although a common trade policy is still lacking *de jure*, the North American Free Trade Area would definitely strengthen the position of the United States in the event of a conflict between the two blocks.

It is certainly not evident whether the regional or the multilateral approach leads to the highest possible welfare of free trade. Indeed, the danger of an escalating trade war between the regional blocks is still a matter of importance. Therefore, it is necessary to find mechanisms which allow a multilateralization of regional integration.

10 The European Union

In the European Union, nation states have given up sovereignty in a number of policy areas and subjected themselves to joint decision-making with other nations. The core of European integration is the Single Market (section 10.1). With respect to the role of government, fiscal federalism is at the heart of European integration (section 10.2). The decision structure in the policy area is quite complex (section 10.3). Monetary union is a major step in the process of European integration (section 10.4). The rigidity of the national labor markets contrasts with the requirement of more flexibility in the monetary union (section 10.5). Eastern enlargement will be an issue for the next few years (section 10.6). Decision making in an enlarged union raises difficult questions to be solved (section 10.7).

10.1 The four freedoms and the Single Market

As an economic union, the European Union aims at establishing a common market by harmonizing important aspects of the institutional framework of the national economies. But European integration goes beyond establishing a common market in the strict sense. A set of economic policy areas is no longer in the hands of the nation states but is either shifted to the European level or requires some type of joint decision-making of national governments. Joint decisions go together with different decision procedures (Commission, Council) and may require different majorities (Nugent 1994; Armstrong and Bulmer 1998).

Free movement of goods

The common market requires the dismantling of all obstacles to the free movement of goods. Barriers to trade include not only tariffs and quantitative restrictions but also national regulations. It has proved to be impossible to harmonize all legal rules of the different countries. Therefore, in the *Cassis-de-Dijon* case of 1979, the country-of-origin principle was established by the European Court of Justice. The *Cassis-de-Dijon*, a fruit liqueur, was widely in use in France. It was not allowed, however, to be marketed in Germany. The German regulation, the monopoly law on spirits (*Branntweinmonopolgesetz*) of 1922 required fruit liqueurs to have an alcohol content of at least 32 percent and thus the alcohol content of 17 percent in the *Cassis-de-Dijon* was 'verboten'. The sense of such a law is a different question. The European Court of Justice ruled that a product legally brought to the market in one country of the European Union also has to be accepted by other countries. This verdict then allowed the export of beer from Belgium that was not brewed in accordance with the German beer purity regulations of 1516/17, and it allowed pasta to be exported that was not made from Italian buckwheat. According to this principle, the different regulations are *de facto* mutually recognized and coexist even if domestic producers are treated less favorably than foreign producers (discrimination against nationals). Only in the cases when products are hazardous and damaging to health, to safety or to the environment does the principle not apply.

Free movement of persons

Workers have the right to work anywhere in the European Union (right of free movement). Individuals have the right to establish businesses everywhere in the European Union (right of establishment). Discrimination based on nationality is to be abolished.

Free movement of services

Services offered in one member country can also be supplied in the other member countries. Thus, the *Cassis-de-Dijon* verdict of the European Court of Justice not only holds for goods, but also applies to services, for instance to banking and to insurance. The country-of-origin rules are mutually recognized. This principle has proven to be a can opener for national regulations. The free movement of services is especially linked to the right of establishment.

Free movement of capital

Until the late 1980s, capital flows were still controlled in some countries. With monetary union in the making, national controls of capital movements could no longer be justified. Consequently, they had to be given up.

Trade policy

Since the European Union is also a customs union, it has a common external tariff which now is at 2.8 percent for all trade in industrial products. Other trade policy instruments are applied uniformly. The EU has a Common Commercial Policy *vis-à-vis* non-members, for instance the United States or in the WTO.

Competition policy

In a single market, competition policy (antitrust policy) has to apply to the market as a whole. Competition policy has to prevent cartels and to ensure that dominant positions within the common market do not arise. Thus, the abuse of market power in the EU and the creation of new dominating positions (monopolies) by mergers have to be controlled on the European level, where the Commission has taken a lead position.

Subsidy control

Competition in the single market should not be distorted by national subsidies. The Commission controls national subsidies and has established a respected power in this domain.

Agricultural policy

Agriculture receives special treatment. It is shielded from the market by Common Agricultural Policy (CAP) which defines reference prices. Agricultural prices in the EU are shielded from the world market by variable import levies. If prices in the world markets for agricultural products are low, a variable import duty lifts the price of agricultural imports to the EU level. Inside the European Union, agricultural prices are guaranteed by market interventions. Agricultural policy is undertaken on the European level and absorbs nearly half of the EU budget.

Indirect taxation

Indirect taxes including value-added taxes may create unnecessary distortions in the common market. Minimum rates have been set.

Monetary policy

With monetary union, monetary policy has been centralized for the EU-11 countries (section 10.4).

EU finances

The budget of the European Union is financed by import duties and contributions of the member states. Contributions by member states consist partly of the value-added tax resource; 1 percent of national returns of the value-added tax are transferred to the EU budget. The other EU revenue is the GNP resource, calculated as a proportion of national GNPs. It is intended to shift EU financing more to the GNP resource in the future. There is a cap on the tax base of the value-added tax resource of 50 percent of GNP. Therefore, contributions are *de facto* related to GNP. The EU has no right to tax or to incur debt. The EU budget accounts for 1.27 percent of GDP of the member states.

EU expenditures

EU expenditures amounted to 86 billion euros in 1998. Of this, 47 percent was spent on agricultural policy, 36 percent on structural and regional funds.

Degree of centralization

This short survey in Table 10.1 indicates some areas of potential centralization.

10.2 Fiscal federalism and the subsidiarity principle

The economist's answer to the issue of the optimal degree of decentralization or centralization is the subsidiarity principle. According to this concept, an economic activity should be assigned to the lowest organizational level that can efficiently deal with that activity. The reasoning behind this principle is that a more decentralized unit has better information on preferences and on the structure of problems. Higher levels of an organization tend to have less information, distortions in collecting information are likely. The lower level can deal better with local or regional issues, it can respond more flexibly.

For the organizational set-up of states and other political units, fiscal federalism can be interpreted as an expression of the subsidiarity principle. According to the approach of fiscal federalism, the central governmental level should be in charge of public goods with a spatial dimension extending over the whole political area, lower levels should be responsible for those public goods that are spatially less extended. Note that the spatial dimension of public goods is also discussed under the heading of the spatial extent of technological externalities or spillover effects. Assigning public goods of different spatial dimensions to different levels of governments implies that the revenue side has to follow the expenditure side (fiscal equivalence, Olson 1969).

For the EU, this means that economic problems of a European dimension such

Table 10.1 Degree of centralization

Centralization	Trade policy
	Agricultural policy
	Competition policy
	Control of state subsidies
	Monetary policy
Shared responsibility between the EU and nation states	Environment
	Consumer protection
	Transfrontier movement of labor
	Energy
	Transport
Decentralization	Wage and income policy
	Social security systems
	Health
	Education

as trade policy should be dealt with at the European level, problems with a national dimension should be decided at the national level, and regional problems should be under the responsibility of the regional authorities.

10.3 Decision making in the European Union

Giving up some national sovereignty

The European Union is not a confederation with an intra-state pattern of rules and it also is not an association of completely sovereign nation states. The Treaty on the European Union is a multilateral arrangement by which sovereign nation states give up some sovereignty in favor of joint decision making on the European level. The Community has been empowered by the individual member states through the treaty. Their power is to establish secondary law. New law can only be created in the context of the treaty, if it is according to the stipulations of the treaty. The treaty can only be changed in the same way that it was originally concluded, namely by negotiation and ratification by the individual member states. Thus, the member states are the masters of the treaty.

The EU treaty is not a constitution (Grimm 1997). If the EU had a constitution, the fundamental decisions would not be made by the Council but by the sovereign, that is, by the people or by a parliament representing the people. Lacking one of the decisive elements of a constitution, namely the European people as a sovereign, the EU is also not a state.

Institutions

The system of governance of the European Union is a multi-level system. Decisions are taken in a complex web of decision-making bodies.

Council of the European Union

The Council of the European Union, also known as the Council of Ministers, is the central decision-making body. It is made up of the member states and meets in more than 25 different forms, for instance, as heads of states or as ministers for a specific portfolio (Foreign Affairs, Economy and Finance, Agriculture, Transport, etc.).

The European Commission

The Commission is the administrative arm of the European Union. Its main function is to administer policy, to initiate policy and to mediate between member states. Many of the measures of the Council are only (and can only be) taken upon the recommendation of the Commission. It also represents the Union in international negotiations.

The European Parliament

The Parliament is involved in decision making (including law making) in different ways, in form of consultation, in cooperation and assent (co-decision).

The European Court of Justice

The European Court of Justice is concerned with the interpretation of EC law. The Court also provides the judicial safeguards necessary to ensure that the law is respected. The types of actions include actions brought before the court by a member state against a member state and by the Commission against a member state.

Types of legal rules

Community law, adopted by the Council – or in the case of co-decision procedure by Parliament and Council – can only be established in those areas which have been defined for joint decisions. Where unanimity is required, the power to legislate still rests with the individual member state. Article 308 of the EU Treaty[1] is a general clause for the Commission to become active; however, this does not imply that the Community has the right to go beyond the creation of secondary law.

Community law may take different forms. Regulations are directly applied; there is no need for national measures to implement them. Directives bind member states with respect to the objectives to be achieved. It is up to the national authorities to choose the appropriate means to implement the directives. Decisions are addressed to any or all member states and are binding. Informal procedures and rules of the game play an important role in the decision making of the European Union.

Different types of majorities

For decisions of the Council, there are three different types of majority according to Article 205 (Seidel 1997):

- If not stated otherwise, the majority of votes of the member states is needed. This is 8 out of 15 member states.
- For a qualified majority in a specific competence, the majority of the weighted votes of the member states is required, i.e. 62 out of 87 if the Council acts in response to a Commission proposal, and in addition to the 62 votes at least the votes of 10 members if the Council does not respond to the Commission.
- Unanimity is required in the most important policy areas. Besides, in the case of qualified majority there seems to be a consensus, whenever a vital interest of a member state is involved, not to take votes and to continue negotiation.

Allocation of votes

The allocation of votes does not correspond to population in a strict sense (Table 10.2).

Policy areas and majorities

Simple majority is required very seldom. It is used, for example, in the Governing Council of the European Central Bank. Qualified majority is required in such areas as agriculture and trade policy in a narrow sense (on the operative level). Basic decisions require unanimity. The most important areas where unanimity is required are: admitting new members (Article 49), indirect taxation (Article 93), direct taxation (Article 95), the budget of the European Union (Article 269) and fundamental rules (Articles 94, 95; Seidel 1997). Unanimity is also required in international treaties in commercial policy (Article 133), cultural policy (Article 151), industrial policy (Article 157), social cohesion policy (Articles 157, 161), research and development policy (Article 166) and environmental protection (Article 175). Of course, the unanimity principle in the area of taxation is at the heart of the question of national sovereignty and political union. Table 10.3 exhibits some policy areas and the required majority in a very simplified presentation.

10.4 Monetary union

Introducing the euro is a project of historical importance. As a common currency, the euro is intended to bring the peoples of Europe closer together. From

Table 10.2 Allocation of votes in the EU

	Votes	Population (in million)
Germany	10	81.6
United Kingdom	10	58.3
France	10	58.2
Italy	10	57.3
Spain	8	39.2
The Netherlands	5	15.5
Greece	5	10.2
Belgium	5	10.1
Portugal	5	9.9
Sweden	4	8.8
Austria	4	8.1
Denmark	3	5.2
Finland	3	5.1
Ireland	3	3.6
Luxembourg	2	0.4
	87	371.5

Table 10.3 Required majorities

Policy area	Required majority
European Central Bank Council	Simple majority
Agriculture Internal market Environment Transport Trade policy in the narrow sense	Qualified majority
Harmonizing the legal framework Indirect taxation Direct taxation Regional and social funds Admittance of new members Entering into international agreements including trade policy in the wider sense Culture	Unanimity

this point of view, monetary union is politically motivated. In addition, monetary union abolishes the cost of exchanging currencies. The transaction costs for the trade of goods, the exchange of services, the movement of people and the flow of capital – for the four freedoms – will be reduced; the Single Market will be completed from the monetary side. Thus, the process of European integration will receive a new impetus.

Institutional design

Monetary union means that monetary policy will be shifted to the European level. The institutional set-up can be explained as follows. In the European System of Central Banks, decisions on monetary policy are made by the European Central Bank (ECB). The decision-making bodies of the ECB are the Governing Council, the Executive Board and the General Council (Figure 10.1).

The Governing Council comprises all the governors of the national central banks of the member states of the monetary union and the six members of the Executive Board. Each member of the Governing Board has one vote, giving the governor of a central bank of a small country the same weight as that of a large country. The governors of the National Central Banks are appointed by the national governments for a minimum of five years; the appointment is renewable. The main task of the Governing Council is to formulate monetary policy and take decisions on the strategy as well on the monetary policy instruments such as the key interest rates.

The Executive Board comprises the President, the Vice-President and four other members. They are appointed by a common accord, i.e. by unanimity, of the governments of the member states at the level of the heads of state or government, on a recommendation from the European Council after it has consulted the European Parliament and the Governing Council of the ECB. The members

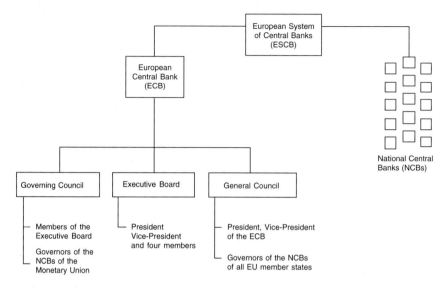

Figure 10.1 Set-up of the ECB

of the Executive Board are appointed for a non-renewable term of eight years. This gives them personal autonomy. The main responsibility of the Executive Board is to implement monetary policy in accordance with the guidelines laid down by the Governing Council of the ECB.

The General Council comprises the President and the Vice-President and the governors of all the National Central Banks of the European Union including those EU countries which are not members of monetary union. Its task is to deal with issues related to the preparation of countries for EMU membership.

Formally, the ECB is part of the European System of Central Banks which also consists of the EU National Central Banks. The National Central Banks of those countries which do not participate in the euro area nevertheless are members of the European System of Central Banks, albeit, with a special status. They do not vote on issues of the monetary union.

The institutional set-up is decentralized with a large weight of eleven votes of national central bankers relative to the six votes of the members of the Executive Council. This weight will tilt even more to the favor of national central banks if new members are admitted. This formal structure points to the fact that the position of the ECB in the European system is different from the Bundesbank's Central Council in the German system where the state central banks had only nine votes relative to the eight votes of the directorate. In the Open Market Committee of the Fed (Federal Reserve Board), only five governors of regional reserve banks are represented relative to seven Washington-based members. Practical questions are whether committees dominated by the national central banks will play an important role and whether the small number of the ECB employees (less than 1,000 in 1998) will be strong enough to stand up against the 60,000 employees of the national central banks. A more fundamental question is whether such a decentralized system will eventually lead to too strong a national influence on a European institution and to an unreliable monetary policy.

The European Central Bank is independent from other institutions in the EU (Article 108). Neither the ECB nor any member of its decision-making body may take instructions from national governments or the EU. The statute of the ECB can only be changed by a new treaty which would require unanimity.

The task of the ECB

Article 105 defines the main objective of the ESCB: 'The primary objective of the ESCB shall be to maintain price level stability'. Other targets such as supporting employment are only secondary and conditional with respect to the target of price level stability. 'Without prejudice to the objective of price level stability, the ESCB shall support the general economic policies in the Community with a view to contributing to the achievement of the objectives of the community as laid down in Article 2' (Article 105). Article 2 defines the task of the Community in general, namely 'to promote . . . a harmonious and balanced development of economic activities, sustainable and non-inflationary growth respecting the environment, a high degree of convergence of economic performance, a high level of employment and of social protection, the raising of the standard of living and quality of life, and economic and social cohesion and solidarity among Member States'.

The role of the ECB is to define monetary policy, i.e. to develop a strategy and to implement this strategy. The ECB has defined the target of price level stability as a change of the price level below 2 percent. It has announced that it will not pursue inflation targeting but will follow monetary targeting with a reference value for the expansion of the money supply. In addition to defining and implementing monetary policy, the ECB will also conduct foreign exchange rate operations, manage the official reserves, support the authorities supervising financial institutions and ensure the smooth operation of payment systems. It has legislative power; its regulations are binding.

Instruments

The main instrument in controlling money expansion are open market transactions under repurchase agreements (repo) similar to the Bundesbank's two-week repo rate. Furthermore, overnight liquidity can be obtained by banks (standing facility). Minimum reserve accounts with the ECB will be required.

Conflict between price level stability and employment

There can be a conflict between the objective of a stable money and other objectives of economic policy such as reducing unemployment. One should not have the illusion that the Phillips curve postulating a trade-off between the rate of inflation and unemployment can be a basis for monetary policy and that an excessive increase in the money supply can stimulate employment in the medium run. People would anticipate the inflation rate and they would require higher nominal interest rates, the value of money would deteriorate and the ECB would lose its reputation. Eventually, the ECB would be forced to put on the brakes, and a 'stabilization recession' would be the result. An excessive expansion of the money supply may also lead to an asset price inflation without affecting the consumer price index as happened in Japan in the late 1980s. When the bubble bursts, the real sphere of the economy will be affected negatively.

Conflict with the European Council in exchange rate policy

The European Council, the central decision-making body of the EU (see above), has the right to conclude formal agreements on exchange rate systems with non-EU members (by unanimity) and it may (by qualified majority) formulate the general orientation for exchange rate policy (Article 111). As a rule, the European Council consists of the economics and finance ministers (ECOFIN). In the area of exchange rate policy, a conflict between the ECB and the Council can develop.

Incompatibility of exchange rate orientation and a stable money

Exchange rate decisions or orientations of the European Council can be incompatible with an independent central bank. If the ECB were forced to maintain a predetermined exchange rate *vis-à-vis* other currencies, this would mean an exchange-rate-oriented monetary policy. In this case, the central bank would not be free to determine its monetary policy. The exchange rate would be the nominal anchor instead of price level stability. Hopefully, this conflict between policy makers and the central bank is softened by the requirement of Article 111 that exchange rate policy must be consistent with the objective of price level stability.

Stable exchange rates?

Politicians occasionally give the impression that the euro will bring about stable currency relations in the world economy. There is ample evidence that the much-conjured international cooperation – G-7 meetings and accords – has not been able to secure stable exchange rates in the past. The proposals to strive for exchange rate targets have not proven feasible. Stable exchange rates in the world can only be established if monetary policy provides for a stable internal value of the currencies and if all other aspects of economic policy, and fiscal policy in particular, do not give rise to negative expectations about currency stability. For this reason, one can only warn against overloading the monetary policy of the European Central Bank with the objective of pursuing exchange rate targets for the euro against leading world currencies.

Strategic external value versus internal value of a currency

Some want to use the exchange rate of the euro against other currencies of the world – like the dollar or the Japanese yen – strategically in the interest of the European export industry by driving down its external value in order to stimulate European exports. This is a misleading idea. Disruptions and quarrels in the international division of labor, turmoil in the financial markets and reactions of other players in the world economy would ensue. What is more important, a lower external value of a currency can only be brought about if this currency is supplied more generously than other currencies. That is, the expansion of the aggregate money supply has to exceed by far the growth of the production potential (plus the tolerated inflation rate and a correction factor for the velocity of money). This, consequently, causes the internal value of the currency to fall. External value and internal value of a currency are two sides of the same coin.

Conflict with the European Council in economic and budget policy

The European Council is responsible for common economic and budget policy. It may coordinate these policies (Article 99); it also is responsible for the stability pact (Article 101). An informal group of EU-11 finance ministers has been created to coordinate economic and fiscal policies of EMU members. Here is another area of potential conflict with monetary policy.

Shielding the Central Bank from political pressure

Central banks are always exposed to political pressure. Political pressure on the European Central Bank may originate from countries facing severe economic problems. This holds particularly true for countries with excessive deficits and high indebtedness. Countries with high government debt are interested in low interest rates, a rather lax monetary policy and a slightly higher inflation rate than the one anticipated by financial markets, because all this would ease their budgetary situation, especially because debts would melt away in real terms. Such a policy becomes even more attractive when political maneuvering space in the future is restricted by a high interest burden. Political pressure on the European Central Bank will be further increased if the economy of a highly indebted state is taken by recession and if it faces severe financial difficulties. The issue is not that a country will deliberately follow a policy of excessive deficits in order to eventually force the European Central Bank to step in as lender of last resort. The problem is that a long-run process of accumulating debt may occur as a result of political weakness so that eventually the European Central Bank has no other option than to monetize the public debt by a lax monetary policy. Consequently, the criterion of a sustainable public budget within the monetary union is well-suited to shielding the central bank from political pressure.

Control of unreliable fiscal policy with the stability pact

Sustainability of the governmental financial condition is therefore an important precondition for a monetary union (Article 104). The overriding target is that the governments remain solvent; usually, this is interpreted as requiring stationarity of the debt. This means that the debt/GDP ratio has to remain constant. In the EU Treaty, this limit for debt in relation to GDP has been set at 60 percent. This restraint for debt is associated with a limit for an excessive deficit of 3 percent of GDP if nominal GDP growth is 5 percent. The intention is to limit political pressure on the European Central Bank. Such a constraint on fiscal policy becomes especially necessary if countries have institutional arrangements which are not conducive to solid governmental finances. A case in point is a constitutional weakness with respect to limiting governmental expenditures as in Italy.

The general rule of the stability pact is that a budget deficit surpassing 3 percent of GDP is considered excessive. This only holds if GDP falls by less than 0.75 percent. In other cases, there are exceptions: a real decrease of GDP on a yearly basis of at least 2 percent is viewed without any further argument as an exception. In the intermediate range between 0.75 and 2 percent, a set of discretionary decisions of the European Council will have to be made. The determination of an excessive budget deficit remains undecided if a member state, after being put into delay by a formal resolution, indeed takes appropriate measures. Whether measures taken are appropriate is also decided by the European Council. It should also be noted that initially only a non-interest-bearing deposit is required. This will be converted into a fine after two years if the budget deficit remains excessive. These discretionary steps raise the question whether the stability pact will be effective. Moreover, there is a conflict of roles, since those who are responsible for the excessive budgetary deficit will also be the ones to define it and to vote on the fines.

No-bail-out clause

According to Article 103 of the EU Treaty, the EU is not liable for the financial difficulties of any member state with a budget deficit, nor are other member states liable for this state's difficulties. Nevertheless, the political pressure for transfers granted by the European Union or by member countries will become perceptible in the future. Thus, if transfers have to be made after all – in spite of liability being excluded – the donor of transfers, as well as the recipient, may develop an interest in keeping these transfers as low as possible, replacing them by a rather lax monetary policy.

Common monetary policy and national decision-making

Common monetary policy must be oriented towards price level stability in the monetary union as a whole. Consequently, it cannot take into consideration specific national conditions. In a monetary union, the monetary 'suit' is no longer custom-tailored for each nation, the one size must fit all. Thus, if nations are in a different position in the business cycle, one being in a boom and another in a recession, if countries experience an asymmetric shock and if they get stuck in a self-inflicted crisis, they must cope with the same monetary policy. Nevertheless, monetary policy is still judged in national political decision-making processes, since a political union does not come into existence simultaneously with a monetary union. Thus, a potential for conflicts inevitably arises between a common monetary policy and national economic interests. Quite a bit of political discipline is required from a country in crisis to accept a monetary policy that is oriented towards European price level stability. If, however, the country in crisis could have its way in getting an easy monetary policy adopted, inflation in Europe would result.

By entrusting an independent European Central Bank with the authority to steer the money supply, i.e. to set the interest rates and determine other monetary policy instruments, the EU Treaty has taken monetary affairs out of the hands of politics altogether; it has depoliticized the process of money creation.

It is an imperative requirement for the monetary union to establish a long-lasting consensus on the very essence of the European Monetary Union, namely on the depoliticization of the common currency. Thus, policy makers have to respect the decisions of the European Central Bank, above all, in situations where these decisions are unfavorable for a single country or its government – for instance, in times preceding an important governmental election or when a country is facing unfavorable economic conditions.

10.5 Monetary union and the labor market

In a monetary union, exchange rates are no longer available as a mechanism of adjustment. This has implications for the labor market. There are two lines of argument which describe specific requirements for the labor market and for wage policy in the monetary union: one relates to diverging labor productivities, the other to the role of wages as a substitute for the exchange rate.

Diverging labor productivities

The differences in labor productivity per head of total employment in the countries of Euroland (EU-11) are quite impressive. Let us define labor productivity as the nominal GDP in ECU, calculated with the central rate, per head of total employment. West Germany is set equal to 100. In 1997, Belgium reached a similar level to West Germany; France (95.3 percent) and Austria (90.9 percent) had a somewhat lower labor productivity. The other countries differ considerably from the West German level, with the Netherlands at 85.4 percent and Italy at 85.3 percent. Ireland (69.5 percent), Spain (62.0 percent) and Portugal (34.5 percent) are quite apart from the others. East Germany reaches roughly 60 percent of the West German level. Using the actual central rate for the British pound, the UK is at 71.7 percent (Figure 10.2).

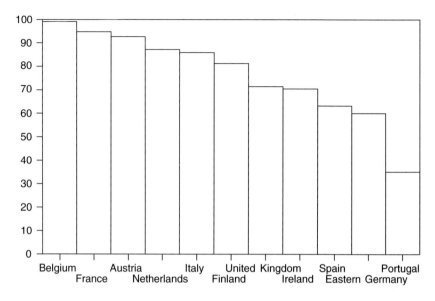

Figure 10.2 Labor productivities in Euroland and the UK[a], 1997
[a]Nominal GDP per person employed
Source: OECD and own calculations; Western Germany = 100

In a monetary union, trading costs are reduced and market segmentations disappear. As a stylized fact, Jevon's law of one price will prevail. This equilibrium condition for the goods market translates into an equilibrium condition of the labor market. Diverging national labor productivities in the currency union are consistent with full employment only if national labor productivities are not exceeded by national labor costs. This means that labor costs have to be differentiated in the monetary union in line with productivity differences.

Wages as a shock absorber

In a monetary union, wages have to take over the role of exchange rate adjustments which can no longer be used as an equilibrating mechanism if economic development between countries diverges. An important case of diverging development is when a shock affects countries asymmetrically, that is when a member country is struck by a negative exogenous shock more intensively than other countries in the currency union. Prior to the monetary union, the country could have devalued its currency to regain competitiveness. Within a monetary union, a member country fully experiences the asymmetric shock: In the case of a negative disturbance, production falls, the utilization of the production potential decreases and unemployment rises. The economy now has to adjust by using mechanisms other than the exchange rate (Siebert 1998c).

Moreover, the exchange rate can no longer be used in other instances: when some countries have weaker growth than others, when the business cycle in the European Union is out of synchronization, when homemade problems evolve in some countries, when some countries respond more flexibly to a shock that is symmetric to the European Union as a whole and when the unemployment rates diverge strongly between countries.

Three substitution mechanisms for the exchange rate

A first mechanism of adjustment which can be taken into account as a substitute for a depreciation of the currency is the migration of labor. If workers leave a country which has been struck by a crisis and move to more prospering countries, unemployment decreases in the crisis area. The per capita income of the country in question will rise again. Nevertheless, this is a 'passive' cure. Moreover, under European conditions, one can assume that this form of adjustment will not be accepted by the countries from which people emigrate nor from countries to which workers would have to migrate. The willingness to absorb workers from abroad will generally be low. Moreover, language barriers and cultural diversity will limit the mobility of people. Even though the free movement of labor is one of the four freedoms of the Internal Market, it seems realistic that labor migration will play a minor role as an equilibrating instrument in the divergent structural development in Europe. Unlike the United States, where labor mobility is generally high and where migration between regions as a reaction to an economic shock plays a central role (Blanchard and Katz 1992), labor mobility in Europe cannot be expected to be a sufficient substitute for exchange rate changes.

If labor migration is ruled out as an alternative to exchange rate adjustment, relative prices will have to do the job. In the case of a negative shock, a real depreciation will bring about improved competitiveness. This means that the relative price of non-tradables must fall, in order to stimulate the production of tradables. In bringing about this change in relative prices, wages, i.e. the price of the immobile production factor, will have to bear most of the burden of adjustment. Under static conditions, a decline in national wages makes a country regain its competitiveness. Under conditions of a growing economy, which is more realistic, wages should not rise as much as before. The decline in wages, or their reduced increase, stimulates the economy in the same way a devaluation would. There is one difference, however: a devaluation re-establishes competitiveness for all goods, a fall in wages favors labor-intensive production and thus re-establishes the competitiveness of jobs.

If wages do not react flexibly, differences in unemployment between the countries of the currency union are likely to develop. Then transfers are the only remaining mechanism to help nations adjust to a crisis (see below).

Thus, a cascade of equilibrating mechanisms exists which can be used to replace an exchange rate adjustment. First, the migration of labor can take the place of a devaluation of the home currency. If this is not possible, prices of the immobile production factor, predominantly wages, can adjust. Alternatively, if this also is not possible, financial transfers have to take over the shock-absorbing role of a devaluation.

Implications for wage policy

Since labor productivities diverge considerably between the countries of the European Monetary Union and can be expected to diverge in the future, labor costs will have to be differentiated between the member states of the monetary union since national labor costs must be borne by national productivities. Otherwise, unemployment will increase. Moreover, we know from empirical studies that convergence of productivities takes a long time.

Future wage policy in the individual countries should orient itself at the national labor productivities. Wage harmonization in the European Monetary Union should not be aimed at. People must understand that the level of national wages must reflect the differences in national labor productivities.

Institutionally, wage formation should not be Europeanized, even if people now compare their wage in a single currency and thus money illusion will no longer segment wage-bargaining behavior of unions. Political demands of 'the same wage for the same type of work' that are likely to be articulated are not well founded with diverging differences in labor productivity. Europeanizing wage formation would definitely increase the unemployment rate in the European countries. What is needed is a decentralization of wage formation, shifting wage formation from the economy-wide or sector level to the regional and to the firm's level. Wage formation, especially in the major countries of the continent, should follow more closely the market process.

Implications for social union

Labor costs also include the contributions to the social systems paid by the firms. These labor costs, too, have to be borne by the national productivities. The divergence in labor productivities makes clear that the costs of social security systems in the different countries must also be different. This means that social security benefits cannot be harmonized. With such a divergence of national productivities, a social union cannot be realized and the Europeanization of social policy should be avoided. The territorial principle of social insurance in Europe, according to which benefits can only be obtained from the system to which contributions have been paid, is quite appropriate.

Monetary union and transfers

Large economic regional units are usually characterized by some type of transfer mechanism. Transfers replace the exchange-rate adjustment mechanism when labor is not sufficiently mobile and when wages are not sufficiently divergent between countries. Taking as an example the US – an area with a common currency – transfers are made between different regions via the allocation of revenue between federal and state authorities and via the social security system. Additionally, the assignment of competences for expenditure and taxation to the various regional administrative bodies – the different hierarchical levels of the state – plays an important role in regional adjustment processes. In principle, a political union will be accompanied by higher transfers. As a rule, competences for expenditure and taxation will be assigned in a way that financial transfers between the different regions only have to net out major discrepancies in revenue.

One must therefore be aware that the monetary union will necessarily be associated with a strong political demand for an additional transfer mechanism and for more tax revenue competences at the central level unless labor markets become more flexible. The demand for transfers may lead to a severe political clash in the monetary union in the future. However, such a transfer mechanism may be acceptable in a political union but it is hardly conceivable among still sovereign nation states. Thus, since the European Monetary Union will not be accompanied by a political union, the willingness at the European level to agree on transfers and on a centralization of tax revenues should be lower than it is in the nation states. In addition, increase in the budget of the European Commission is limited, since decisions on tax policy have to be passed unanimously. Furthermore, the assignment of the right to tax to a central level requires democratic legitimization. Finally, transfers eat away some of the efficiency gains that can be expected from intensified European integration.

10.6 Eastern enlargement

The Czech Republic, Hungary, Poland, Estonia and Slovenia are negotiating for membership of the European Union. Integrating these countries will have an impact on the new members as well as on the European Union.

Trade

Except for agricultural and some so-called 'sensitive' products that are protected by the EU, such as iron and steel, textiles and clothing, regional integration is already taking place due to the EU's agreements with ten reform countries, namely the individual members of the Visegrad 5 (and not CEFTA, their free-trade association), the Baltic States, Romania and Bulgaria. The agreements more or less establish a free-trade area with the EU in which tariffs and quantitative restrictions are largely abolished.

- Exports of the five EU candidates range between 41 and 57 percent of their GDP in 1997 (Table 10.4). With respect to trade, they have reached higher degrees of openness than Western European countries. This means that these countries are quite outward oriented.
- The share of exports going to the EU relative to total exports varies between 51 (Estonia) and 68 (Slovenia) percent; the EU candidates are integrated into the EU with a similar percentage as the EU members. In terms of trade, they

Table 10.4 Some data on EU candidates, 1997

	GDP per capita in percent of EU average	Exports in percent of GDP	Exports to the EU in percent of total exports	EU exports to countries in percent of total EU exports	Inflow of foreign direct investment 1993–1997, mil. US$
Czech Republic	48.5	57.6	67.8	2.2	6,821.8
Estonia	34.8	47.8	51.1	0.3	218.8
Hungary	36.6	53.2	62.7	1.9	12,073.0
Poland	30.8	41.3	66.3	3.5	16,655.0
Slovenia	60.6	47.0	68.1	0.9	922.8

Source: PlanEcon 1998; OECD, *Short-Term Economic Indicators, Transition Countries*, Paris 1998; IMF, *International Financial Statistics* CD-ROM 1998; Eurostat; *Internal and External Trade of the EU* 1998; EBRD, *Transition Report 1998*, London 1998

are *de facto* already EU members. Thus, free access to the EU market is critical for the reform countries (Baldwin 1994; Baldwin *et al.* 1997).

- Meanwhile, the market of the EU candidates is becoming important for the European Union with 8.8 percent of EU exports (extra-EU exports). For some countries, Central and Eastern Europe is an especially interesting market. Germany accounts for almost 43 percent of the EU exports to the five EU candidates and it exports 6 percent of its total exports (intra- and extra-EU exports) to these countries.

- With respect to the product mix of trade between the EU and the CEECs-10 (Central and Eastern European Countries), in two product categories, namely in 'chemicals and rubber and plastic goods' and in 'other machines and equipment', the EU is a net exporter (Baldwin *et al.* 1997). There is only a slight net surplus in transport equipment whereas the CEECs have a net surplus in 'other manufactures'. This suggests that the EU has a comparative advantage in capital- or technology-intensive products (and the CEECs-10 in labor-intensive 'other manufactures'). It is quite surprising, however, that in all the other product groups, trade between the EU and the reform countries is more or less balanced, namely in food and agricultural products, other primary goods, textiles, clothing and footwear, iron and steel and semi-processed goods. This means that there is already quite a lot of intra-industry trade, albeit with a vertical structure so that Western Europe exports the more capital-intensive products.

Capital flows

The opening up of new regions means new investment opportunities. If uncertainties for investors can be kept low, the new regions will attract capital. The EU candidates have attracted an accumulated stock of foreign direct investment of 37 billion US$ in the period 1993–1997.

Hungary, Slovenia and the Czech Republic have reached FDI levels comparable to those of emerging markets in Latin America and in Asia. Foreign direct investment, though rather volatile over time, has accounted for roughly 20 percent of total investment in Hungary, more than 10 percent in Poland and a little less than 10 percent in the Czech Republic since 1992 (see Table 3.3). These levels, which are not in line with the findings in the Feldstein–Horioka (1980) tradition, are of course corrections to the isolation from the world capital market in the past 50 years. It can be expected that capital inflows will continue, though not at the current level. An important condition for capital inflows is that political uncertainty be further reduced. Of course, integration with the EU would be a major event in reducing uncertainty.

We cannot exclude that in the future capital inflows may temporarily die down or even reverse, and balance-of-payments crises may ensue. Witness the Czech Republic in 1997. Countries may get into a credibility crisis due to an unconvincing stability policy. High absorption relative to domestic production, wage increases surpassing productivity growth, short-termism of economic policy, social policies, budget deficits and government debt, distributional targets and populist policies all may be causes for instability, implying a depreciation of the home currency, lower capital inflows and a lower growth rate of the production potential.

Migration of people

Differences in gross wages between Poland and the Czech Republic on the one hand and Germany on the other hand are now (1998) estimated to be 1 : 6 at market rates; they were 1 : 10 in the early phase of the transformation process. In purchasing power parity, GDP per capita in Poland and the Czech Republic is put at 31 or even 48 percent of the EU level. In Romania and Russia, wages at market rates reach only 7 and 8 percent of the German level, respectively (and 15 percent at purchasing power parity).

Under normal conditions, income differences are a factor that leads to the movement of people. We know, however, that it is not only income differences in the Harris–Todaro tradition (Harris and Todaro 1970) that can explain migration. The decision to migrate must be understood as an intertemporal maximization problem where the potential migrant searches for a maximum lifetime income, i.e. maximizes the expected present value of his or her income during life (Siebert 1993). Migration is to be compared to an investment decision. As a matter of fact, it is an investment relating to human capital. Consequently, expectations on how a migrant's future income will develop both abroad and at home come into play. If it can be expected that the economic situation at home will improve, the incentive to migrate is reduced. In that case there is a positive option value of waiting because over time differences in income per capita will become smaller.

An exemption from the free movement of labor

Even though migration pressure seems to be smaller than feared initially, with the existing wage differences between Western and the most progressed Central and Eastern European countries, enlargement cannot immediately include the free movement of labor. This important freedom has to be phased in over time. Keeping in mind that convergence is a very slow process and that income per capita can be expected to differ for quite some time, the transitional period cannot be short, i.e. it should be in the range of 10–15 years. Possibly, quotas defining the right of entry to a national labor market in Western Europe might have to be introduced; these quotas which can be auctioned off in the new EU member countries, should increase over time.

Different adjustment mechanisms

If the movement of people is considered undesirable, it is not the right policy to erect obstacles against the mobility of workers. It is necessary to reduce the economic pressures which will engender migration. As water follows the law of gravity people will follow economic opportunities. One important mechanism that can ease the pressure is capital mobility. Here, it is in their own interest for the new market economies to make themselves attractive to foreign capital. As they succeed in luring capital from abroad they improve the productivity and wages of their workers and reduce the incentive to migrate. They must also aim to raise the savings rate at home. The other mechanism is to make exports more competitive in order to take advantage of the EU market. If real income in the new market economies rises, the advantage of migrating becomes smaller. Thus, there is a cascade of adjustment mechanisms. *Ceteris paribus*, i.e. if nothing else is done, people will have a strong incentive to move. This mechanism will become less important if capital can be attracted, and even less so if product markets in the European Union are completely opened up.

Common Agricultural Policy

A major stumbling block for EU enlargement is common agricultural policy. It is true that the MacSharry reform of 1992 attempted to bring price floors in the EU somewhat more in line with world market prices by paying compensations per unit of land and also per head of cattle or sheep (as a means of income). These compensation payments are, however, not yet uncoupled from production. Moreover, compensation should have been conditioned to the development of world market prices. Possibly, the EU will come under stronger pressure in the WTO negotiations starting in 1999 to further reduce production-stimulating compensations especially after the US has abolished its deficiency payments in 1996.

In any case, common agricultural policy is still a machinery producing excess supply relative to market conditions. If this machinery is extended to the reform

countries we can expect a sizable increase in productivity of the agricultural sector there, especially since these countries tend to produce the heavily subsidized
'northern' products. It is apparent that an extension of common agricultural policy to Central and Eastern Europe in its existing form will conflict with the WTO
commitments of the new members, add to the already existing inefficiency and
require additional funds. Estimates of yearly additional budget costs of an
enlargement by the Visegrad-4 countries range from 4 billion ECU to 37 billion
ECU (Baldwin *et al.* 1997; Tangermann 1997). Baldwin *et al.* (1997, p. 154) put
the consensus estimate at 10 billion ECU. Tangermann (1997) expects CAP
expenditure for the Visegrad-4 to be around 13 billion ECU in 2005 (in 1993
prices).

There seem to be two options for agricultural policy in enlargement. One is
that agricultural policy of the EU is reformed before enlargement takes place.
The other option is to exclude agriculture from enlargement completely or to
practice a phased-in enlargement for agricultural products. The problem with
such a waiver for agricultural products or a phasing-in is that agricultural production would operate under different conditions in two parts of an enlarged
European Union. To have different prices using border controls would be a
severe obstacle to a common market in the non-agricultural goods. A different
approach to agricultural policy would imply quantity controls on production in
the new member countries or keeping farm income in the CEECs low by other
instruments (such as producer price reductions in the event of oversupply). Both
approaches create severe problems for the development of the agricultural sector
in the new EU members. To sum up, a reform of the European Common
Agricultural Policy is a precondition for enlargement; at the minimum, a reform
should be credibly under way before enlargement begins. Setting such a
condition cannot mean, however, that the agricultural lobby is put into the position of preventing the enlargement of the European Union. Care must be taken
to prevent giving an increased threat potential to the agricultural sector in the
political bargaining of enlargement.

10.7 Decision making in an enlarged Union

Enlargement implies that it will become more difficult to make decisions. In an
enlarged European Union, the veto power that each country has due to the principle of unanimity becomes a powerful hindrance, eventually meaning that no
decision can be taken at all. For a qualified majority, the EU becomes more heterogeneous. The common denominator gets smaller and smaller, eventually
becoming meaningless. Therefore, the institutional framework of decision making has to be redesigned. This, however, will not be easy for a number of reasons.

- First, it is questionable whether renouncing unanimity would ultimately con-
  solidate the integration process (Seidel 1997). The 'optimum majority rule' is
  intended to minimize decision costs, i.e. the costs arising from the inability to
  reach decisions as well as the costs of disregarding the minority interests of

countries. Thus, the long-standing debate on the pros and cons of the unanimity principle reflects the dilemma of European decision-makers who are caught between the inefficiency of the consensus principle and the protection of vital national interests. A second-best solution to this dilemma may be the introduction of the 'unanimity-minus-one rule'. In this model, unanimity is deemed to exist in spite of the veto of one member state. It reflects the idea that no single member state should be in a position to veto a unanimity-based decision.

- Second, Europe does not have a constitution; decisions with a qualified majority of the European Council or a 'unanimity-minus-one rule' can run into conflict with national constitutional law in areas of 'vital interest'. Thus, it is not possible in the opinion of Germany's Constitutional Court to legitimize – in a sufficiently democratic way – decisions of the European Council that have been adopted against the will of Germany. This position makes the rule 'unanimity minus one' impossible.

Without major changes in the democratic legitimization of the European decision-making process relating to the role of the European Parliament and a European 'people' as a sovereign (Grimm 1997), the unanimity principle cannot be given up. In contrast to the area of unanimity, it may be easier to find a solution in the arena of qualified majority. Assuming that in an enlarged EU the allocation of new voting rights will follow the established pattern (compare Baldwin *et al.* 1997), Poland with a population of 40 million will have 8 votes (like Spain), the Czech Republic and Hungary 5 votes (like Belgium), Slovenia and Estonia 2 votes (Table 10.5). Altogether, the new EU members will have 22 votes out of 109 votes in the EU Council. Applying the same percentage for a qualified majority as in the EU-15, qualified majority would be at 77 votes with a blocking possible by 33 votes (Table 10.6). In order to make decisions possible, the qualified majority will have to be put at a somewhat lower percentage than in the EU-15.

It is feared that a mere continuation of the current weighting of votes after an Eastern enlargement would mean that Council decisions could be taken by a qualified majority of member states against a minority of other member states representing a majority of the European population (Seidel 1997). This would indeed hold for a second wave of enlargement, but with the first wave a qualified

Table 10.5 Allocation of votes to new members

	Votes	*Population (in million)*
Poland	8	38.6
Czech Republic	5	10.3
Hungary	5	10.2
Estonia	2	1.5
Slovenia	2	2.0
	22	

Table 10.6 Qualified majority

	Votes	Qualified majority votes	in percent of votes
EU-12	76	58	76
EU-15	87	62	71
EU-20[a]	109	77	71

[a]Assuming the same percentage as in EU-15

majority of the smaller member states (Czech Republic, Greece, Netherlands, Poland, Spain and Italy) with 79 votes would still represent 54 percent of the population (Stehn 1997). Nevertheless, one of the next intergovernmental conferences will have to reweigh the votes in the Council. Several models are currently being discussed to this end, most importantly of all the introduction of a so-called 'double majority'. According to this model, for a majority decision to be valid, not only a majority of states but also a majority of the European population represented by these states would be necessary.

Note

1 Articles are quoted according to the most recent version (Amsterdam Treaty).

Part IV

National economic policy versus a world economic order

Again and again, conflicts arise between national interests and the welfare of the world as a whole, i.e. of all countries together, with regard to the international division of labor. National interests may be rather short-term or even be linked to the advantage of particular groups in one country only, opposed to long-term benefits for that country or the world as a whole. Thus, the conflict between protectionism and free trade comes to life again and again (chapter 11). With locational competition between countries, the mobility of capital has opened up a new dimension of international interdependence where countries are competing for the mobile production factors of capital and technology (chapter 12). The utilization of the environment, a subject that will become more important in the future, is another field where national interests and worldwide concerns also can collide (chapter 13). To prevent the strategic behavior of states, the countries have to commit themselves to a set of rules for the international division of labor that excludes non-cooperative behavior as far as possible. Such an international order includes rules for the exchange of goods, for factor migration and for utilizing the environment (chapter 14).

11 National protectionism versus world wide free trade

For a variety of reasons, the international division of labor has been tampered with through trade policy measures. Historic periods of protectionism were followed by epochs of free trade and vice versa (section 11.1). A whole arsenal of arguments for taking trade policy measures have been put forward. A number of arguments have a defensive orientation (section 11.2), others are rather aggressive (section 11.3), and yet other arguments concern retaliation (section 11.4) and the creation of equal conditions for competition (section 11.5). These arguments are critically reviewed. Finally, the reasons for a free international division of labor are summarized (section 11.6).

11.1 Periods of protectionism and free trade

In the international division of labor, periods of liberalization and of protectionism have alternated in economic history. The beginning of the 19th century, with the Napoleonic Continental Blockade against Great Britain, was protectionist. In 1815, the British Corn Laws took effect. Intensely discussed in the literature, these laws aimed at assuring autarky in agricultural goods in case of another conflict. The first half of the century was then marked by the intention of reducing trade barriers; the Corn Laws were abolished in 1846. A phase of liberalization began. Until the First World War broke out in 1914, there was a time of free trade, especially in the exchange between Great Britain and its colonies and its former colonies; important capital flows went into the newly independent states and the colonies. But the continental countries also reduced their trade barriers, e.g. in the German Tariff Union (1834). This phase of liberalization was accompanied by largely stable currency conditions in the framework of the gold standard.

With the First World War, the phase of integration in the world economy came to an end. The hyper-inflation that hit Germany and other European countries in 1923 and the Great Depression starting in 1929 seriously disrupted the world economy. Tariffs and other trade barriers increased; the 1930s saw devaluation races in which states tried to stimulate their exports by devaluing their currencies and thus improving their employment possibilities ('beggar-thy-neighbour policy').

After the Second World War, a framework for the world economy was created with the GATT (General Agreement on Tariffs and Trade) in 1948. Based on this framework, the international division of labor could develop beneficially, without trade barriers. Until 1971, the currency system of Bretton Woods succeeded in keeping foreign currency rates relatively stable. With the World Bank and the International Monetary Fund, international organizations that aimed at a stronger integration of all countries into the world economy were created (see chapter 14).

A snapshot of this development is given in Figure 11.1. From 1900 on, the US tariff rate declined until the First World War, then it went up again until the 1930s. From then on, it was continuously reduced. World trade, in nominal terms, has risen continuously in the last fifty years.

11.2 Arguments for trade policy interventions: protection of domestic production

Trade policy interventions are justified with a variety of arguments. The motives can be either defensive or aggressive. They can be geared to an economy as a whole (or an economic region) or to single sectors. They can refer to national instruments or to international rules. We will first examine the arguments that deal with the protection of domestic production, especially of import substitutes.

Figure 11.1 Tariffs and world trade in economic history
Sources: For the US tariff rate (calculated as US tariff revenue in relation to the value of US imports): Magee *et al.* (1989), chapter 13 and Department of the Treasury of the United States Government, *Monthly Treasury Statement of Receipts and Outlays* (1990–1998); for world trade: International Monetary Fund, *International Financial Statistics* CD-ROM 1998

Autarky

Under the label of 'autarky', political and also military arguments have been put forward. During the second half of the 19th and the first half of the 20th century for instance, this motive served to justify the protection of German agriculture as well as the special position of German hard coal and of the steel sector. Today, the autarky argument reappears in the somewhat refined form of supply risk, i.e. of being cut off from imports. However, in the modern world economy, the sources of supply for import goods are dispersed worldwide so that single-sided dependencies hardly exist. The risk of being cut off from deliveries is thus reduced. The globalization of the markets counteracts the dependency of countries *vis-à-vis* exclusive suppliers. Furthermore, a high-cost self-sufficiency has considerable disadvantages for those domestic export sectors that use these goods as inputs for their production. Suppose that a country isolates itself from the import of, say, semiconductor products, to protect its domestic semiconductor producers. This will hamper its own export sectors (like engineering) that use semiconductors intensively in their products. And finally: even if we assume for a moment that reducing the supply risk was a goal of economic policy, this does not necessarily imply the protection of domestic producers; this goal can be better attained by piling up stocks. Autarky thus entails considerable welfare losses.

Protection of established industries

Another assertion is that existing domestic sectors have to be protected against foreign suppliers. In general, the starting point is a loss in competitiveness for a domestic sector producing import substitutes; the relative prices for the domestic producers become less favorable. In this situation, policy makers try to hold on to the production and employment of the domestic sector. To achieve this, a number of instruments are at hand.

Import duties

A tariff on the imported good 2 makes this good more expensive. The incentive to produce becomes stronger for the domestic producers, whereas, due to the higher price, the domestic consumers demand less. The domestically produced quantity of the import substitute increases, the imported quantity declines. Let $\tilde{p}_2 = p_2(1 + t)$ denote the domestic price after the introduction of the tariff (where t is the tariff rate). With a tariff, the relative price $\tilde{p} = p_1/\tilde{p}_2 = p_1/p_2(1 + t)$ falls. The production point moves from P to P′ (Figure 11.2). This price ratio also determines the consumption point, C′. We assume that the tariff revenues are redistributed to the households as a lump-sum payment, moving the budget line to the right. On the world market, the home country (as a small country) continues trading at the world market price ratio, p. For giving away P′D in exports, it receives DC′ in imports. The domestic price ratio is DE/DP′. The tariff rate is EC′/DE; EC′ is the government's tariff revenues.

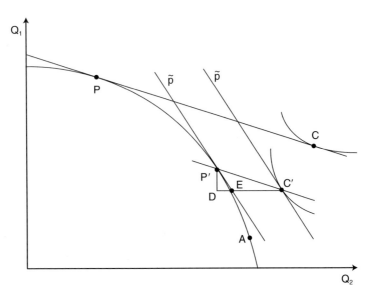

Figure 11.2 Effects of a tariff on imports

The tariff on imports protects the domestic import substitutes sector, but the opportunity costs are considerable:

1   The export sector (producing good 1) shrinks as the import substitutes sector attracts production factors. Protecting one sector thus weakens the other sector. In a dynamic economy, import protection hampers the development of export opportunities. For instance, by protecting agriculture and coal-mining, more modern sectors, like engineering or the semiconductor industry, are penalized. If we enlarge the model to comprise monetary effects as well, this also follows from a tariff-induced revaluation of the domestic currency, as the protection against imports reduces the demand for foreign currency.

2   If the production of import substitutes is concentrated in a particular region of a country, protection against imports hampers the development prospects of this region in a number of ways. One example is that protected sectors tend to pay high wages, impairing the development of new enterprises and also of the export business. Furthermore, the incentives to increase efficiency are weaker, and finally – leaving the allocation model – the protection against imports leads to a reduced demand for foreign money and thus to a revaluation of the domestic currency, causing a negative effect for the export business.

3   Consumers reach a lower welfare level in the consumption point C' (instead of C).

Subsidies

Besides a tariff on imports, the protection of the domestic (or import-substituting) sector can also be realized through a subsidy. If, as an example, a production subsidy (s) is paid for the (domestically produced) import substitute, the producers face a change in the price ratio, as the producer price ($\widetilde{p}\,_2^p$) for the domestically produced import substitute rises. The domestic producers' incentive to produce becomes stronger. The relative price facing the producers,

$$\widetilde{p}^{\,p} = \frac{p_1}{\widetilde{p}_2} = \frac{p_1}{p_2(1 + s)} \, , \text{ declines. The production point is thus relocated from P to}$$

P′ (Figure 11.3).

In contrast to a tariff on imports, consumers still face the world market price despite a subsidy: there is no market segmentation, and – if the country is small – they trade according to the world market price line that has to be drawn through point P′, as it was for the tariff. The difference, however, is that a subsidy for an import substitute leads to a split between the consumer price (DC′/P′D) and the producer price (DE/P′D) in the home country. The trade triangle is determined by C′, the point of tangency between the indifference curve and the world-market price line. Subsidizing the import substitute makes this trade triangle shrink, and the country incurs a welfare loss. The point of consumption, C′, is situated on a lower indifference curve than C, and the trade triangle P′C′D is

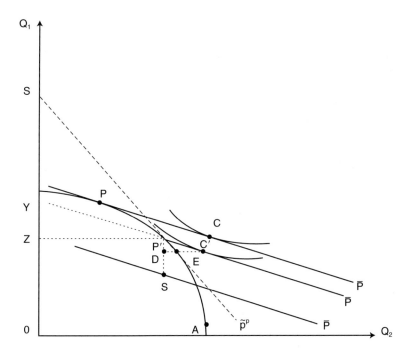

Figure 11.3 Subsidy for import substitutes

smaller than that without the subsidy (not shown in Figure 11.1, but with points P and C).

If we now take into consideration that the subsidy has to be financed, further effects arise, for instance if sector 1 is taxed to finance the subsidy. With taxation of sector 1, the price ratio would yet again change in favor of sector 2. The production point then wanders down the transformation curve, starting from P′. In production as well as in allocating factors, taxes may distort the allocation and cause efficiency losses. The production point moves into the interior of the transformation area (point S), and the country incurs further losses. The difference between a subsidy and a tariff on imports is that a production point S would represent a less favorable economic situation compared to P′. The world market price line ($\bar{p}$) then runs through point S.

Quotas

The domestic sector can also be protected by the use of quotas. Assume that the import quantity should not exceed DF, the permitted trade triangle is limited to PDF (Figure 11.4). If we move this permitted trade triangle along the transformation curve, the curve FF′F″ describes the trade points allowed. A quota can be chosen to yield just the same result as a particular tariff on imports, and vice versa. Under certain conditions a tariff and a quota are thus equivalent. We might choose a tariff rate so that the import quantity DC′ in Figure 11.2 corresponds to the quota DF in Figure 11.4. This equivalence of effects occurs only if the government sells the import quotas (import licenses) in an auction and redis-

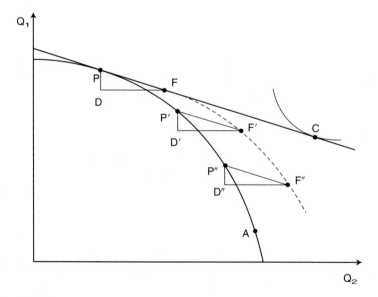

Figure 11.4 Quota

tributes the revenues (which correspond to the tariff revenues EC' in Figure 11.2) to the households.

If the quotas (licenses) are distributed otherwise, different effects will occur. For instance, let DC' in Figure 11.2 represent the quota. Then the households cannot reach the consumption point C' with a quota DC' if the import licenses are distributed according to the 'grandfather clause' (who imported in the past?), the first-come-first-served mode (who submits the application form first?) or political viewpoints, as happens from time to time in developing countries (who has a good friend?). These distribution modes make it impossible to redistribute the revenue from the licenses uniformly to the households, and the households' budget line does not move outward by EC' as in Figure 11.2.

Voluntary export restraints

With an agreement on restraints for exports, governments agree on a maximum import quantity (from the point of view of the importing country) or a maximum export quantity (seen from the exporting country). Exporting countries enter export restraints under the threat of facing even harder entry barriers for their exports. An importing country could basically auction a quota among the exporters of a foreign country; as a rule, however, the distribution of the allowed export quantity among the exporters is left to the exporting country. This means that the exporting country receives the rent of the agreed quota, leaving the home country with an additional welfare loss compared to a self-managed import quota. If the foreign government leaves these rents to its home companies, these have higher profits. As a rule, quotas cause foreign firms to export products of higher quality (upgrading). This can lead to further competitive distortions in the importing country. An example is the voluntary agreement on export limitations for cars between the European Union and Japan in effect until the end of 1999. This agreement was initially intended to protect firms in the lower product segment, but the upgrading of Japanese car exports brought increased competition in the upper segments of the European car market. According to new WTO rules, voluntary export restraints are no longer allowed.

Variable levy

This type of tariff lifts a low world market price to a guaranteed reference price at home. The lower the world market price, the higher is the levy. This system, for instance, is practiced in the framework of the European Union's agricultural policy.

Stretching structural change

The argument of protecting certain sectors also appears in the form of stretching structural change. The assertion is that old industries like coal and steel should be helped to adapt to a new situation, but experience shows that subsidies tend to become irremovable over time.

Protecting infant industries

Many countries are not yet fully integrated into the international division of labor; they are still at the beginning of a development process. In these countries, the argument goes, import duties and other trade barriers should protect newly founded industries, so-called infant industries, until they become competitive. This process comprises making use of falling average costs by accumulating production know-how over time and by exploiting future economies of scale in production. Various measures can be applied: tariffs, quotas, or preferential access to the domestic market for capital.

The basic intention is a temporary protection against imports until the domestic sector has reached a sufficiently strong position on the world markets. However, experience shows that such a protection tends to become entrenched in the course of time, contrary to its intended temporary character. This is confirmed by Latin America's experience in the four decades 1950–1990 with its import substitution policy that aimed at replacing the imports with domestic production. As this policy neutralized competition, cost control and incentives to find new economic and technical solutions were non-existent. The centrally planned economies also tried to make use of economies of scale by concentrating their production facilities at a small number of locations and isolating themselves from the international division of labor. They even tried to implement a division of labor from the top by making the specialization of the national economies a political decision. This method has proved a failure as well.

11.3 Arguments for political trade interventions: the maximization of profits from external trade

A different type of argument focuses on strategically maximizing a country's gains from trade. International trade causes gains; the idea is to redirect these gains into a certain country's pockets. In this case, the opportunity costs of the trade intervention do not arise in the country itself but elsewhere. Optimal tariffs and strategic trade policy belong to this category.

Optimal tariff

In contrast to a small country, a large country can influence the prices on the world market. As its market position is influential, it does not have to take prices as given by the world market.

Influence on the terms of trade

If a large country demands less of its import good (good 2) as a result of the tariff (making its offer curve shift to the left) there will be an excess supply at the previous price, and the price p_2 has to fall. The relative price $p = p_1/p_2$ rises, meaning that the terms of trade for the tariff-imposing country improve. With better terms of trade, domestic welfare improves, as the home country receives more import goods for its exports. The gradient of the straight line OS in Figure 11.5 represents the world market price ratio, p; the line runs steeper as p rises. Through its trade policy, the country shifts the equilibrium solution from point S to point S′.

Tariff rate and welfare

Figure 11.6 shows the effects of a tariff on national welfare, depending on the tariff rate. It is assumed that the foreign country does not react to an increase in

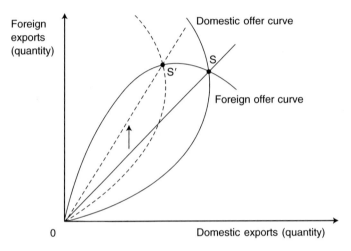

Figure 11.5 Tariff effects on the terms of trade

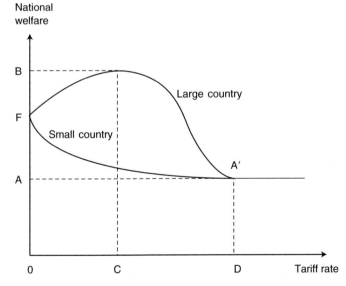

Figure 11.6 Tariff effects on a country's welfare

the tariff. At a tariff rate of zero we have free trade, and the country reaches a real income OF that serves as a welfare indicator. A large country can increase its welfare by raising the tariff rate. OC is the optimal tariff, with a welfare level OB. Further tariff increases make the welfare fall because the quantity effect – the limitation of trade – now overcompensates the positive terms of trade effect on welfare. If the tariff is raised sufficiently (OD), the autarky situation results: the welfare level OA in this situation is lower than with free trade.

According to the assumptions, a positive terms of trade effect does not occur if the country is small. A rising tariff makes the trade triangle shrink; welfare decreases (along the FA' curve in Figure 11.6).

Tariff and opportunity costs: the large country case

At first sight, the argument concerning the optimal tariff appears striking. A country is able to increase its welfare by measures of trade intervention. But opportunity costs arise as well.

1   First of all, a position of market influence for our large country has to be assumed. Monopolistic positions, however, are often not defensible in the long run as processes of substitution take effect on the demand side. OPEC is a good example for this effect. Even if the short-term import demand for a product may be inelastic, the long-term demand will become more elastic. In particular, markets that are contestable in the long run make it impossible for a country to pursue an optimal tariff strategy.

2   A tariff, whether on imports or exports, always entails long-run inefficiencies. What is optimal in a static model may prove absolutely wrong under the dynamic conditions of real life. The tariff-protected companies flag, and eventually their competitive advantage disappears. The rents, i.e. non-functional incomes, are no incentive for efficiency, and rent-seeking develops (see below).

3   The home country's welfare gains may prove elusive if the outside world reacts to the domestic tariff by imposing a tariff of its own: this makes the foreign trade curve shift as well, to the right. With such a retortion tariff, the former equilibrium situation S before tariffs (Figure 11.7) develops into the new equilibrium S'' instead of S' (single-side tariff imposition by the home country). This non-cooperative behavior makes world trade shrink. The lens of potential trade gains becomes smaller (Figure 11.7). The form of the two countries' trade curves determines where this tariff war will finally end. In general, both countries lose.

Strategic trade policy

The basic model

In an approach similar to the argument concerning infant industries, strategic trade policy also has the goal of improving the domestic sector's position in for-

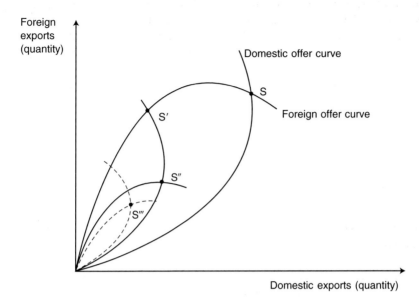

Figure 11.7 Tariff war

eign trade. This is based on the idea that the government can help a domestic company to reach a monopolistic position on the world market or a stronger position in an oligopoly. In the models of strategic trade policy (Brander and Spencer 1985), this can be attained by export subsidies (or subsidies for research and development) paid by the state, giving the domestic firm – at least in the model – an earlier start and helping it to reach a monopolistic position. The profits linked to this activity flow into the home country (rent creation). If another supplier is already present on the foreign market, the government may strengthen the domestic company's market position, e.g. by paying export subsidies. This gives the domestic firm the Stackelberg leadership in a duopoly, and profits are shifted from the foreign country into the home country (rent shifting).

Criticism

The approach described above is based on extremely simple models, like the one of Brander and Spencer (1985) where two duopolists from two different countries produce for the market of a third country, i.e. the world market. It has to be doubted whether models of such simplicity can yield sufficiently well-founded recommendations for economic policy.

1　The simple model is not robust with regard to the modeling of competition in a duopoly. In a model with Cournot quantity competition, an export subsidy is recommended for economic policy. If, on the other hand, the duopoly is modeled as a Bertrand price competition, even the export sector has to be taxed to shift rents to the home country.

2   World-wide monopolies and worldwide oligopolies are rare. As a rule, markets are contestable; this contestability has been intensified by globalization. It is extremely difficult to find examples of oligopolistic structures on the world markets. The automobile industry is characterized by a worldwide dispersion, the market for semiconductors is competitive simply due to the short lifespan of its products. A duopolistic structure can only be found in the market for large passenger airliners, with two suppliers (Airbus and Boeing).

3   Similarly to the optimal tariff argument, the models of strategic trade policy assume that the foreign government does not react, but reality looks different (compare the disputes of the US vs. Japan and of the US vs. European Union). When governments retaliate with subsidies for their own companies, strategic trade policy results in welfare losses for all countries.

4   With respect to the concepts of 'rent creation' and 'rent shifting' we need to add the further concept of 'rent seeking'. Let us assume an environment where the government actively tries to shape the conditions for its export industries, according to each sector's specificities. In this context, companies invest a good deal of energy and considerable resources to get favorable conditions for their export sector. They will thus become active in the political arena instead of concentrating on the entrepreneurial task of pushing through new factor combinations and on creating new products. This binds resources, which cannot be used in production. A large share of the rent, or even the rent as a whole, is thus lost in the process of rent-seeking. An efficiency loss is inevitable.

5   Most of the models are partial (and naive), as they finance the governmental subsidies 'out of nothing' (as a lump-sum tax taken from the households). The negative effects that arise from financing the subsidies through distorting taxes are not considered in this partial equilibrium framework.

6   If the state wants to help companies into a Stackelberg leadership position in the context of strategic trade policy models, it needs to know which products will thrive on the world markets of the future. Governmental offices and parliaments do not have this information. The information provided by industries about expected technological developments is biased by these industries' vested interests. Strategic trade policy thus lacks the necessary information base that is assumed in the models. Competition as a method of discovery in the sense of Hayek (1968) is given up.

11.4 Arguments for political interventions in trade: retortion as a necessary answer?

Anti-dumping

A frequently repeated argument is that a country cannot rest passive if another country's firms offer their products below production costs or below the domestic price on the world market but that it has to answer with anti-dumping measures such as quotas or import tariffs. It cannot be denied that an explicit dumping represents a distortion to the international division of labor; consequently, it is prohibited according to Article VI of GATT. It is equally true, however, that in many anti-dumping cases, protectionist goals gain the upper hand. Anti-dumping then can easily develop into a protectionist division (Messerlin 1989).

Sliding into a non-cooperative trap

Unfortunately, retaliation entails the danger that a trade war develops. This would bring a less favorable welfare situation for both countries. It is therefore important to find, in the framework of the WTO, rules for the international division of labor that limit strategic behavior of particular economies. This also holds for anti-dumping measures, which must not be instruments of protectionism. Free trade is always advantageous for a country, as is shown in the following.

The Free Trade for One theorem

Free trade is beneficial for a (small open) country even if the other country or the rest of the world behaves in a protectionist way (Free Trade for One theorem). For example, the foreign country can put an import duty on its import good (good 1), i.e. the home country's export good. This decreases the foreign demand for good 1. The world market price p_1 of good 1 falls and the terms of trade $p = p_1/p_2$ of the home country deteriorate. This would also be valid if the foreign country puts an export duty on its export good (good 2); this would make this good's price rise on the world market. As a small country, the home country has no possibility of reacting and the world market price line is relevant. This line runs steeper and the home country shifts its production from point P to point P′ (Figure 11.8). Due to the protectionist policy of the foreign country – e.g. if the foreign country applies its optimal tariff – the home country suffers a welfare loss as the new consumption point C′ represents a lower welfare level than point C of the free-trade situation. But the home country is still left with an advantage from trade, as long as the consumption point C′ is situated above the welfare level of the autarky point, A.

However, the theorem of the advantage of free trade for one must not deceive about the fact that a single-sided activity of a particular country influences the distribution of gains from trade between the countries. If a country is large, it can seek to influence the terms of trade on its own by imposing a tariff. This may cause conflicts that finally lead all countries into a prisoner's dilemma of trade policy that they cannot get out of on their own.

11.5 Arguments for interventions in trade: creating a level playing field

Industry and trade unions of the industrialized countries demand a worldwide equalization of conditions under which firms (and labor) compete (a level playing

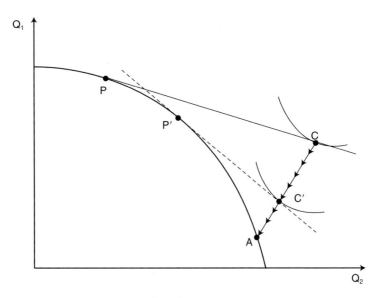

Figure 11.8 A country's advantage from free trade

field), focusing often on equal social and environmental standards. As an example, demands are voiced that employees in newly industrializing countries should have the same social conditions as their counterparts in the industrialized countries.

As far as they are members of the International Labor Organization (ILO), the countries of the world have already laid down minimum standards for working conditions, like the ban on child labor. To level out further social standards and to extend the industrialized countries' social standards to developing countries and newly industrializing countries would be amiss, however. Just as wages in China cannot be raised to the German level, a rich industrialized nation does not have the right to impose its social standards on a newly industrializing country. The decision how much social security a country wants to allow itself must be left to that country, as the purpose of the international division of labor is precisely to exploit the differences in factor endowment conditions. If everything were harmonized, there would be no need for an international division of labor. This reasoning holds analogously for environmental standards.

11.6 Arguments for a free international division of labor

The arguments in favor of a free international division of labor are not only arguments against protectionism. More powerful are the arguments in favor of free trade.

Welfare gains for the world

The world as a whole gains from free international trade. This follows from the fact that free trade overcomes national restrictions: the more restrictions are overcome, the more leeway for economic decisions results, and this causes efficiency gains. If the production of one good remains constant, the possible production quantity of the other good rises. This argument can best be understood if we start from free trade and if then additional national restraints are introduced. This limits the choice set. Free trade takes away such restraints.

Figure 11.9 shows two situations: A is characterized by trade-restricting measures, while F represents free trade. In the initial situation, A, the price lines p and p^* intersect, indicating unexploited arbitrage opportunities and efficiency gains. The condition $p < p^*$ means that Home can specialize in producing good 1 and Foreign in the production of good 2 if the trade barriers are lifted. In point F, the price ratios in the two countries are equal. The total worldwide production rises (shift from point $0'$ to $0''$) and the production of at least one good is higher now.

Welfare gains for a particular country: allocation-driven gains

Regarding welfare gains for a particular country, we distinguish between allocation-driven gains (or static gains) and dynamic gains.

Increased utility

Imports allow consumption at a lower price than in autarky. External trade permits specialization in producing the good for which a country has a comparative

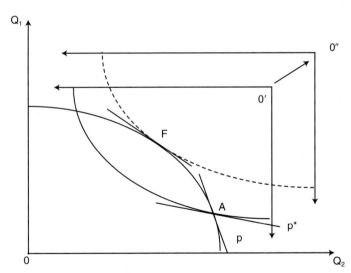

Figure 11.9 Welfare gains for the world

advantage. By shifting its production from point A to point P (Figure 11.10), a country can reach a higher welfare level in point C, as the households have more goods at their disposal than they had before trade. External trade enlarges the consumption space: whereas the consumption space was limited by the transformation curve before trade was opened, it is now – with free trade – determined by the world market price line (budget line) running through point P. The production value, which is at the same time the gross domestic product, as measured in units of the import good, rises from 0D to 0E. An alternative representation with the simple market diagram of supply and demand shows that the households receive a higher consumer surplus by imports.

In detail, the welfare effect can be split into three effects. First, the quantity or volume effect represents the country's ability to buy more imports at given prices. The new price ratio on the world market is represented by a price line that would, other things being equal, run through point A (this line is not shown in Figure 11.10). Second, the price effect stems from lower opportunity costs and from terms of trade that are more favorable than those in autarky. Finally, we have a specialization effect. The combination of the quantity effect and the effect on the relative price can be called the 'trade effect'; its origin lies in the possibility of trading at a free-trade price ratio that differs from the ratio in autarky. The specialization effect results from adjusting production to the new price ratio, i.e. by moving along the transformation curve.

The effect on factor incomes

Due to the rise in the gross domestic product, the overall real income of the production factors increases. However, the real income of a particular factor (here:

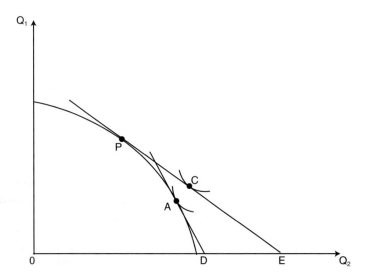

Figure 11.10 The welfare effect of external trade

labor) may decrease if the country (partially) specializes in producing goods whose production is characterized by an intensive use of the other production factors (not labor).

The variety effect

If we consider preferences for different varieties of a product, external trade enlarges consumers' consumption possibilities. On the production side, the variety of inputs allows for higher efficiency due to a more specialized intermediate import use.

The scale effect

Average costs fall with rising output. Factor and resource input per unit of output decrease.

The profit effect

In models with imperfect competition – i.e. with a product price above marginal cost – a rise in output means that the value of the additional production exceeds its production costs. Firms have higher profits; national welfare rises. However, trade can make markets contestable; this reduces market segmentation.

Dynamic welfare gains

In the long run, the dynamic effects of free trade can be considered to be more important than the effects, according to a comparative-static context.

The competition effect

Free external trade ensures intensified competition between suppliers. The domestic producers have to face up to the foreign supply. This triggers a tendency to cut cost. Competition controls cost and ensures efficiency. It also forces economic actors to find new economic solutions and to discover new products. In the sense of Hayek (1968), competition is thus a method of discovery. External trade disposes of national monopolies; free trade is the best competition policy.

The innovation effect

External trade stimulates technological progress, as the strengthened international competition induces a search for cheaper production possibilities and for new products.

The accumulation effect (Baldwin et al. 1997)

Through the import of capital goods trade allows a larger stock of production factors, and it is also an incentive for accumulating a larger factor stock. This accumulation effect holds for physical capital (including infrastructure capital) and human capital. The innovation effect is one form of the accumulation effect because a larger knowledge is accumulated, enabling producers to use the given production factors more effectively.

Whoever is still not satisfied with all these effects may take a look at the experience of those regions of the world that isolated themselves from international competition: Latin America in the four decades until 1990 and the centrally planned economies until the end of the 1980s.

12 Locational competition

Countries compete for the mobile factors of production on a global basis (section 12.1). The essential channel of locational competition is the mobility of capital (section 12.2). The economic instruments used are the supply of public goods and taxation (sections 12.3 and 12.4). Locational competition has a major impact on the position of the immobile factor labor and restricts the maneuvering space of national economic policy (sections 12.5 and 12.6). Furthermore, it can be interpreted as institutional competition, that is competition between different institutional set-ups (section 12.7). It is quite controversial, in how far locational competition will lead to a race to the bottom (section 12.8). Locational competition controls excessive government power, the Leviathan (section 12.9). Especially the smaller countries of the world economy are exposed to locational competition (section 12.10).

12.1 On the concept of locational competition

Competition in the world economy occurs on three different levels. First, firms compete in the world product markets. Second, countries compete in the world market for capital, for technological knowledge, for high-skilled mobile labor, and, to some extent (for instance in historical cases), for residents. Third, there is a complex and intricate system of interrelations between the immobile production factors of countries, especially labor, by which these immobile factors also compete on a worldwide scale (Figure 12.1).

Firms aim for higher profits by selling their products in markets of other countries. They enhance their competitiveness by producing goods in high demand, by developing new products or by providing a good at lower costs. Governments attempt to maximize the utility of their residents, i.e. the income of the immobile factors of production. In a scenario without factor mobility, national governments can induce an increase in the supply of factors of production such as (i) capital through savings, (ii) human capital through education, training and learning on the job and (iii) technological knowledge through invention and innovation. In a scenario with factor mobility, countries can augment the income of the immobile factors of production by attracting mobile capital and mobile technological knowledge and by inducing mobile factors not to leave the country. This improves the factor endowment of the country which in turn increases the productivity of the immobile factors. Besides firms and governments, workers

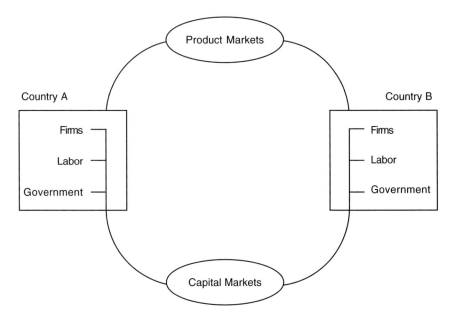

Figure 12.1 Levels of locational competition

strive to maximize their utility by searching for jobs with a higher income and with more secure employment. At first sight, they compete on the national labor markets. But the demand for labor is a derived demand, being linked to demand for the goods that workers produce. Thus, national labor markets are linked through global product markets, albeit through intricate mechanisms.

These three levels of international competition – firms, governments and workers – are interdependent. Whether a firm is competitive depends, among other things, on the framework which is provided by the government. Whether it is worth investing in a country depends on all conditions that influence firms. Whether the reward of labor is high or low depends on the capital endowment of workers in a country. The higher the capital stock the higher the marginal productivity of labor. Additionally, the marginal productivity of labor is influenced by technological knowledge. Finally, the position of workers depends on the competitiveness of their firms, because the demand for labor is derived from the demand for goods.

Our concept of locational competition is thus a broad concept combining each of the three interdepending levels of competition (for another view see Krugman (1994)). The traditional theory of trade is more focused on analyzing just one element, i.e. competition between firms on the world product market, of that broad concept of locational competition, including the implications of the Heckscher–Ohlin theorem for the income of factors of production. In contrast to this traditional approach, locational competition means that the immobile factors of production in a country compete for the mobile factors of production of the world. The issue is to what extent countries are able to keep mobile factors of production at home or whether they can attract mobile factors of production from abroad. In such a Tiebout (1956) context, countries provide public goods and semi-public or meritorious goods, e.g. infrastructure capital, internal and external security, quality of the educational system and cultural amenities, thereby attracting mobile factors of production such as high-quality labor, capital and technology. These goods, however, have to be financed by taxes, fees and prices. Countries have to find the optimum mix between the supply of public, semi-public and meritorious goods and the opportunity costs of financing them. An ample supply of these goods may not be too desirable if it requires too high taxes. Conversely, very low taxes may not be attractive after all if the supply of public goods is extremely poor.

12.2 Channels of locational competition

Locational competition operates through different channels. In this paradigm, the main channel of interdependence between countries is the mobility of factors of production, especially the mobility of physical capital and of new technological knowledge. Additionally, the exchange of commodities leads to locational competition. A special kind of interdependence results from the mobility of portfolio capital. In extreme situations, people start to migrate. Finally, communication processes can lead to international demonstration effects. These mechanisms are explained now.

The mobility of physical capital

Mobile capital can be relocated if conditions for investment change. We have to distinguish physical and portfolio capital. Physical capital is completely mobile *ex ante* when capital is not yet embodied in machines; thus the mobility of physical capital mainly refers to new capital, i.e. to investment (or to clay in a putty-clay model). But even physical capital in place can be turned into funds *ex post* when depreciation allowances for physical capital are earned in the market and not reinvested in the same machinery but reallocated to other uses. Then sunk costs no longer play a role. Thus, even *ex post*, the movement of new capital is a powerful force of interdependence between countries. This also holds if it is taken into account that real capital movements only represent a mechanism netting out excess demand or supply of national capital markets in the sense of the Feldstein–Horioka (1980) hypothesis. Moreover, empirical studies suggest that the importance of the global capital markets is increasing and that the segmentation has been reduced (chapter 3). Furthermore, capital movements of different periods are gaining weight if accumulated in the long term. Finally, we know the importance of marginal changes in economics that are able to begin new long-term processes. Therefore there is no reason to neglect the importance of capital mobility.

The mobility of portfolio capital

Apart from physical capital, portfolio capital is another important channel of interdependence between countries. When the agents on the financial markets lose confidence in the monetary and economic policy of a country, they reverse capital flows and induce a depreciation which signals to the voters the poor evaluation of national economic policy by the markets. As a result, financial markets and competition between currencies act as a controlling mechanism for the soundness of a stabilization policy in an economy.

The exchange of commodities

It is not correct to relate locational competition to capital mobility alone. In principle, capital movements represent a similar mechanism to the movement of goods, which means that the movement of factors and the movement of goods can create similar effects. Suppose capital and technological knowledge are totally immobile internationally. Locational competition will still take place through the exchange of goods. Consider a country that is making production less attractive, for instance by a sharper regulation of business activities or by substantial increases of capital taxes. Consequently, the competitiveness of its exporting firms will deteriorate, absolute and comparative advantage will be reduced, exports will decrease, and in the long run other countries in the same economic sector will gain a comparative advantage. As a result, the country with heavy regulation and high taxation will suffer from its politics. In the long run, it will be less attractive to accumulate capital in the exporting sectors and in the sector producing import substitutes (of course, it will also be less attractive to accumulate capital in the sector of non-tradables. But competitive pressure will be especially strong in the tradable sector). The country will have a reduced capital stock which is not due to capital leaving the country but to a slackening capital accumulation especially in the area of tradable goods because investment in this area has become less attractive. It is true, however, that the impact of changes in commodity flows is less noticeable than the impact of capital flows.

Migration

The importance of migration and its potential impact became obvious in the breakdown of central planning in Eastern Europe at the end of the 1980s. The mobility of people was an enormous factor in locational competition between the economic systems. The socialist planned economies were weakened politically when people started to exit, specifically when 600 East German tourists broke through the Hungarian border at Sopran on 19 August 1989 and Hungary did nothing to hold them back. It is therefore reasonable to relate the collapse of the communist systems to the exit of people. As already pointed out by Tiebout (1956), the exit option of people has a controlling function for national governments.

The demonstration effect

Finally, another channel of locational competition is a demonstration effect which must not be underestimated. By observing the performance and success of others, people are able to gain experience, or, as Mark Twain mentioned: 'There is nothing so annoying as a good example.' This demonstration effect was of crucial importance in the competition between East and West.

As the global integration of economies further increases the mobility of physical capital and technological knowledge, locational competition is intensifying as well. The globalization of markets implies that the concept of locational competition becomes more important.

12.3 Instruments of locational competition

With the concept of locational competition, the comparative advantage of firms and sectors of an economy is not only an advantage due to natural conditions but it is also an acquired comparative advantage which is influenced by political decisions. Whether a country is able to attract mobile factors not only depends on its natural resources, but also on the skills of its workers (the quality of human capital) and the efficiency of its infrastructure. All these factors can be influenced. At least in the long run, i.e. over 10, 20 or 30 years, these endowment conditions can be improved substantially by investment in education and training as well as in transport and communication systems (acquired comparative advantage).

Which are the instruments governments can use to attract mobile factors and induce them not to leave the country? On the one hand, a state can increase the attractiveness of a location by the supply of public goods. On the other hand, any government activity has to be financed and raises the tax burden. In this respect, it is necessary to weigh up the advantages of the supply of public goods and the burden of financing them; a generous supply of infrastructure does not increase the attractiveness of a location unless taxes on mobile factors are kept at a reasonable level. But a country that levies very low or even no taxes on economic activity can also be unattractive for mobile factors if the infrastructure is not sufficiently developed. Obviously, there is a conflict of targets, which can be solved by comparing costs and benefits.

Apart from competition in taxation and in the supply of public goods (competition in infrastructure), there is also competition between institutional arrangements of countries. Indeed, a large part of locational competition is institutional competition in the regulatory framework that determines the way things are carried out in a society. These institutional rules can be formal aspects such as the constitution, the independence of the central bank or the right to free collective bargaining as well as informal aspects such as non-codified, habitual behavior, e.g. to start collective bargaining in a pilot region and then to generalize it to the other regions and the economy as a whole (as in Germany).

12.4 Competition in taxes and public goods

The effects of taxes and infrastructure

Mobile capital has the option to leave a country when conditions become less favorable, e.g. in case of tax increases. Consider an investment decision of a firm that maximizes profits. A source-based tax, e.g. a corporate capital tax, is levied at a tax rate t per unit of capital. Profits[1] are maximized if the marginal productivity of capital (F_K) equals the real interest rate (r/p) and the tax (t/p) per unit of capital in real terms, i.e. $F_K = r/p + t/p$. In Figure 12.2, line RR is the real interest rate, given by the world capital market, which means that we are considering a small economy. Line PM is the marginal productivity of capital. OK is the country's capital stock that is built up before levying a tax. The rectangle ORHK denotes capital income, whereas the area OPHK denotes national output. The triangle RPH indicates the income of labor. A tax levied on capital reduces the marginal productivity of capital: the net productivity curve of capital is shifted downward (P′M′). In the new equilibrium I, less capital is employed in the country. Capital LK leaves the country. Interpreting the area under the capital productivity curve as national output, the country experiences a reduction of gross domestic product of LJHK. Gross national product additionally includes capital income LIHK from abroad. Gross national product is reduced by IJH.

Figure 12.2 depicts the isolated impact of taxation. Assume taxes are used to finance public goods such as infrastructure G. If an improved infrastructure raises the marginal productivity of capital, the productivity curve of capital is shifted

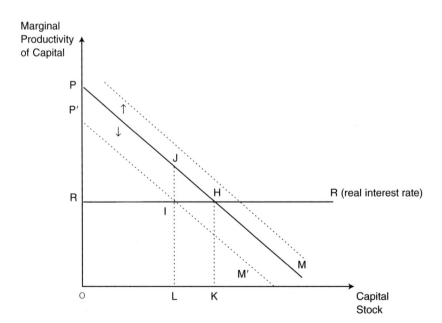

Figure 12.2 The impact of a source tax on capital

upward, and there is a higher incentive to accumulate capital. Thus, there are two opposite effects: taxation reduces capital accumulation and induces capital to leave the country whereas infrastructure attracts capital. Obviously there is some kind of trade-off between the two effects.

The optimal supply of infrastructure

It is necessary to find out which level of infrastructure and taxation is optimal. Figure 12.3 depicts the marginal benefit curve (MB) and the marginal cost curve (MC) of a public good like infrastructure G, which is financed by taxes. The positive effect of infrastructure, the marginal benefit, decreases when the provision of infrastructure is increased. However, the more infrastructure is provided, the higher are its marginal costs. The optimal quantity of infrastructure (OA) is determined by the point where both curves intersect, i.e. where marginal social benefits and marginal social costs of infrastructure are equal. OZ is the price of using one unit of infrastructure which is equal to its marginal costs at the optimum.

When explicitly taking infrastructure into account in the production function, i.e. $Q = F(L,K,G)$, then, from the point of view of society, the supply of infrastructure is optimal if the marginal productivity of infrastructure F_G equals the marginal cost of infrastructure (in real terms) $C'(G)/p$:

$$F_G = C'(G)/p. \tag{12.1}$$

In contrast to this view of society or the economy as a whole, firms view marginal benefits of an input provided by the government (or by someone else) as

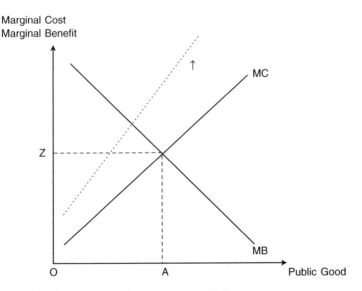

Figure 12.3 Marginal benefit and marginal cost of infrastructure

increasing their revenue, i.e. as marginal revenue; marginal costs of a unit of the input are given by the price the firms have to pay for the input, for instance in the form of taxes. For firms, the optimal condition is that marginal profits are positive. In the case of benefit taxation, the beneficiaries of a public good and its payers are identical: there is no divergence between social and private costs and benefits.

Effects on the tax base

Consider now an open economy instead of a closed one, i.e. an economy with capital mobility instead of an economy without capital mobility. As a result, the marginal cost of supplying infrastructure also comprises the effect of capital leaving the country. Capital may leave a country if the price of infrastructure is more favorable in the foreign countries or if the price (taxes) to be paid in the home country does not correspond to the benefits for the firms. If capital leaves a country because of a tax,[2] e.g. a corporate capital tax, the tax base is reduced. This has to be taken into account in the equation of the optimal amount of infrastructure as a loss in the objective function.[3] It means that the marginal cost curve of a public good shifts upward in comparison with the closed economy, because the opportunity costs of capital leaving the country have to be considered as additional costs (Figure 12.3). Let t be the tax rate per unit of capital and $dK/dt < 0$ the outflow of capital due to a tax-financed infrastructure. Let $\eta_{Kt} = (dK/dt).(t/K)$ be the elasticity of capital with respect to the tax rate. Then the condition for the optimal supply of infrastructure is given by

$$F_G(G) = \frac{C'(G)}{p(1 + \eta_{Kt})}. \tag{12.2}$$

The marginal benefit (F_G) has to equal the revised marginal costs [$C'(G)/p(1 + \eta_{Kt})$]. If the capital stock declines with an increase in the tax rate, the revised marginal cost is *ceteris paribus* higher than in a closed economy (equation 12.1). If t is chosen too high, then $F_G(1 + \eta_{Kt}) < C'(G)/p$ and the cost of supplying infrastructure is too high. This is as an incentive for capital to leave. Consequently, the mobility of capital can change the cost–benefit calculation of governments.

With the introduction of capital mobility, another reason for the outflow of capital could be a better provision of infrastructure abroad at lower marginal costs due to differing natural conditions such as the existence of natural waterways. In such a case of better endowment due to natural conditions, capital movements induce a more efficient global allocation.

Other policy areas

The necessity of comparing benefits and costs is relevant not only for infrastructure, but in a similar way it also holds for other government activities. If, for example, the government finances basic research, then the marginal productivity curve of capital in Figure 12.2 moves upward. But since technological knowledge does not fall from heaven, it has to be produced somehow and the state has to find a method of financing it, e.g. by taxation. As a result of taxation, the marginal productivity curve moves downward again. It is obvious that there are positive marginal benefits of basic knowledge as well as marginal costs of its supply (Figure 12.3). The efficient supply of new basic knowledge is reached at the point where its marginal benefit just equals its marginal cost.

Environmental policy is another example of a government activity influencing the marginal productivity of capital. Consider an environmental tax on production processes. There are two effects. First, the marginal productivity curve of capital shifts downward (Figure 12.2). Second, even if the improvement of environmental quality induced by such a tax is not necessarily an advantage for mobile capital in the strict sense, there may be an indirect advantage by increasing the attractiveness of a location for a firm, e.g. through improved living conditions (environmental quality) for its employees. This shifts up the marginal productivity curve of capital.

12.5 The impact of locational competition on labor

Another important matter is the question of how the distribution of income is affected by capital mobility. This can also be shown in Figure 12.2. In the initial position (H) national investment is financed by internal savings. With the outflow of capital, savers and capital owners receive the same income as before the introduction of the capital tax. But now they earn income ORIL at home and income LIHK abroad. The income of the factor capital does not change: capital is able to avoid the capital tax entirely.

Labor income falls from RPH to RP′I, which is a substantially smaller triangle.[4] With the outflow of capital, labor as a production factor loses, its real income decreases.

This illustrates an important principle of taxation: mobile factors are able to avoid a tax put on them. In the long run, such a tax always hits the immobile factor, which means that a tax on internationally mobile capital always affects labor.

The bargaining position of trade unions aiming at a high income for their members and at secure employment are affected by capital mobility. Assume they succeed in pushing for a wage increase above productivity growth. In an open economy with capital mobility, capital will leave the country, and labor productivity will be reduced. Either wage income falls or, with the previous wage remaining constant, more people will be unemployed. The opportunity costs for trade unions rise, and they must change their strategy except when social policies of the government accommodate the unemployed. Thus, the globalization of markets and the increased capital mobility have altered the relative bargaining position of trade unions.

Locational competition may also have an implication for the institutional set-up of wage bargaining because the bargaining equilibrium between employers' associations and trade unions is affected by the increased mobility of capital.

Firms have an exit option, and this may lead employers' associations not to resist wage increases too strongly. Then, delegating the wage formation process to the social partners (as in the German concept of *Tarifautonomie*) will no longer yield positive results for the economy as a whole with respect to employment. This implies that locational competition requires the redefinition of the checks and balances of wage bargaining.

It is thus quite conceivable that locational competition has affected – among other factors such as deindustrialization or the reorganization of the work process – the position of trade unions in Europe. For instance, the German Trade Union Federation (DGB) lost about 3.6 million members in the period between 1991 and 1997, leaving 8.62 million members at the end of 1997.

12.6 A change in opportunity costs for national politics

Locational competition changes the cost–benefit calculus of national politics.[5] The exit option of capital redefines the opportunity costs of economic policy measures in the usual cost–benefit analysis. It has an impact on the constraint set, the maneuvering space, of the government. Locational competition reduces governmental power. The best example is the emigration of people from the centrally planned states of Central and Eastern Europe. Emigration affected the maneuvering space of decision makers so much that the political systems either collapsed or were compelled to adapt themselves entirely to the new situation.

Another example for the impact of locational competition on the maneuvering space of national governments is the controlling function of capital markets in the case of portfolio capital which can be reallocated at will. Consider stabilization policy (monetary policy, fiscal policy) and assume that a country expands its money supply in excess of the growth of the supply side. Then, purchasing power parity indicates that the national currency will be devalued and market participants will anticipate the devaluation. Thus, purchasing power parity affects exchange rate expectations. A similar effect also holds if public debt is increased and if therefore exchange rate expectations are affected. This mechanism (an interplay of purchasing power parity forming exchange rate expectations and interest rate parity determining portfolio adjustments) represents a check on governments' having a lax stability policy. This could be witnessed in 1983, when France had to reverse its economic policy, which had aimed at stimulating internal demand during the first two years of the Mitterrand presidency. The very fine controlling mechanism, an interplay of purchasing power parity and interest rate parity, of the European System of Exchange Rates (chapter 5) implied that persistently high inflation, combined with an increasing current account deficit and rising foreign debt finally brought a devaluation of the French franc. This then required the change of policy.

12.7 Institutional competition

Locational competition also takes place as institutional competition, i.e. competition over regulations such as mechanisms of licensing or other regulations (Siebert and Koop 1993). For historic reasons, each state has developed its own institutional design, e.g. its legal system. These institutional rules can induce different effects on economic events, including for instance a slowing down of growth or an impediment to employment. For that reason, it is necessary to compare internationally the way things are (to be) handled within a country. Some regulations will persist in this competition, others will have to be adapted.

The best example for institutional competition still is the *Cassis-de-Dijon* verdict of the European Court of Justice (chapter 10). This verdict started the recognition of the country-of-origin principle which automatically leads to institutional competition. Not only in Europe, but all over the world there is institutional competition beyond the demonstration effect described above, taking place in the sense that everybody poses the question of how others behave in a similar situation and whether others might accomplish the same tasks much more easily by doing things differently (benchmarking).

The alternative to the country-of-origin principle, according to which the country-of-origin rules are also applied to the importing country, is the country-of-destination principle. This means that the importing country defines the standard for an imported product. In the international exchange of goods, the country-of-destination principle would cause distinct impediments (chapter 14). If every importing country were allowed to define its own product standards, this would represent numerous barriers to trade, especially the risk of a protectionist abuse of product requirements. Therefore the rules of GATT and WTO attempt to apply the country-of-origin principle in order to prevent the rise of further barriers to trade.

12.8 Locational competition – a race to the bottom?

Some fear that locational competition leads to a race to the bottom in the supply of public goods, e.g. infrastructure, as capital mobility induces the marginal cost of the supply of public goods to rise. It is feared that individual countries might vie with each other in the creation of favorable conditions for private capital, e.g. by lowering taxes, which could cause the supply of public goods to fall to an inefficiently low level, possibly even to zero.

This is not true. First, if capital is leaving and if locational competition has an influence on the infrastructure that is supplied, the marginal benefit curve still defines a lower floor below which the supply of infrastructure cannot fall. This is due to the users of infrastructure, who – in spite of capital mobility – are willing to bear a higher tax rate in order to get the advantage of an improved infrastructure. It is therefore not correct to state that locational competition will lead to a zero supply of public goods.

Second, consider such goods as roads, ports and airports. They can be financed quite often by user charges and market prices. In this case no tax on the capital invested is necessary, so that the opportunity costs of providing infrastructure are not influenced by an outflow of capital. Indeed, by assuming an equivalence of the supply of infrastructure and user prices, the government cannot require revenues to be higher than the funds which are used for the supply of infrastructure.[6] Thus, there are a number of possibilities of how to secure an efficient supply of infrastructure even in the case of international competition. For example, benefit taxation could be introduced, which means that someone who takes advantage of a certain good has to pay the corresponding tax according to the equivalence principle. Additionally, it is possible to privatize parts of the previously publicly supplied infrastructure in order to set scarcity prices for infrastructure. A further variant is the interpretation of infrastructure as a club-good, which leads to the concept of fiscal equivalence (Olson 1969). In this respect, it is quite realistic to consider public goods as having different spatial spreadings. A theatre for instance is important only for the residents of a certain region. As a result – assume the costs of organization to be irrelevant – a specific form of organization is needed for each public good with a certain spatial spreading, which allows the supply of the public good as a club-good enabling the use of corresponding prices or charges.

Even though there is only a weak correlation between taxes and the supply of public or merit goods in the sense of the equivalence principle, firms are still able to recognize positive effects from taxes as long as the advantages from the supply of a public good exceed the tax burden. For instance, this is true in the case of a good system of education. Firms are still ready to pay for public or merit goods such as social coherence or the cultural environment, which have no direct influence on the production function of a company. Therefore a race to the bottom does not necessarily take place.

12.9 Checking the Leviathan

Locational competition restricts the scope of action of the state: when the state is considered as an insurance against low incomes (H.-W. Sinn 1996), possibly under the veil of ignorance concerning the individual's income (Rawls 1971), then the ability of the state to finance such an insurance by taxes on capital and companies is indeed limited by capital mobility. Accordingly, the social security contributions paid by the employers make labor more expensive, thus decreasing the return on capital. Since investors are able to elude payment by leaving the country, demand for labor diminishes and the revenues of the social insurance system are reduced. The opportunity costs of politics change.

But is this to be deplored? Locational competition – like competition on product markets – is a means to lower costs and to discover new solutions in the sense of Hayek (1968). Competition between states increases efficiency, rent-seeking of groups can be reduced (Lorz 1996). Locational competition can thus be seen as a device of taming the Hobbesian Leviathan (S. Sinn 1992b). This is especially relevant when people vote with their feet and leave their country as some residents of the centrally planned economies of Central and Eastern Europe did in the late 1980s. People in general leave their country only with the greatest reluctance, when they have lost all hope at their previous place of living. In this respect, the exit option controls governments. Thus, locational competition can be seen as an important political mechanism for freedom.

There are proposals to limit institutional competition, e.g. by international cooperation extending the right of a state to levy taxes on its citizens beyond national frontiers. This is quite understandable for fiscal reasons, and it may not be easy to draw the line where some tax coordination in a common market like the European Union may be justified. But on a worldwide scale, proposals of limiting tax competition must not destroy the exit option of people, which is a central human right of freedom. Any form of cooperation destroying the exit option would be a cooperation in favor of totalitarian systems, a cooperation against freedom. This would be in complete contradiction to an open society in the spirit of Popper (1945).

12.10 Locational competition between the regions of the world

Locational competition is also competition between political systems and economic philosophies. The diverging experience of different regions of the world with respect to policy approaches is quite impressive. Regions of the world that have faced locational competition head on have had economic success in the past; regions that have shied away from locational competition have often fallen back.

Eastern Europe had a division of labor from above by managed trade where the exploitation of economies of scale was the leading doctrine. But in essence, Eastern Europe had not been exposed to competition from the world economy. Latin America was misled for nearly four decades up to the late 1980s by the economic doctrines of Prebisch (1950) and Singer (1950) and the policy of import substitution. This approach implied that the tradable sector of the economy was not exposed to world market prices. Eventually, Latin America lost its efficiency, but it changed its policy in the 1990s.

It is worth noting that these efficiency losses are long-run phenomena and that it takes some time for the erosion of efficiency and the slowdown of dynamics to eventually show up. This holds for Eastern Europe where the 1950s basically indicate a normal pattern of the catching-up process relative to the United States, but where eventually the grinding force of paralysis and inefficiency takes over. A similar story holds for Latin America where with the lapse of time the restrictions imposed by the policy of import substitution eventually showed their fatal result.

The Pacific Rim countries have followed the opposite route. They were outward oriented and they did not distort relative prices between export goods and import goods. Thus, their infant industries had to compete from the start with the world economy and find the markets for their products. This proved to be an incentive to make the national economy more efficient. A country or a region of the world not participating in this 'beauty contest' will eventually fall behind.

Some innovators in worldwide institutional competition are small countries like New Zealand and Chile. Due to a high degree of openness, which is a distinct attribute of small economies, there is great pressure to adapt to institutional competition. New Zealand undertook a complete change of all aspects of economic policy in 1983. Incidentally, this had been induced by a Labour government. It seems as if New Zealand has solved many of the problems which arose in the past. Chile switched to a capital-funded national pension system during the 1980s. Two European examples of small economies that have been successful in locational competition, are Ireland and the Netherlands.

But even the big regions of the global economy have to face locational competition. The US has always been an open economy, which means that the US always had to adapt to the needs arising from locational competition. Continental countries in Europe, though open in most of their product market, have been slow to adjust in some areas, especially in the labor market.

Notes

1 Profits are defined as revenue, i.e. price (p) times quantity (Q), minus costs. Costs include capital cost (real interest rate as price of capital times capital input, rK) and labor cost (wage rate times labor input, wL). A company maximizes its profits taking into account taxes ($Pi = pQ - wL - rK - tK$), subject to the output constraint given by the production function ($Q = F(L,K)$). By differentiating the Lagrangian function $\mathcal{L} = pQ - wL - (r + t)K - \lambda [Q - F(L,K)]$ with respect to Q, the optimum condition is: $p - \lambda = 0$, which means that the shadow value λ equals the market price. By differentiating with respect to K we have: $F_K(\cdot) = (r + t)/p$.

2 Capital leaves a country if the net marginal productivity is reduced due to a tax increase, i.e. if

$$\frac{d\{p \cdot F_K(K,L,G) - t\}}{dt} < 0.$$

Because of the budget restraint of the state, $C(G) = t \cdot K$, there is an interrelation between the supply of infrastructure G and tax revenues tK: $G = C^{-1}(t \cdot K)$. The optimal tax rate in the case of capital mobility is characterized by profit maximization subject to tax revenues (tK) and the cost of capital (with r defining the interest rate in the world capital market, which is – for simplicity – supposed to be constant):

$$p \cdot F\{K(t),L,C^{-1}[t \cdot K(t)]\} - t \cdot K(t) - r \cdot K(t).$$

The resulting first-order condition is:

$$[p \cdot F_K - t - r]\frac{dK}{dt} + \frac{p \cdot F_G[K + t \cdot dK/dt]}{C'(G)} - K = 0.$$

In the equilibrium of the capital market, the first term equals zero. This yields:

$$F_G = \frac{C'(G) \cdot K}{p \cdot [K + t \cdot dK/dt]}.$$

Dividing the denominator and the numerator of the right side of the equation by K, equation 12.2 results.

3 If capital moves out, income of the immobile factor labor will be reduced because labor productivity falls when workers are less well endowed with capital. Lower labor income also implies a lower tax base.

4 If the state redistributes its tax revenues P′PJI among the households, then labor loses only IJH.

5 It is an interesting observation that institutional changes exert considerable influence on the allocation of power. A telling example is the transition from fixed to flexible exchange rates. With the use of flexible exchange rates, the balance of power between fiscal and monetary policy has shifted. Now monetary policy exerts a greater influence than fiscal policy (Siebert 1994, ch. 16).

6 Additionally it has to be taken into account that the state has to balance its budget. There are tax revenues, but there is also expenditure on infrastructure. With falling average costs of infrastructure (due to high fixed costs) this creates the problem that the budget might not be balanced with prices equaling marginal costs (Sinn 1996). Note, however, that the immobile factor (labor) also has an indirect advantage arising from the supply of infrastructure, namely if capital is attracted and if consequently labor is better equipped with capital and thus has a higher productivity.

13 Using the national and the global environment

For the economist, the environment is a scarce good. Environmental systems have a spatial dimension. The environment can be a national or a global good (section 13.1). If the environmental endowment of countries differs, then the traditional theories on the international division of labor hold (section 13.2). For global goods, new institutional solutions should be found, in order to avoid non-cooperative behavior (section 13.3).

13.1 The economic paradigm of the environment

The environment is the set of the natural conditions of the human biosphere; it includes the quality of air, of rivers, lakes and the sea, of the soil and the quality of the living environment (e.g. biodiversity). From the point of view of an economist, the environment is a scarce good, but a good with its own specific features.

The environment as a scarce good

The environment has two competing functions for the economic system (Siebert 1998b): it is a public consumption good (arrow 1 in Figure 13.1) and it absorbs waste from consumption and production (arrows 2 and 3). These two roles are in conflict. Emissions from consumption and production are transformed into pollutants ambient in the environment by natural processes (diffusion) which influence the quality of the environment (damage function, arrows 6 and 7). In addition, the environment supplies inputs for the production process (arrow 5). Competing uses are linked to externalities. Indeed, arrows 2, 3, 4, 7 and 1 in Figure 13.1 describe an externality in greater detail, by introducing the intervening variables, emissions and pollutants ambient in the environment.

In its role as environmental quality, the environment is a public good, that is, it is used to the same extent by all. Nobody can be excluded from the consumption of this good (non-excludability), and there is no rivalry in consumption (non-rivalry). In its role as an absorber of waste, the environment is not a public good, but a good for which exclusion rights can be defined (private good). With respect to environmental quality, the supply of a public good cannot be determined by the market system, because no institutional arrangement is available to aggregate the consumers' willingness to pay. Thus, the optimal supply of a public good

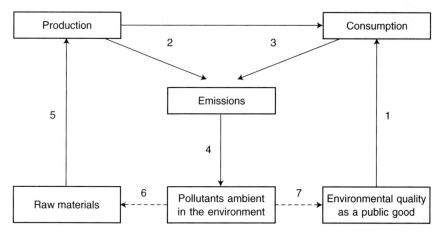

Figure 13.1 The economic system and the environment
Source: Siebert (1998b)

must be determined in a political decision-making process. Once the desired quality of the environment is set, user rights can be defined for nature as an absorber of waste. With these user rights market processes can develop. In this way, prices can be put on emissions either by introducing transferable emission permits or by taxing the emissions. The public good should not be mixed up with a free good for which no price is charged. Historically, the environment was used as a free good in its capacity as an absorber of wastes; this implied a deterioration of environmental quality as a public good. Instead of the term 'free good', the term 'common property resource' ('the commons') is used for a situation in which no property rights are defined.

The spatial dimension of environmental goods

Environmental systems always have a spatial dimension. With respect to their dimension in space, environmental goods can be divided into three categories. The first comprises national environmental goods, i.e. those that fall completely within the borders of one nation as a river system or the tributaries of a river may. The second group is formed by cross-border environmental goods, which are shared by (at least two) countries like transfrontier pollution (e.g. acid rain). The third category consists of global environmental goods, i.e. goods that pertain to the Earth as a whole like the ozone layer. Of course, environmental problems are mostly related to several environmental systems but the separation into these three groups is very helpful for the analytical solution of the problem.[1]

The environmental problem is characterized by an extensive casuistry: pollutants are bound in products, they are emitted from stationary or mobile sources (like cars), they accumulate over time and, finally, there is a difference between the use of non-renewable and renewable resources (Siebert 1998b). All these issues pose specific problems for the international division of labor. In the following, we will assume that emissions originate from production processes by stationary sources and are delivered into air and water.

13.2 Environmental abundance as a national factor endowment

As far as the environment is a national good, its scarcity can be different from country to country due to the following reasons:

- The absorption capacity of the environment as a receptacle for emissions may vary between countries because the assimilation capacity can differ due to natural conditions.
- The population of one country may have stronger preferences for environmental quality than that of another country, consequently assigning a higher value to the environment. Even if international preferences are equal, a higher income per head can lead to a stronger demand for environmental quality. Finally, institutional rules also influence the demand for environmental quality, as they affect political decisions by which the desired state of the environment is determined.
- The demand for environmental assimilation services may be different because of the level and structure of consumption and production, but also due to abatement and disposal technologies for emissions and waste.

The different abundance of the environment means that the goals for environmental quality, set by the political process, differ. Defining U as environmental quality, the domestic environmental quality U is different from the foreign U^*, and thus $U \lessgtr U^*$. Different abundance also means that the absorption capacity for emissions E in different regions of the world is not equal: $E \lessgtr E^*$. This holds even if environmental quality as a public good is identical.

Different environmental qualities have to be considered in the same way as differences in factor abundance. The Heckscher–Ohlin approach can thus be applied. Countries with a relative abundance in environmental quality will export commodities which use the environment intensively in their production. If the environmental endowment is not equal, prices will differ as well, due to the differing scarcity. Through trade, prices will tend to become more equal over time, because in the country with the relatively abundant environment, the production of the good which uses the environment intensively will rise, and therefore the demand for assimilation services of the environment will increase. In the country where environment is relatively scarce, the production of the good which uses the environment intensively will fall, and therefore the prices for emissions will do so as well. If capital is mobile, these effects will occur through capital movements from one country to the other.

Insofar as the environment is a national good and its scarcity can be expressed by market prices, environmental endowment and environmental policy signaling the preferences of the citizens are no reasons for international regulation. The environment must then be treated like any other factor endowment. When we consider the large casuistry on environmental problems, environmental political instruments can work as trade barriers (chapter 14).

13.3 Global environmental problems

Looking at global environmental problems, the environment appears as a public good which covers the whole world and which everyone uses to the same amount. Examples are the atmosphere and the ozone layer. One of the current hypotheses of physicists is that the global climate is warming due among other factors to the increased concentration of carbon dioxide. Another hypothesis is that the emission of chlorofluorocarbons (CFCs) damages the ozone layer. These effects do not occur overnight; instead, they occur after several decades.

Let us consider two economies. The environmental quality U^W is a global public good, so that $U = U* = U^W$. As environmental quality is a public good, it cannot be assigned to a single nation. The total emissions of the world E^W are composed of the emissions of both countries, $E + E* = E^W$. They have a negative influence on global environmental quality, so that $U^W = G(E^W)$.[2]

The decision problem for allocating global environmental goods consists of two interwoven questions:

- Which environmental quality of the global environmental goods should we aim at?
- How should the costs of reaching the desired global environmental quality be divided among the individual countries?

Analytically, the approach to determining the target level for public environmental goods is to derive the aggregate willingness of nations to pay. The problem is that sovereign nations can behave as free-riders. The corresponding institutional difficulties surface when it comes to determining the benefits that arise from the protection of global environmental goods for individual countries, say the (monetary) value of prevented environmental damage, and to assigning the costs for the attainment of the protection, say the prevention of waste. According to the polluter-pays principle, cost assignment would be fair in terms of pollution caused. However, this principle requires a sovereign authority that does not exist for the world as a whole.

For these reasons, nations have to find mechanisms by which they bind themselves in using global environmental goods. In the end, this is a question of a contractual rule governing the use of global environmental goods in the way the Coase theorem on environmental agreements has suggested (Siebert 1998b), with the additional difficulty that sovereign states are doing the bargaining. In this process, the interests of important polluters and the preferences of countries with higher environmental awareness will play an important role, as well as income per head and a variety of other variables. Consider China, for example, a country with large coal reserves, that will want to use these resources for its development, without worrying too much about how this might influence the concentration of carbon dioxide in the world's atmosphere. As individual countries will behave strategically, it will be difficult to come to (and to implement) a self-restriction of sovereign states in using global environmental goods. Besides the problem of realizing multilateral solutions, another issue lies in the necessity that multilateral agreements should remain stable in the long run. Once a multilateral agreement is signed, it should be made sure that sovereign states have no interest in reneging and walking away from the contract.

Looking at possible institutional solutions, an example is an agreement on a worldwide certificate system for carbon dioxide emissions (Heister *et al.* 1995). In this agreement, the total quantity of worldwide allowed emissions is fixed. But difficulties arise when a consensus has to be reached on who will be entitled to these certificates, as they determine a user right, more precisely the right to use the global environment and indirectly the natural resources that generate carbon dioxide. Possibly, a proportional reduction rate for the given emissions is a starting point for industrial countries. Developing countries will require an increasing rate. Unfortunately, such an approach starts from the current level of emissions and does not take into account that the level of emissions increases with the economic growth of the newly industrializing countries.

Notes

1 Cross-border environmental problems are not discussed in detail (Siebert 1998b, chapter 12).
2 With cross-border environmental problems an interdependence exists such that the environment transports emissions from one country to another. The diffusion function is: $E = T(E^*)$ or $E^* = T^*(E)$.

14 An institutional order for the world economy

After having discussed several areas where national interests and world interests can clash, like trade policy, locational competition and environmental allocation, we now look at the institutional design for the world economy. The issue is how strategic and non-cooperative behavior of nation states can be channeled into a system of rules defining a global frame of reference. Countries can behave strategically in their national policies, in order to derive the greatest national benefit out of the international division of labor. In their trade policy, they can levy an optimal tariff or they can attempt to implement strategic trade policy in favor of certain sectors. Countries can also behave as free-riders towards global public goods. All these cases imply non-cooperative behavior of countries, which eventually leads to a welfare loss for the world as a whole and possibly even for the individual countries involved. Consequently, an institutional order has to be created which prevents countries from falling into the trap of non-cooperative behavior. Furthermore, mechanisms should be established that enable countries to get out of a situation of non-cooperative behavior. Strategic behavior in trade policy is explained in section 14.1; other areas of non-cooperative behavior or of externalities are discussed in section 14.2. The world economy needs a system of rules (section 14.3). We then look at the history of the WTO and how it works (section 14.4). A number of new problems have to be addressed, e.g. free market access versus national regulation, competition policy and aggressive trade policy (section 14.5). Moreover, as an implication of the paradigm of locational competition, rules for the mobility of production factors are receiving increasing attention in the discussion of economic policy (section 14.6). Social norms are a major matter of debate (section 14.7). The integration of the environment in the world trade order represents a specific problem (section 14.8). The mechanisms to stabilize and strengthen the world order are analyzed (section 14.9). The role of the IMF is treated in section 14.10. Finally, the main elements of the global economic order are summarized (section 14.11).

14.1 Strategic national behavior

States can behave strategically against other states. Trade policy is a major area where non-cooperative or strategic behavior of nation states can be observed. The goal is to influence the gains from trade.

Cooperative and non-cooperative trade policy

Countries can improve their terms of trade if they are sufficiently large. When one or several large countries implement such a strategic policy, the gains from the international division of labor dwindle for the other countries. For our analysis, we consider a two-country case and first introduce a situation of free trade as a reference point, in which both countries gain from international trade. As a simplification we assume that both countries are identical but are in different autarky positions before trade starts. In Figure 14.1 these autarky situations are depicted by points A and A*. Gains from trade, i.e. the gains in welfare in comparison to autarky, will then be equal for both countries. We assume that the trade benefits in a situation of free trade amount to (17,17*). In the following, the first number of such a set denotes the domestic trade benefits, the second number indicates the foreign trade benefits. These numbers do not denote the level of utility, but the change in the level of utility in comparison to the autarky situation. In Figure 14.1, the free-trade situation is characterized by the point I (17,17*), which is the tangential point of the indifference curves of the two economies. In point F_1 , the transformation curves of both economies are tangent to each other, and the straight line p denotes the equilibrium world price ratio.

When the domestic country behaves strategically by levying an import duty or an export duty or intervenes in other ways, then the domestic gains from trade can be increased; the gains from trade of the foreign country decrease. Such a situation II can be achieved by using the optimal tariff. Point II (20,7*) denotes the distribution of gains from trade. It is important to notice that the domestic pro-

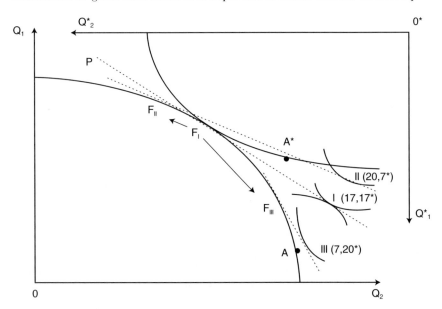

Figure 14.1 Gains from trade with strategic behavior

duction point moves to point F_{II}. The system of coordinates related to F_I of the foreign country is not valid any more.

Alternatively, the foreign country could raise an optimal tariff in order to increase its gains from trade, while the domestic gains from trade decrease. This is point III with bundle (7,20*). The domestic production point moves to F_{III}. In this case again, the system of coordinates for the foreign country is not valid any more.

Also, a situation IV (9,9*; not shown in Figure 14.1) can occur, in which both countries are implementing a tariff policy. Finally, in the extreme case in which both countries take protection to the limit and are in the autarky situation A and A*, the gains from trade are (0,0*).

Figure 14.2 depicts the trade benefits, that is the increase in benefits U, U^* relative to the autarky situation. The area within the curve through 0, II, I, III is the area of the possible gains from trade. Assume both countries to be in the initial position in situation IV, with trade benefits amounting to (9,9*). Then the area between the curve and above point IV defines the possible trade benefits for both countries.

In the initial position IV, both countries can benefit from the transition to free trade. If they cooperate, they will proceed to situation I, where each of them reaches a welfare maximum and where the gains in total utility are maximized. However, in the case of non-cooperative behavior, they will not reach the optimal situation I. Both countries strive for the positions II and III, but instead they

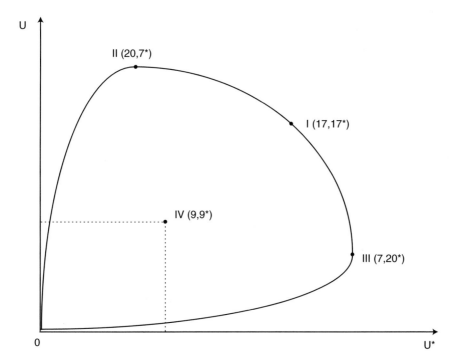

Figure 14.2 Trade benefits area

Table 14.1 The prisoner's dilemma: welfare levels with free trade and tariff policy

Domestic country \ Foreign country	Free trade	Tariff policy
Free trade	I (17,17*)	III (7,20*)
Tariff policy	II (20,7*)	IV (9,9*)

remain in situation I or even move closer to the origin. This is the prisoner's dilemma. They cannot agree, because one country will always expect that it will have greater benefits in a situation different from situation I. The situation considered above corresponds to a game with four possible outcomes. In Table 14.1, the gains from trade represent a pay-off matrix for the players. In the case of free trade (situation I), both countries can benefit.

Trade benefits due to liberalization

A pay-off matrix with the welfare effects of liberalization and protectionism for the world as a whole and for the different regions was calculated before the conclusion of the Uruguay Round which took place from 1986 to 1994 (Table 14.2). The world would lose if North America or the European Union implemented a protectionist policy (−214 billion US$ a year). The protectionist region itself would also lose. If only one region liberalized trade unilaterally, not only would this region benefit from the policy as postulated in the free-trade-for-one theorem (chapter 9) but the other regions would also benefit. Gains are considerably larger when both regions pursue free trade policies. The gross world product could rise by about 5 percent.

Different concepts of trade policy

So far, we have outlined only two possible trade policies, i.e. free trade and tariff policy. However, in reality we can observe a great diversity of approaches to international trade policies. In Figure 14.3, these approaches are ordered on a

Table 14.2 Pay-off matrix of protectionism and liberalization of the EU and North America[a]

	North America is protectionist		North America liberalizes	
EU is protectionist	EU −132		EU 42	
	Asia–Pacific −18	World −214	Asia–Pacific 38	World 133
	North America −64		North America 53	
EU liberalizes	EU 37		EU 211	
	Asia–Pacific 7	World 50	Asia–Pacific 63	World 397
	North America 7		North America 124	

[a]Change in gross domestic product in billion US$ (in real values of 1988)

Source: Stoeckel *et al.* (1990)

| Autarky | Division of labor from above | Protectio-nism | Import substi-tution | Strategic trade policy | Aggressive trade policy | Regional integration | Free trade |

Figure 14.3 Different concepts of trade policy

continuum that spans from free trade to autarky. In the situation of a centrally planned division of labor from above, as practiced in the former COMECON until the late 1980s, the allocation of production factors and goods was executed along political lines. Moreover, the economic area remained more or less closed to the outside world. Protectionism, import substitution and strategic trade policy intervene in different forms. Aggressive trade policy strives for the opening of foreign markets and is not afraid to use protectionist measures to achieve this goal. Regional integration approaches the free trade situation.

14.2 Free-rider behavior, public goods and externalities

Strategic behavior in trade policy is possible when a country is large enough to acquire a monopolistic position. Additionally, strategic behavior can occur when there are other interdependences apart from trade, e.g. the case of global public goods, that is those goods that are consumed in equal amounts by all. An example of a world-wide public good is global environmental media. Public goods are strongly related to technological externalities. These interdependences do not represent interdependences via markets, but via 'technological' systems. Thus, in the case of global warming the global atmosphere is such a system. Technological external effects are interdependences in the output and input space of production and utility functions of economic agents.

If we consider strategic behavior towards public goods, then countries may behave as free-riders. They use a public good without contributing adequately to its production. A country could use the high quality of the global environmental good, but at the same time heavily burden this good through its emissions. In a similar way, a country could enjoy the stability of international trade rules, but break them at the same time, and in this way undermine this stability. Whenever global public goods are concerned, rules for the world economy have to be developed.

14.3 The world trade order as a system of rules

Nations autonomously pursue a trade policy in order to promote their welfare. Such an economic policy can get into conflict with a free international division of labor. Consequently, a rule system is needed to reduce transactions costs, most prominently to diminish uncertainty arising from the behavior of market participants or originating from the non-cooperative conduct of sovereign nation states. The basic idea of such a world economic order for the trading system is to provide an institutional framework that allows the participating economies to capture the potential welfare gains from the international division of labor.

A system of rules for the behavior of governments takes the place of *ad hoc* negotiations between governments. A central element of such a rule-based institutional framework for the world economy is that sovereign states voluntarily commit themselves to respect rules which prevent strategic, i.e. non-cooperative, behavior by individual countries. The contractually binding commitments, made freely by governments, are ratified through domestic legislative processes. Strategic behavior of national governments would destroy the international order as a public good, representing a negative externality for the rule system. The rules must prevent such strategic behavior. Self-commitment by states limits national governments' choice of actions in the future and in this sense represents a 'negative catalogue', a restraint on government behaviour. It protects the international division of labor against national governments (Tumlir 1983). The self-commitment of states is also a shelter from the power of protectionist groups in the individual economies. Moreover, the rules must induce nation states to act cooperatively in certain areas (Haggard and Simmons 1987) and to develop the system further. The World Trade Organization (WTO) is not only about respecting rules but also about making rules. An international order thus provides a skeleton of an international economic constitution for sovereign nation states in the area of international exchange.

Despite the game-theoretic character of international negotiations on rules for the division of labor and the related possibility of strategic behavior, countries have succeeded in concluding a multilateral agreement for trade for a variety of reasons. First of all, there is the historic experience that the way out of the prisoners' dilemma induces welfare gains to all, and that a tariff war is by no means advantageous for any single country. Second, an agreement on rules is not a solitary event, but only part of a sequence of agreements on rules. In such a repeated game with an infinite time horizon, gains are divided again and again. From this point of view, cooperation can pay off, because countries will care about their reputation. Finally, the uncertainty on future gains from new negotiations can lead to a less aggressive, more cooperative behavior.

14.4 The WTO – how it works

A little bit of history

The first attempt to establish an International Trade Organization (ITO) in 1947 failed. As a compromise, the GATT (General Agreement on Tariffs and Trade) was founded in 1948 by 23 countries. In 1995 it was followed by the World Trade Organization (WTO). At the time when the GATT was established, after the protectionist experiences of the 1930s, the goal was to create a stable framework for international trade in order to provide the preconditions for growth and an increase of prosperity. Membership increased continuously over time (Table 14.3). In the period 1986–1998, 44 countries joined the GATT/WTO. As of 1999, the WTO has 134 members, and 30 states are applying for membership, among them Russia and China.

Rounds of liberalization

GATT succeeded in eight liberalization rounds in significantly cutting tariffs and reducing other barriers (Table 14.4). In the years before the Geneva Round of 1947, the tariffs of the industrialized countries were as high as about 40 percent of the import value (on average). After the Uruguay Round, they were brought down to about 4.3 percent. The first five GATT rounds were concentrated on tariff cuts. The last rounds, all of them lasting several years, embraced new themes. The Kennedy Round, for example, developed an anti-dumping code, although this was not ratified by the US. In the Tokyo Round, a proposal for a new anti-dumping code saw daylight, but an improved code on subsidies was left behind. Finally, the Uruguay Round extended the agenda with new rules on services, intellectual property and property rights, and a dispute settlement procedure.

This tendency to liberalization was opposed by some developments that are rather protectionist. The United States obtained a waiver for agriculture in 1955; this then became very important for European agricultural policy. In 1961, the Short Term Arrangement on Cotton Textiles was introduced during the Dillon Round. It included the right for countries to impose unilateral import quotas. In 1988, the US introduced the 'Omnibus Trade and Competitiveness Act' (Super 301) and created the legal possibility of retaliating in the event of trade-restricting measures by other countries. The European Union developed its 'Trade Defence Instrument' in 1994 (see below).

Decision structure of the World Trade Organization

The WTO is an international organization based on a multilateral agreement. The central decision making body, the ministerial conference, is responsible for general questions (Figure 14.4). The WTO council, the general director and the

Table 14.3 GATT/WTO membership,[a] 1948–1999

1947	23
1960	38
1970	78
1980	85
1990	100
1999	134

[a]End of year

Source: GATT/WTO, *International Trade, Trends and Statistics* (several issues)

Table 14.4 Liberalization rounds and protectionist counters

	Liberalization rounds	Average tariff reduction for industrial goods in percent		Protectionist arrangements
1947	Geneva Round	19		
1949	Annecy Round	2		
1950–51	Torquay Round	3		
1955–56	Geneva Round	2	1955	The US attains an exceptional arrangement for agriculture (waiver)
1960–61	Dillon Round, Geneva Round (all five rounds on tariff cuts)	7	1961	Quantitative restrictions on trade in textiles
1963–67	Kennedy Round, Geneva Round (anti-dumping code)	35		
1973–79	Tokyo Round (new anti-dumping code, subsidy code)	34		
1986–94	Uruguay Round (rules on services and intellectual property, dispute settlement)	40	1984	New trade policy instrument of the EU
			1994	Trade Defence Instrument
			1998	Omnibus Trade and Competitiveness Act of the US. Retaliation instrument

Source: GATT/WTO, Annual Reports

general secretary are the operative bodies. They have a dispute settlement body and a trade policy review body at their disposal. The member countries of the WTO are legally bound by three multilateral agreements, GATT (General Agreement on Tariffs and Trade), GATS (General Agreement on Trade in Services) and TRIPs (Trade-Related Aspects on Intellectual Property Rights). Three councils are assigned to the three multilateral agreements.

The WTO is different from GATT in several respects. First, member states have formally ratified the WTO agreements, whereas GATT was simply signed by governments. GATT only dealt with trade in goods; in addition, the WTO covers services and intellectual property as well. Third, the dispute settlement mechanism is more effective. Note, however, that the GATT rules referring mainly to trade remain valid as an element of the WTO framework.

Figure 14.4   The decision structure of the WTO

The basic principles

The world trade order is based on three main principles: the principle of liberalization, the principle of non-discrimination and the principle of reciprocity. More specific principles support and specify those main principles.

Liberalization

The simple idea of GATT/WTO is to reduce trade barriers. This principle is a general point of reference. Nations have to abstain from raising existing tariffs or from levying new ones. In addition, quantitative restrictions or non-tariff barriers are forbidden. The eight liberalization rounds since the foundation of the GATT in 1948 are proof that the concept of liberalization works.

Non-discrimination

Trade policy measures should not differentiate between countries, countries should be treated equally. In particular, there must be no discrimination between domestic and foreign products. This principle can be explained very well with Thailand's cigarette case, decided by GATT in 1990. Thailand had raised a tariff on imported cigarettes, referring to health policy reasons, but without taxing domestically manufactured cigarettes. In the Thailand cigarette case, it was ruled that it is consistent with the world trade order for a country to take measures for health reasons (Article XX), but it must not make a difference between domestic and foreign products and it should not discriminate against imports.

Most-favored-nation

The most-favored-nation principle is an expression of the non-discrimination principle (favor one, favor all). The obligation towards a general, positive and unconditional most-favored treatment, which is included in Article I of the GATT treaty, implies that a tariff reduction that is granted to one country has to be granted to all countries. In this way bilateral tariff reductions are multilateralized. While the non-discrimination principle is a negative mechanism banning discriminating behavior, the most-favored-nation principle is a positive mechanism strengthening free trade.

Reciprocity

The principle of reciprocity requires that concessions have to be granted mutually. This means that a tariff cut in one country has to correspond to an equivalent cut in another country. This is practiced by a bilateral demand–supply system. For example, a country will offer a concession x when another country has offered a concession y. However, a country can only ask for a concession for a specific product if it is in the position of the principal supplier, which means that it provides the main part of the imports of the partner country (principal supplier rule).

Bound tariffs

When countries agree on reduced tariffs, they bind their commitments. Changing the bindings requires negotiating with the trading partners and compensating them for loss of trade. Thus, binding creates opportunity costs of non-compliance.

The concept of reciprocity of concessions is based on the mercantilist idea, according to which the reduction of trade barriers is a sacrifice. This contradicts the theory of the international division of labor, according to which a country can raise its welfare by unilaterally reducing its tariffs. The notion of concession stems from the public opinion on international trade. It can possibly make the political realization of tariff cuts much easier.

Single undertaking

The single-undertaking nature of the WTO reflects the concept of packaging the benefits arising in different areas of the international division of labor. In the past, plurilateral agreements, introduced in the Tokyo Round, allowed a subset of GATT members to sign contracts for specific areas, for instance the Agreement on Civil Aircraft and the Agreement on Government Procurement. Such a procedure, though easing a contract among at least some GATT members, represents an *à la carte* approach and entails the risk of fragmentation of the multilateral trading system. In principle, it can be expected that the single-undertaking nature of WTO will strengthen the rule system because it forces countries to swallow less favorable rules in one area if they are compensated by rules allowing higher benefits in other areas. The approach of packaging is also helpful in focusing bargaining when a liberalization round is being concluded. However, the 'offsetting' between the advantages of suborders should not be carried too far. If in the course of time the advantages of countries shift asymmetrically in the individual suborders, a fragile structure of acceptance could collapse like a house of cards. To avoid domino effects, it makes sense that the suborders should basically legitimize themselves on their own and not be conditionally accepted.

The most important articles of the WTO

Preamble: 'Recognizing that their relations in the field of trade and economic endeavour should be conducted with a view to raising standards of living, ensuring full employment and a large and steadily growing volume of real income and effective demand, developing the full use of the resources of the world and expanding the production and exchange of goods, . . .'

'Being desirous of contributing to these objectives by entering into reciprocal and mutually advantageous arrangements directed to the substantial reduction of tariffs and other barriers to trade and to the elimination of discriminatory treatment in international commerce, . . .'

Article I: '. . . any advantage, favour, privilege or immunity granted . . . to any product originating in or destined for any other country shall be accorded immediately and unconditionally to the like product originating in or destined for the territories of all other contracting parties . . .'

Article III: '. . . internal taxes and other internal charges, and laws, regulations and requirements affecting the internal sale, . . . should not be applied to imported or domestic products so as to afford protection to domestic production . . .'

Article VI: '. . . dumping, by which products of one country are introduced into the commerce of another country at less than the normal value of the products, is to be condemned . . .'

Article XI: 'No prohibitions or restrictions other than duties, taxes or other charges, whether made effective through quotas, import or export licences or other measures, shall be instituted or maintained . . .'

Article XII: 'Notwithstanding . . . Article XI, any contracting party, in order to safeguard its external financial position and its balance of payments, may restrict the quantity or value of merchandise permitted . . .'

Article XIII: 'No prohibition or restriction shall be applied . . . on the importation of any product . . . or on the exportation of any product . . . , unless the importation of the like product of all third countries or the exportation of the like product to all third countries is similarly prohibited or restricted . . .'

Article XX: '. . . nothing in this Agreement shall be construed to prevent the adoption or enforcement by any contracting party of measures: . . . necessary to protect human, animal or plant life or health; . . .'

Article XXIV: '. . . the provisions of this Agreement shall not prevent . . . the formation of a customs union or of a free-trade area . . .'

Further rules of the WTO

Further rules relate to other aspects of trade barriers such as waivers, anti-dumping and subsidies. Other aspects refer to national regulation. The general aim is to restrain trade-restricting or trade-distorting activities of nations by a set of rules.

Voluntary export restraints

All voluntary export restraints which were used to circumvent tariff liberalization should be eliminated by the year 2000. No new forms of quantitative restrictions should be allowed.

Waivers

Within the framework of the international trade order there are a number of exceptions. A waiver from the non-discrimination principle and from the most-favored-nation clause holds for regional integrations according to Article XXIV, although they discriminate against third countries. It is assumed that regional integrations inducing free trade within a spatially limited area will eventually lead to global free trade. This exception relates to customs unions, free-trade areas and preference zones.

Another waiver is valid for agricultural products: market access may be restricted by import regulations and exports can be strengthened by subsidies. In the Uruguay Round quantitative import restrictions were partly replaced by tariffs. This tariffication of quantitative restraints will allow the reduction of tariffs by a flat rate later on. Agricultural tariffs have been reduced by 38 percent in industrial countries and by 24 percent in developing countries. New negotiations have to be launched.

The third waiver is the world textile agreement (Multi Fiber Agreement). Bilateral agreements between individual countries (including tariffs, quantitative restrictions and voluntarily export restraints) and trade restraints have been allowed internationally. Until the year 2005, the new world textile agreement shall be integrated into the WTO rules.

Anti-dumping and countervailing duty measures

Though defensible in a framework of theoretical models, these instruments can easily develop into a severe impediment for trade (administered protection). They are defined by national legislation and can be captured by national interest groups. They represent a way around bound tariffs and (now) forbidden quantitative restraints. Even if they are not actually applied, the threat of using them entails uncertainty and may already lead to the 'appropriate' export behavior. In economic categories, contingent protection represents effective protection. This 'administered protection' (Krueger 1998, p. 8) seems to have become more important as a protectionist device of US trade policy. The task for the WTO will be to contain the protectionist impact of this approach. Standards have to be defined which must be respected by national anti-dumping laws.

Country-of-origin versus country-of-destination

When product norms are applied, we distinguish between country-of-origin rules and country-of-destination rules. The country-of-origin principle accepts the rule of the country of origin whereas the country-of-destination principle leaves it to the importing country to set the domestic standard as the yardstick for its imports. The result would be a potpourri of diverging standards representing barriers to trade. Moreover, such regulations can easily be captured by interest groups. The attempt of GATT has been – and the aim of the WTO must be – to push back the role of the country-of-destination principle. Which regulations are set for the production of goods should be left to the discretion of the country of origin. The different regulations of national countries of origin should rather have equal standing competing with each other. A weakening of the country-of-origin principle and a strengthening of the country-of-destination principle will inevitably harm the multilateral order. The goal of the world trade order is therefore that countries mutually accept the regulations of the country of origin for product quality and production processes in order to minimize transaction costs. Thus, competition between rules can thrive. Only in precisely demarcated cases, for example, public health protection, should the country of destination and its standards take precedence over the norms of the country of origin. But even then the measures adopted should involve neither discrimination nor protection.

National treatment

For services, the principle of national treatment is applied. Foreign suppliers have to be treated in the same way as domestic suppliers. This principle is much weaker than the principles applied in trade of products. For services, the country-of-origin principle has not been acceptable so far. It has been used within the European Union, but not world-wide.

Dispute settlement

The member countries of the WTO have voluntarily agreed to a dispute settlement system. If a country violates the rules, the WTO is allowed to demand a change in the trade policy decisions and to impose sanctions.

Relative to GATT, the dispute settlement procedure has been strengthened. Whereas the ruling of a Dispute Panel can be appealed before the Appellate Body, the decision of the Appellate Body is binding unless all parties are against its adoption. When the Dispute Settlement Body (DSB) has adopted the panel or the appellate report, the losing party must either propose a suitable implementation of the report's recommendations or negotiate compensation payment with the complaining party. If there is no agreement on compensation or if the losing party does not implement the proposed changes, the DSB can authorize the other party to impose retaliatory measures such as counter-tariffs. The retaliation can occur in the same sector, in other sectors or even in other agreements.

The dispute settlement mechanism seems to have found acceptance. Since the formation of the dispute settlement mechanism, WTO members have requested consultation 150 times in 114 distinct matters (if India, Malaysia, Pakistan and Thailand file a complaint about the import prohibition of shrimp products by the United States, this is counted as four requests and one distinct matter). Twenty-nine of these consultation requests in 27 distinct matters were made by developing countries. The two major trading blocks have used the WTO settlement procedure frequently. The EU has brought cases to the WTO panels 21 times and the US 35 times. This shows that developing and developed WTO members rely on the settlement procedure. Furthermore, the losing parties have until now always accepted the final decision of the dispute settlement mechanism. The US has lost four cases in the WTO panels and has each time accepted the outcome. A debate has, however, developed over the WTO dispute settlement panel decision from September 1997 concerning the EU import system for bananas. The EU has partly changed its banana regime, but the change falls short of US desires.

14.5 New areas for the world trade order

These are a number of new areas in the international division of labor for which rules have to be developed.

Strategic trade policy and subsidies

When tariffs and quantitative restraints will lose importance in the future, governments may be tempted to use subsidies in order to lower their producers' production costs, thus establishing an artificial price advantage and distorting the international division of labor. A conceivable response to this would simply be to ignore domestic subsidies, since a subsidizing country does not employ its resources optimally, and thereby accepts a loss of its own efficiency and welfare. This is especially prevalent for old industries like coal. One cannot, however, be too complacent about domestic subsidies. Subsidies by one country take market shares away from the corresponding sectors of other countries and lead to political demands for retaliation. Thus their effect resembles those of protectionist measures. Moreover, strategic trade theory could, in the future, become more appealing to practical politics and provide a rationale for subsidizing 'new' sectors, albeit on the basis of rather restrictive (and naive) models. We may see more of this interventionist approach in some European countries as a reaction to globalization. This may lead to political demands for retaliation. Thus, the effect of subsidies may be as detrimental to international trade as traditional protectionist measures. They may also be part of an aggressive bilateralism.

According to the WTO rules, trade-distorting subsidies for export goods and import substitutes are forbidden and product- and industry-specific subsidies are inadmissible if they harm the trade opportunities of other members. Even so it is difficult to demarcate subsidy practices from other admissible policies such as research assistance and aid in adapting to new environmental technologies. It is likewise difficult to penalize and stop violations in the framework of monitoring processes. Furthermore, important sectors such as agriculture and the aviation industry either explicitly or implicitly still enjoy special treatment. Therefore, the existing subsidy code, of which the core is present in the world trade order, must be further developed in order to prevent subsidy competition between governments. How difficult it is to monitor subsidies is shown by the European Union's aid supervision.

Free market access and national regulation

The trade order is essentially oriented to denying governments (or integrated regions) tariff and non-tariff instruments with which the governments could directly intervene in trade flows at their borders. Such instruments have been outlawed through a negative catalogue. However, this still does not guarantee that there will be free access to markets. If we want to ensure free market access, it will be necessary that national regulations do not limit access for goods and firms.

Therefore, multinational barriers, due to national legislative and informal practices that effectively limit access to markets should be dismantled. These barriers include policy measures in the broadest sense, such as licensing procedures for economic activities, for facilities and for products, technical standards, arrangements for public procurement and interlocking ties between firms (as with Keiretsu in Japan) on the same or different levels of the vertical production structure, whereby outsiders are excluded (Ostry 1995). By accepting the country-of-origin principle instead of the country-of-destination principle, market access is made easier.

Open services markets

Services comprise an extensive and diverse spectrum. They include cross-border supply, consumption of a service abroad, commercial presence and presence of natural persons. The diversity of services becomes apparent by the WTO classification list with 7 main categories and 62 subcategories (see chapter 1). A rule system for the international exchange of services should hold for the whole variety of services. Since the phenomena to which rules are to be applied are so divergent, it is difficult to establish an all-encompassing international rule system. A major distinction is between border-crossing and local services analogous to that between tradable and non-tradable goods. Within these categories, another distinction becomes relevant, namely between 'person-disembodied' and 'person-embodied' services (Bhagwati 1984; Klodt *et al.* 1994). Disembodied services are not 'embodied' in persons, for example, detail engineering using computer-supported programs, the development of software and accounting. For the international trade order, disembodied cross-border services are not very different from material goods. Just as commodities are carried by the transport system, disembodied services cross national borders by means of communication media. As a consequence, markets must be open for them just as they must be open for commodities. Border-crossing disembodied services should be treated like commodities.

National treatment in the case of person-embodied services

In the case of person-embodied services (consumption abroad, commercial presence, presence of natural persons), non-discrimination can be obtained through national treatment, i.e. equal treatment for foreigners and one's own nationals.

The General Agreement on Trade and Services (GATS) establishes for the first time a framework for the notification of existing rules, but it has a long way to go before a rule system for all forms of international services with free market access is fully developed (Snape 1998). Markets are yet to be opened in many respects: barriers discriminating against foreigners or non-discriminatory barriers erected by competition policy will have to be torn down, the product coverage must be extended. So far, these are exemptions to the most-favored-nation (MFN) treatment. The conditionality of the most-favored-nation clause prevalent in services must be extended to an unconditional use. National treatment as a central principle only applies to services where a country has made a specific commitment; exemptions are allowed. Moreover, the present approach is to find agreements for specific services. For instance, in financial services a multilateral agreement was reached in December 1997 with 70 WTO members; other sector agreements relate to telecommunications and information technology. This sector-by-sector approach raises the risk that sector-specific aspects will dominate. It has the disadvantage that it does not sufficiently harness the export interests of the economy as a whole in order to dismantle barriers of trade (Krueger 1998).

International competition policy

Markets should not be closed through the market power of firms. Globalization makes markets more contestable, and in this sense free trade is the best competition policy. All measures that improve market access support competition policy. However, firms may try to create monopolistic positions in the global markets, if possible, and to exploit them by setting prices to the disadvantage of buyers.

In the past, competition policy was a national affair (and in the European Union it is an EU matter). In the new global environment, national competition policies face a new challenge. National competition policy should not be oriented towards the advantage of domestic firms or home-based multinationals and should not permit firms to build up or exploit monopolistic positions internationally. Competition policy should also oppose business practices intended to reduce global competition. It should prevent the exploitation of market power, and help to improve the contestability of the world product markets.

Therefore, it is necessary to change the orientation of national competition policies. Interactions between competition policies of different countries have to be taken into consideration. For instance, mergers in one country (Boeing and McDonnell Douglas) have an impact on the market structure elsewhere (Airbus in Europe). Therefore, the competition policy of different authorities is involved and mergers need the agreement of different authorities (like the EU and the US). Another issue is the misuse of market power. Thus, the question arises whether a country harmed by another country's competition and antitrust policy should have the right to obtain changes in the objectionable policy. An institutional consultation and sanctioning mechanism must be created (Graham 1995). Under consideration are the effects doctrine with an international right to extraterritorial legal application (Immenga 1995), treaty agreements – including bilateral treaties between the US and Europe – on the concession of mutual competencies (Ehlermann 1995), on the harmonization of international competition law (hard law) on the basis of national regulations (Fikentscher and Immenga 1995), and on the mutual recognition of institutional rules, that is a *Cassis-de-Dijon* approach with an international interpretation (Nicolaides 1994). An alternative proposal is to give parties injured by anti-competitive practices or competition policies a right to take their case to an international court or an international competition authority empowered to enforce competition rules (Scherer 1994).

Presently, it is not foreseeable that an international institutional framework for competition policy will be established which can effectively restrict the misuse of monopolistic market positions and discourage competition-limiting mergers. Thus, at present we can only expect to establish a few minimal competition policy rules for countries or regional integrations (such as the European Union), either in the framework of the World Trade Organization (Immenga 1995), in the OECD or in multilateral agreements, as between the EU and the US. We also have to consider the option that, initially, only some of the rules would be agreed upon by the most important OECD countries, because there are fundamental differences in their legal systems, as between Anglo-Saxon and Continental European law.

Aggressive trade policy versus the multilateral order

When important trading nations or regions of the world pursue an aggressive trade policy, they endanger the multilateral system. The US and the EU have built up an arsenal of new trade-political instruments, which they can use to open markets or as a retaliatory measure, without considering the mechanisms of the world trade order. The US, for instance, can react immediately on trade-restricting measures of other countries by imposing trade-restricting measures of its own with its powerful instrument 'Super 301'. Trade-barrier reductions already agreed on can be deleted, import restrictions can be imposed and bilateral export-restriction agreements can be pursued. Above all, trade policy restraints are supposed to serve as a lever for opening markets. With the 'Trade Defence Instrument' the European Union has created a similar apparatus, to counter the trade policy of other countries.

By creating these trade policy weapons, the two trading blocs, in the sense of result-oriented bilaterally conceived policies (Dornbusch 1990), have exempted themselves from the rules of the multilateral world trade order; they violate the most-favored-nation principle. The risk exists that bilateral measures will escalate. The two large players are forcing other countries to make concessions, and they threaten unilaterally by denying market access in the US. An aggressive trade policy of one country (unilateralism) and the reaction of other countries, or even the agreement of two countries at the cost of a third country (bilateralism) lead to a destabilization of the multilateral order. Therefore, unilateralism and bilateralism have to be limited. The trade policy instruments of such an aggressive market opening policy have to be integrated in the rules of the world trade order. An outcome-oriented, bilaterally conceived aggressive trade policy for opening markets must not replace a rule-based multilateral order.

14.6 Rules for factor movements and locational competition

Besides the exchange of goods and services, factor mobility is a further important form of interdependence between economies. Countries compete for mobile technological knowledge and for mobile capital. This leads to locational competition in which governments compete for the mobile factors of production, namely mobile technological knowledge and mobile capital (chapter 12). The policy instruments governments can use in order to attract these mobile factors are institutional arrangements, taxes, and infrastructure in the widest sense, including the educational and the university systems.

Property rights for mobile technological knowledge

When countries compete for mobile technological knowledge, property rights become important. These relate to all sorts of intellectual property, copyright and associated rights, trademarks, industrial design, patents, the layout designs of integrated circuits and geographical indications (like appellations of origin). Issues to be solved (and partly included in the Agreement on Trade-Related Aspects of Intellectual Property Rights (TRIPs)) are minimum standards of protection to be provided by the individual countries, enforcement of intellectual property rights, and dispute settlements.

A global system of rules for new technology has to solve problems which are similar to those of structuring a national patent system. On the one hand, user rights to new technological knowledge must be secure, since otherwise there will be insufficient incentives to search for and adopt new technological knowledge. This means that property rights to new knowledge must be respected throughout the world. On the other hand, this property protection must not create permanently exclusive positions and make markets uncontestable. Rather, the diffusion of new knowledge must be possible after a certain passage of time. Accordingly, time limits should be set on the protective effect of user rights. The optimal duration of property rights depends among other things on product life-cycles and the time-frame of research and development phases; this can differ greatly from product to product. Since countries may have an interest in protecting their firms' technological knowledge for as long as possible (although this reduces the incentives for their own technological dynamics), the solution cannot consist simply in mutually recognizing national patent laws. Rather, it may be desirable to set time limits on the validity of national patents. With respect to the other types of property right such as trademarks and geographical indications there is no necessity to let protection run out.

National technology policy should be dealt with in the same way as national subsidies. Thus, the international subsidy code must set limits for industry-specific research subsidies. In contrast, there is no need for controlling the improvement of the general conditions for research and development, for example, when countries generally introduce more favorable tax conditions for research and development, innovation, investment and entrepreneurial activity, as well as organize basic research and further technology transfer so that they can be internationally competitive.

An investment code for capital mobility

It is in the best interest of each country to keep capital at home and to attract more capital from outside. Each country should therefore structure its institutional framework accordingly, i.e. provide for the security of property rights, avoid uncertainty about corporate taxes, develop a tax system and a general economic framework which make the country less risky and more attractive for foreign direct investments.

Even if it is the host country's responsibility to enhance its own attractiveness, it may be helpful to have an investment code in order to minimize disruptions. For instance, foreign direct investments should be protected against expropriation. Capital should be allowed to be repatriated and profits of capital invested should be allowed to be sent to the country of the capital owners. Multilateral agreements can make the direct investments of the sending country more secure. They can make a country appear less risky for direct investments. Moreover, uncertainty for investment may be a cause for uncertainty in trade. Consequently, an investment code is required which surpasses the trade-related investment measures (TRIMs). It is an open question whether a two-speed approach should be recommended for an investment code, with the OECD countries going ahead and the WTO following, or whether an investment code, has better chances to be accepted if it is initiated by the WTO (Krueger 1998, p. 408). Eventually, an investment code should be administered by the WTO.

Another important condition for an efficient international division of labor is that savings should not be prevented from seeking better opportunities abroad. Otherwise countries would force their savers to invest solely at home.

The right of exit for the migration of people

The right of individuals to leave a country, the exit option, can be interpreted as an important element of a liberal order. Every individual should have the right to choose to leave given living conditions which he or she finds unacceptable. This principle should hold even if the exit option conflicts with the claim that citizens of a state must fulfill their tax duties, when they take their residence abroad. The freedom of the individual should be given priority to the tax claims of the state. A credible right to exit is a limit on the actions of the government and implicitly controls the government.

The exit option does not, however, imply the entry option, i.e. the right to migrate *into* a country. States define their identity by setting their immigration policy (Hillman 1994). This creates difficult ethical questions which can be more easily solved if potential countries of immigration – beyond the duty to accept the politically persecuted – are sufficiently open and if regional integrations such as the European Union, although only spatially limited from an international economic perspective, guarantee the freedom of movement within their territory.

For many reasons labor migration should be replaced by the movement of goods and capital mobility. The strengthening of an international economic order for the international exchange of goods and the openness of markets reduces the necessity of migration.

14.7 Social standards

Recently, there have been increased calls to equalize social norms (see chapter 11), and this is supposed to be accomplished through trade policy measures. Countries which do not employ these standards are supposed to be denied access to markets elsewhere.

Except for some minimum standards as agreed upon by the members of the International Labor Organization (ILO), this is a misleading idea. By harmonizing social standards the developing countries would be negatively affected. Because of their lower labor productivity these countries are unable to pay the same wages that industrialized countries pay. For similar reasons, they cannot be expected to adopt the industrialized countries' labor standards or social norms because these standards increase the cost of production in the same way as higher wages do. The industrialized countries have no ethical right to ask the developing countries to implement the social norms of the industrialized countries. Therefore, harmonizing social norms cannot be a promising strategy of the rich countries against globalization. Also in this domain, the country-of-destination principle cannot be practiced in the world trade order. Which regulations are set for the production of goods should consequently be left to the discretion of the country of origin. Besides, trade policy is unsuitable as a means of harmonization. Social norms are not a public good.

14.8 The environment and the world trade order

In the past, the international frameworks for environmental issues and for the world trade order have been developed side by side. In the future, it will become increasingly important to consider more strongly the consistency of these frameworks.

National environmental policy and international rules

If the environment is an immobile national endowment factor, the different environmental scarcities of countries can be expressed by different prices of environmental services. This is relevant when the absorptive and regenerative capacities of national environments vary, when a high population density makes it more difficult to spatially separate residential and recreational areas from environmentally degrading transport and production activities and when the preferences of countries for environmental quality differ. Signaling different environmental scarcities by different prices does not require an international rule system but the pricing can be left to national policies. A market economy approach to environmental policy which taxes emissions or establishes prices for environmental services through licensing is consistent with an institutional framework for the international division of labor. The more successful the integration of the environment in the economic regulations of individual countries, and the more successful welfare can be defined by also taking into consideration nature and the environment, the better environmental policy can be integrated into the international trade order.

Protecting health and conserving natural resources

If prices for national environmental use are not (or cannot be) applied and other measures such as administrative approaches, emission norms or product standards are employed by countries to protect their citizens' health and life and to conserve natural resources (Article XX of the GATT Treaty), those measures must be non-discriminatory. Non-discrimination requires that in the case of market entry restrictions, regulations through production permits, facility permits and product norms must not give preference to domestic producers and domestic goods. Thus it should not be permissible, for example, with the aim of reducing health hazards, as in the Thailand cigarette case (1990), to restrict the import of goods or to tax them unless the same measures are simultaneously applied to similar domestic goods.

The similarity of products should be defined from the demand side, for example in terms of possible harmful effects, and not from the production side. As in the Mexican–American tuna fish case (1991), the principle of similarity should not be applied to the production methods (in the tuna case, methods of fishing which do not sufficiently protect dolphins). This means that the country-of-origin principle should apply. Non-discrimination should also satisfy the condition that policy instruments should accord to the proportionality principle. Measures must accordingly be necessary in the sense that otherwise environmental policy aims or the protection of natural resources could not be achieved. As a rule, these aims are, however, achieved in a better way through specific environmental policy measures rather than through trade policy.

The territorial principle as a restraint for national measures

Trade policy must not be employed to force national preferences on other countries. Any country's environmental policy should not apply to external effects outside its own territorial area. Since countries have different amounts of environmental resources and also different environmental preferences, those with stronger environmental preferences should not be entitled to impose their environmental preferences on other countries by means of trade-restricting measures (Siebert 1996b). The thesis that the country-of-origin principle should be fundamentally recognized for national environments can be generalized. If harmful effects appear outside a country's territorial area and if they do not affect a country's territory, i.e. if there are no cross-border externalities, countries should not have the right to use trade policy to influence the production methods of a country of origin. Also, the protective clauses for health, life and exhaustible resources found in Article XX should in the case of national environmental goods be applied only within a country's own territorial area. Thus countries should not have the right to employ unilateral measures to protect the environment in other countries. A different matter, however, is if transfrontier pollution occurs. Then, a Coasian solution has to be found.

Global environmental goods

Global environmental goods, i.e. public goods with a worldwide spatial dimension, require an agreement of all countries as to what amount and what quality of these public goods should be supplied. It is not sufficient to decide about which emissions should be reduced, it is also necessary to decide about the appropriate distribution of costs of emission reduction among individual countries (see chapter 13). It is difficult to reach an international consensus, because countries have different preferences and because they have different per capita incomes and thus have different willingness to pay. In addition, the cost functions for disposal differ from country to country. Moreover, a nation can behave as a free-rider. Thus, implementing the polluter-pays principle for global goods runs into difficulties. To what extent a stable international environmental framework with voluntary commitments by states can be created under these conditions using compensatory payments is a complex issue and has been the subject of numerous studies (Siebert 1998b).

Consistency between the international environmental order and the international trade order

Environmental policy aims at protecting the natural living-conditions, i.e. it deals with scarcity. An institutional order for the international division of labor attempts to make it possible to increase the prosperity of all countries through exchange, i.e. it also deals with scarcity. Both orders attempt to do away with distortions and they represent institutional frameworks dealing with allocation. Since environmental policy and international trade intersect at many points, the rules of the two frameworks should not conflict. In principle, the aims are not contradictory, since scarcity must be defined by taking the natural living conditions into account. If we start from the premise that the valuation of the goods on which affluence is based as well as the valuation of environmental quality must depend on national preference, contradiction between the regimes can be avoided. The more successfully the environment as a scarce good is integrated into the economic order of individual countries and the more affluence is defined by taking into account nature and the environment, the sooner congruence of targets will be achieved between the two orders.

Compared to the administrative approach using regulations, the market economy approach to environmental policy provides more consistency between the two sets of rules. The sooner the polluter-pays principle is accepted as a guideline by all countries, the easier it will be to achieve consistency of the two orders in the case of global environmental concerns. This clearly holds for national environmental goods. For global goods, implementing the polluter-pays principle has to overcome the difficulties mentioned above like the differences in preferences, in willingness-to-pay and free-rider behavior. What would be needed is a consensus on the conditions under which the polluter-pays principle can be applied to global goods; this is equivalent to a consensus regarding the conditions under which compensations must be used.

Inconsistency between the two rules system should be prevented. The following aspects can help to minimize conflicts:

- The group of countries signing international environmental agreements should not be too divergent from those who are members of the WTO.
- Even if the international environmental order and the international trade order have consistent aims in principle, the rules of the two orders should not be contingent upon each other. Making the rules mutually conditional would cause considerable uncertainty, not only in the international division of labor, but also in the production of environmental goods. Institutional orders should not be uncertain.
- It appears ill-advised to create a temporary waiver for the environment as an

exception to the world trade order. One reason is that the previously created exemptions for the agricultural and textile sectors have become resistant to change and have led to a permanent infringement of the most-favored-nation principle. If an exceptional regulation is questionable even in the case of very specific and internationally declining sectors like agriculture, then a similar procedure appears still less desirable for an area like the environment that is pervasive in all sectors of the economy and that will become increasingly important in the future.

- The sets of instruments of the two orders should be kept separate. Trade policy instruments should not be employed for environmental policy purposes. Countries should not have the right to apply their environmental policy outside their own territory. Non-discrimination and the priority of the country-of-origin principle over the country-of-destination principle should be guiding principles.
- A similar mechanism to the WTO dispute settlement mechanism should be developed for the environmental domain.
- In the case of global environmental goods a consensus should be developed regarding the conditions under which the polluter-pays principle and when compensations should be applied.

14.9 Stabilizing and strengthening the WTO

The WTO is a multilateral agreement of sovereign states. It is essential that sovereign states abide by the rules to which they have agreed and do not renege. A set of mechanisms stabilizes and strengthens the WTO.

Sanctions

An important mechanism in international contracts is sanctions which can be taken if rules are violated. The WTO dispute settlement procedure serves this purpose.

Positive mechanisms

Besides sanctions in dispute settlement, the world trading order contains mechanisms that attempt to strengthen the institutional arrangement and help to expand it. One such mechanism is the most-favored-nation clause which extends reductions of trade barriers to third parties and thus multilateralizes liberalizations. Another mechanism is reciprocity of concessions requiring that the tariff reduction of one country must be answered by other countries (even though the concept of reciprocity has its roots in a mercantilistic philosophy). Yet another mechanism is to bind tariffs so that the results of liberalization rounds are 'chiseled in stone' and countries cannot easily walk away from agreements that have been reached. A country that wants to raise the bound tariff has to negotiate with the countries most concerned. It has to compensate for the trading partners' loss of trade.

Strengthening support from private groups

In order to restrain national interest groups, the World Trade Organization needs the support of the private sector. In the past, export interests were harnessed against protectionist groups. In order to attract the support of the private sector, it should be made clear what advantages households and enterprises can obtain from the international framework. New rules should be tailored such that they get the support of the private sector. Thus, strengthened intellectual property rights and improved exchange conditions for services can be attractive for the private sector.

The prospect of an increase in future benefits

An essential condition for an international economic order is that the institutional framework should be acceptable to all countries, that all countries can expect to gain from it. For each country the advantages of membership must exceed the advantages of non-membership. It is crucial that benefits are expected in the future. It pays to stick to the rules because there will be a reward in the future. The individual country's cost–benefit calculations should not shift asymmetrically over time. The net advantage for each country should increase and in no case worsen. If this condition is not fulfilled, there will be an incentive not to honor the treaty, but instead to withdraw from it.

From an intertemporal perspective, the global rule system is a relational contract (MacNeil 1978) in which countries interact along a time axis and in which a strategic gain from non-cooperative behavior today must be confronted with the opportunity costs of retaliation in future periods. Honoring a rule system or violating it must be interpreted as a repeated game in which an agent accumulates or destroys reputation and in which the preparedness of the other agents to cooperate tomorrow is affected by the agent's behavior today. These intertemporal linkages help to prevent reneging on the contract and to give stability to the system.

Preventing institutional domino effects

An economic order may be conceived as existing of several suborders (Eucken 1940). The interdependence of suborders raises other issues. One is that the suborders may contradict each other. Clearly, they must be mutually consistent. One suborder must not lead to behavior on the part of economic agents which contradicts and undermines some other suborder. As a consequence, suborders must have the same or similar objectives or philosophies. An important example of this consistency issue is the relation between the world trade order and the world environmental order (see above). In any case, the interdependence of suborders must be taken into consideration when an overall rule system is developed.

Another issue is to what extent the withdrawal of benefits from one subor-der can be used as a threat or sanction to abide by the rules of the other sub-order. In a game-theoretic approach, threatening with the withdrawal of benefits from one rule system may be an effective inducement to join (and to respect) another rule system. However, this approach makes one suborder con-tingent on another suborder. If one institutional system falls, the other falls too. This raises the risk that the overall rule system is endangered. Therefore, the advantage of threatening the withdrawal of benefits of one suborder must be weighed against the risk of destroying the overall rule system. If the WTO is understood as a single undertaking, suborders cannot be singled out for strategic purposes.

A possible approach to this question is to explicitly distinguish between two dif-ferent stages, namely the creation of an institutional arrangement and the imple-mentation of the rule system associated with it. In establishing a new institutional framework, withholding benefits to non-members from another subsystem is a strong sanction that is positive for establishing the new order. Once an institu-tional arrangement is established, however, the validity of one suborder should – as a principle – not be contingent on the functioning of some other suborder in order to prevent institutional domino effects. This means that the instrumental levels should be clearly separated. As a rule, economic policy instruments avail-able to an international organization should be limited to specific suborders. Trade policy instruments should not be employed for environmental policy pur-poses. The instrumental level should thus be subdivided into different modules which should be clearly demarcated.

Multilateralizing regional integrations

In order to prevent regionalism from becoming inward looking or degenerating into an aggressive bilateralism (chapter 9), regional integrations should be multi-lateralized. An important precondition for multilateralizing regional integrations is to keep regional integrations open to new members. A strong mechanism for this is for members of integrated regions to grant concessions to third countries, in the sense of conditional most-favored-nation treatment where 'conditional' means that the third countries have to grant similar concessions in order to ben-efit from the trade barriers' reductions achieved within the integrated region (Klodt *et al.* 1994). This could be done on a voluntary basis, but the WTO could also agree on a timetable for multilateralization (Srinivasan 1998). Another approach is to link regional integrations by agreements going further than the WTO system (see below).

Drawing a line for which areas no rules should be developed

We have discussed several areas into which the WTO has to be expanded: ser-vices, investment and property rights. Other areas are debated such as competi-tion policy, labor and social standards and the environment. Quite clearly, the rule system has to respond to new issues. But somewhere must be a line where the WTO is not and should not be in charge.

A more theoretical answer is that the WTO should only be concerned about rules for the international division of labor, including trade of goods and services, international factor mobility and trade restrictions arising from national environmental policy for the national environment. Global environmental issues have to be solved by a different institutional arrangement. A basic principle is that differences in endowments are accepted as the starting point for the international division of labor arbitraged by trade and factor flows. This would exclude protectionism, harmonization and world-wide redistribution. The WTO cannot possibly solve the issue of distribution between nation states. Introducing distributional constraints will make the world order ineffective. Such issues, including the alleviation of poverty, have to be solved in other ways.

A more practical answer is to look at which areas of rules nation states are prepared to hand over to the WTO and which new areas of rules the WTO can absorb into its rule system without losing efficacy.

Extending to new members

Enlarging the membership of the WTO club will generate additional benefits to the old members. The new members will have benefits as well. Enlargement of the membership is therefore an important mechanism to make the system more attractive.

In the long run, the optimal size of the WTO is the world as a whole because then all potential benefits of the international division of labor are exploited. In the short run, however, there is one important condition for the extension of membership. The system of rules should not be weakened but strengthened when a new member enters. The pending accessions of China and Russia illustrate that a new member can have a strong impact on the WTO rule system. New members must accept the rule system as a single undertaking. They must have a track record showing that they have followed the basic WTO philosophy for some time. Moreover, economic conditions in the potential new member countries must be such that the countries are fit to survive in the world market.

Extending the frontier by a WTO-Plus

Another positive mechanism is to allow new problems to be solved by a subset of WTO members. These countries could commit themselves to realize attempted results of the WTO rounds more quickly than planned, liberalize more than agreed and employ the permitted exceptions less often. Such a WTO-Plus, a two-speed world integration, could advance the integration process in the world economy. This also holds for dovetailing various regional blocks by establishing a free-trade zone between the blocks, for instance in a trans-Atlantic economic area. This mechanism, however, is in conflict with the single-undertaking nature of

WTO and the concept of packaging advantages in different areas. Care must be taken where each mechanism should have priority.

14.10   The role of the IMF once more

As discussed in chapter 6, an institutional arrangement preventing financial crises is an important cornerstone of a multilateral order for the world economy. In this context, the IMF has to play its role. The IMF is caught between its short-term role of bridging balance-of-payments disequilibrium or preventing a run on a currency and its long-term task of establishing incentives that prevent a currency crisis from developing. The IMF has to provide more comprehensive information and to improve the early warning system. By signaling problems to the financial markets early on, larger problems can be prevented. Signaling problems is one way of reducing the moral hazards created by extensive costs of intervention by the IMF. Reducing the moral hazard problem also requires that private credits (banks, bondholders) should be adequately involved in the losses of a financial crisis so that they anticipate the risk. The IMF should also address the issue that the size of its operation creates the wrong incentives for sovereign creditors.

14.11   The interdependence of the world institutional order – a summary

The institutional arrangements for the world economy vary with the different types of interdependence among countries. Traditionally, trade policy rules have been intended to facilitate international merchandise trade. Recently, these rules have been extended to services; other areas such as competition policy are discussed. Norms for the mobility of production factors – technology, physical capital and labor – are receiving increasing attention with locational competition between countries becoming more important. Norms for the use of the environment will also acquire greater significance in the future (Table 14.5). Finally, financial transactions, balance-of-payments disequilibria and exchange rate volatility are a matter of concern.

Looking at these and other problems, the institutional design of the world economy is in a process of development. There has to be a division of labor between the international organizations. Trade and factor mobility is clearly the domain of the WTO. Improving structural conditions for long-run growth is the task of the World Bank. The Bank for International Settlements (BIS) in Basle is in charge of securing the functioning of the payment system. The IMF fluctuates between its short-run role of bridging international liquidity gaps or balance-of-payments crises and its long-run role of improving structural conditions. In fact, the assignment problem among international organizations seems to be unsolved.

Table 14.5 Elements of an institutional order for the world economy

Type of interdependence	Possible distortions, disturbances	Rules
Exchange of		
● Goods	Protectionist trade policy (tariffs, import quotas, 'voluntary' export restraints, strategic trade policy, anti-dumping, subsidies, product standards)	Trade rules, above all against new forms of protectionist trade policy. Country-of-origin principle for product norms
	Social norms	No worldwide standardization possible
	Market power of firms	Competition rules. Free access to markets. Effects doctrine
● Services	Discrimination against foreign suppliers	National treatment
Factor migration		
● Capital	Risk of expropriation of foreign investments. Tax competition for mobile capital	Governments compete using their infrastructure, tax system and regulations for mobile capital. National self-interest implies countries make themselves more attractive to outside capital. Investment code
● Technology	Too low incentives for technological progress, due to property rights not respected internationally	Property rights which protect new knowledge but permit gradual diffusion
● Labor	Abrupt mass migrations	Free trade and free movements of capital as a substitute for labor migration. A right to emigrate (right of exit). Openness in immigration policy. Not achievable: a universal right of immigration
Diffusion of pollutants	Transfrontier pollution, free-rider behavior of individual countries with regard to global environmental problems	International rules only for transfrontier and global environmental problems. Transfrontier pollution subject to agreement between countries concerned. National environmental problems are subject to national environmental policy. Separation between environmental policy and trade policy
Financial transactions	Volatility of exchange rates, currency runs	Each country must keep the value of its money stable. Discretionary macroeconomic coordination is not possible unless each country submits itself to rules giving up sovereignty similar to the gold standard

References

Alonso, W. (1964). *Location and Land Use.* Cambridge, MA: Harvard University Press.

Anderson, K., H. Norheim (1993). History, Geography and Regional Economic Integration. *Centre for Economic Policy Research. Discussion Paper,* 795. London.

APEC. http://www.apecsec.org.sg.

Armstrong, K.A., S.J. Bulmer (1998). *The Governance of the Single European Market.* Manchester: Manchester University Press.

ASEAN. http://www.aseansec.org.

Axelrod, R. (1986). An Evolutionary Approach to Norms. *American Political Science Review,* 80: 1095–1111.

Baldwin, R.E. (1994). *Towards an Integrated Europe.* London: Centre for Economic Policy Research.

—— (1998). Trade and Wages. Symposium *'Challenges for Highly Developed Countries in the Global Economy'* of the Kiel Institute of World Economics. March 20.

Baldwin, R.E., J.E. Francois, R. Portes (1997). The Costs and Benefits of Eastern Enlargement: The Impact on the EU and Central Europe. *Economic Policy,* 24: 125–176.

Barro, R.J. (1992). Convergence. *Journal of Political Economy,* 100: 223–251.

Barro, R.J., X. Sala-i-Martin (1992). Convergence across States and Regions. *Brookings Papers on Economic Activity*: 107–158.

—— (1995). *Economic Growth.* New York: McGraw-Hill.

Bhagwati, J. (1984). Splintering and Disembodiment of Services and Developing Nations. *The World Economy,* 7: 133–143.

—— (1989). Is Free Trade Passé After All ? *Weltwirtschaftliches Archiv,* 125: 17–44.

—— (1991). *The World Trading System at Risk.* New York: Harvester Wheatsheaf.

—— (1992). Regionalism and Multilateralism. *The World Economy,* 15 (5): 535–555.

Bhagwati, J., A. Panagariya, T.N. Srinivasan (1998). *Lectures on International Trade.* 2nd edition. Cambridge, MA: MIT Press.

BIS (Bank for International Settlement) (1998). *The Maturity, Sectoral and Nationality Distribution of International Bank Lending. First Half 1997.* Basle.

Blackhurst, Richard (1997). The WTO and the Global Economy. *The World Economy,* 20 (5): 527–544.

Blanchard, O.J., S. Fischer (1989). *Lectures on Macroeconomics.* Cambridge, MA: MIT Press.

Blanchard, O.J., L.F. Katz (1992). *Regional Evolutions.* Brookings Papers on Economic Activity (1): 1–75.

Bode, E. (1998). Lokale Wissensdiffusion und regionale Divergenz in Deutschland. *Kieler Studien,* 293. Tübingen: Mohr.

Bosworth, B.P. (1993). *Saving and Investment in a Global Economy*. Washington, DC: Brookings Institution.

Brander, J.A., B.J. Spencer (1985). Export Subsidies and International Market Share Rivalry. *Journal of International Economics*, 18: 83–100.

British Petroleum Company. *BP Statistical Review of World Energy*. London.

Buch, C.M. (1996). Creating Efficient Banking Systems: Theory and Evidence from Eastern Europe. *Kieler Studien*, 277. Tübingen: Mohr.

Bucovetsky, S., J.D. Wilson (1991). Tax Competition with Two Tax Instruments. *Regional Science and Urban Economics*, 21: 333–350.

Bundesanstalt für Geowissenschaften und Rohstoffe (1995). *Reserven, Ressourcen und Verfügbarkeit von Energierohstoffen 1995*. Stuttgart: Schweitzerbart.

Carstensen, K., G. Hansen (1998). How Important are Real Shocks for the Real Exchange Rate? In: R. Galata, H. Schneeweiss, H. Küchenhoff (eds.), *Econometrics in Theory and Practice*. Heidelberg: Physica: 161–174.

Caves R.E., J.A. Frankel, R.W. Jones (1996). *World Trade and Payments: An Introduction*. 7th edition. New York: HarperCollins.

Central Bank of the Russian Federation. *Bulletin of Banking Statistics*. Moscow.

Cline, W. (1995). Managing International Debt: How One Big Battle Was Won. *The Economist*, 18 February. London.

Coase, R.H. (1960). The Problem of Social Cost. *Journal of Law and Economics*, 3: 1–44.

Datastream.

David, P.A. (1999). The Determinants of Long-Run Economic Growth and Wealth Creation. In: OECD, *21st Century Economic Dynamics: Anatomy of a Long Boom*. Paris.

De Grauwe, P. (1993). The Political Economy of Monetary Union in Europe. *The World Economy*, 16 (6): 653–661.

—— (1996). Monetary Union and Convergence Economics. *European Economic Review*, 40: 1091–1101.

—— (1997). *The Economics of Monetary Integration*. 3rd rev. edition. Oxford: Oxford University Press.

De Long, J.B. (1988). Productivity Growth, Convergence, and Welfare: Comment (on W.J. Baumol (1986): Productivity Growth, Convergence, and Welfare). *American Economic Review*, 78 (5): 1138–1154.

Department of the Treasury of the United States Government. *Monthly Treasury Statement of Receipts and Outlays*. Washington, DC.

Deutsche Bundesbank. http://www.bundesbank.de/index_e.html.

—— *Balance of Payments Statistics*. Frankfurt/M.

—— *Monthly Reports*. Frankfurt/M.

Deutsches Institut für Wirtschaftsforschung (DIW). *Vierteljährliche Volkswirtschaftliche Gesamtrechnung*. Berlin.

Deutsches Institut für Wirtschaftsforschung (DIW), Institut für Weltwirtschaft und Institut für Wirtschaftsforschung Halle. *Gesamtwirtschaftliche und Unternehmerische Anpassungsfortschritte in Ostdeutschland*. Kieler Diskussionsbeiträge. Institut für Weltwirtschaft, Kiel. 18 Reports, various years.

Dixit, A.K., V. Norman (1980). *Theory of International Trade*. Cambridge: Cambridge University Press.

Dornbusch, R. (1976). Expectations and Exchange Rate Dynamics. *Journal of Political Economy*, 84 (6): 1161–1176.

—— (1990). Policy Options for Freer Trade: The Case of Bilateralism. In: R.Z. Lawrence,

C.L. Schultze (eds.), *An American Trade Strategy: Options for the 1990s*. Washington, DC: Brookings Institution: 106–134.

EBRD European Bank for Reconstruction and Development. *Transition Report*. London.

—— *Economics of Transition*. London.

Economist Intelligence Unit (1999). *Country Report Brazil*. London.

Ehlermann, C.D. (1995). The Role of Competition Policy in a Global Economy. In: OECD, *New Dimensions of Market Access in a Globalizing World Economy*. Paris.

Eichengreen, B. (1997). EMU: An Outsider's Perspective. *Irish Banking Review*: 2–13.

Ethier, W. (1995). *Modern International Economics*. 3rd edition. New York: Norton.

Eucken, W. (1940). *Die Grundlagen der Nationalökonomie*. Jena: Fischer. (English Edition: *The Foundations of Economics: History and Theory in the Analysis of Economic Reality*. Berlin, 1992: Springer.)

European Central Bank. http://www.ecb.int.

European Union. http://europa.eu.int.

EUROSTAT. *Internal and External Trade of the EU*. Luxembourg.

Feldstein, M. (1997). The Political Economy of European Monetary Union: Political Reasons for an Economic Liability. *Journal of Economic Perspectives*, 11: 23–42.

—— (1998). Refocusing the IMF. *Foreign Affairs*, 77 (2): 20–33.

Feldstein, M., C. Horioka (1980). Domestic Saving and International Capital Flows. *Economic Journal*, 90: 314–329.

Fikentscher, W., U. Immenga (eds.) (1995). *Draft International Antitrust Code. Kommentierter Entwurf eines internationalen Wettbewerbsrechts mit ergänzenden Beiträgen*. Baden-Baden: Nomos.

Findlay, R. (1995). The Philosophy of Locational Competition. In: H. Siebert (ed.), *Locational Competition in the World Economy*. Tübingen: Mohr: 3–16.

Finger, J.M., M.D. Ingco, U. Reincke (1996). *The Uruguay Round – Statistics on Tariff Concessions Given and Received*. Washington DC: World Bank.

Fischer, S. (1998). IMF and Crisis Prevention. *Financial Times*, 30 March.

Fischer, S., R. Sahbay, C.A. Végh (1996). Stabilization and Growth in Transition Economies: The Early Experience. *Journal of Economic Perspectives*, 10: 45–66.

Frankel, J.A. (1997). *Regional Trading Blocs in the World Economic System*. Washington: Institute for International Economics.

Freeman, R.B. (1995). Are your Wages Set in Beijing? *Journal of Economic Perspectives*, 9 (3): 15–32.

Garber, P. M. (1989). Tulipmania. *Journal of Political Economy*, 97: 535–560.

—— (1990). Famous First Bubbles. *Journal of Economic Perspectives*, 4: 35–54.

GATT/WTO *International Trade, Trends and Statistics*. Geneva.

Giovannini, A. (1989). Capital Taxation. *Economic Policy*, 4: 345–386.

—— (1990). Reforming Capital Income Taxation in the Open Economy: Theoretical Issues. In: H. Siebert (ed.), *Reforming Capital Income Taxation*. Tübingen: Mohr: 3–18.

Government of the Russian Federation. *Russian Economic Trends*: Monthly Update. London.

Graham, E.M. (1995). Competition Policy and the New Trade Agenda. In: OECD, *New Dimensions of Market Access in a Globalizing World Economy*. Paris.

Grimm, D. (1997). Which Constitution for Europe? In: H. Siebert (ed.), *Quo Vadis Europe?* Tübingen: Mohr: 3–9.

Gros, D., A. Steinherr (1995). *Winds of Change: Economic Transition and Central and Eastern Europe*. New York: Longman.

Grossman, G.M., E. Helpman (1991a). *Innovation and Growth in the Global Economy*. Cambridge, MA: MIT Press.

—— (1991b). Trade, Knowledge Spillovers, and Growth. *European Economic Review*, 35: 517–526.

—— (1995). Trade Wars and Trade Talks. *Journal of Political Economy*, 103 (4): 675–708.

Gundlach, E. (1998). Das Wirtschaftswachstum der Nationen im zwanzigsten Jahrhundert. *Die Weltwirtschaft*, 1: 85–107.

Gundlach, E., P. Nunnenkamp (1998). Some Consequences of Globalization for Developing Countries. In: J.H. Dunning (ed.), *Globalization, Trade and Foreign Investment*. Amsterdam: Elsevier: 153–174.

Hagen, J. von, M.J.M. Neumann (1994). Real Exchange Rates within and between Currency Areas: How Far away Is EMU? *Review of Economics and Statistics*, 76 (2): 236–244.

Haggard, S., B. Simmons (1987). Theories of International Regimes. *International Organization*, 41: 491–517.

Harris, J., M. Todaro (1970). Migration, Unemployment and Development; A Two-Sector Analysis. *American Economic Review, Papers and Proceedings*, 60: 126–142.

Hayek, F.A. v. (1968). Der Wettbewerb als Entdeckungsverfahren. *Kieler Vorträge*, 56. Institut für Weltwirtschaft, Kiel.

Heinrich, R. (1996). Central Europe's Place in Global Capital Movements. In: G. Csáki, C. Fóti, D. Mayes (eds.), *Foreign Direct Investment and Transition. The Case of the Visegrád Countries*. Institute for World Economics of the Hungarian Academy of Sciences, Budapest: 31–56.

Heister, J., E. Mohr, W. Plesmann, T. Stoll, R. Wolfrum (1995). Economic and Legal Aspects of International Environmental Agreements: The Case of Enforcing and Stabilising an International CO_2 Agreement. *Kiel Working Papers*, 711. Institut für Weltwirtschaft, Kiel.

Heitger, B. (1993). Comparative Economic Growth: East and West. In: B. Heitger, L. Waverman (eds.). *German Unification and the International Economy*. London: Routledge.

Helpman, E., P.R. Krugman (1990). *Market Structure and Foreign Trade*. Cambridge, MA: MIT Press.

Herberg, H. (1990). Welfare Effects of Non-Tariff Barriers: A General Equilibrium Analysis. *Weltwirtschaftliches Archiv*, 126: 511–522.

Herberg, H., M. Kemp (1991). Some Implications of Variable Returns to Scale: The Case of Industry-Specific Factors. *Canadian Journal of Economics*, 24 (3): 703–704.

Hiemenz, U., E. Gundlach, R.J. Langhammer, P. Nunnenkamp (1994). *Regional Integration in Europe and its Effects on Developing Countries*. Tübingen: Mohr.

Higgins, B.H. (1959). *Economic Development. Principles, Problems and Policies*. London: Constable.

Hillman, A.L. (1989). *The Political Economy of Protection*. Chur: Harwood.

—— (1994). The Political Economy of Migration Policy. In: H. Siebert (ed.), *Migration: A Challenge to Europe*. Tübingen: Mohr.

Hodrick, R.J., E.C. Prescott (1997). Postwar US Business Cycles: An Empirical Investigation. *Journal of Money, Credit, and Banking*, 29: 1–16.

Hoekman, B.M., P.C. Mauroidis (1994). Competition, Competition Policy and the GATT. *The World Economy*, 17 (2): 121–150.

Holtfrerich, C.E., O. Schötz (1988). *Vom Weltgläubiger zum Weltschuldner: Erklärungsansätze zur historischen Entwicklung und Struktur der internationalen Währungsposition der USA*. Frankfurt/M: Knapp.

Immenga, U. (1995). Konzepte einer grenzüberschreitenden und international koordinierten Wettbewerbspolitik. *Kiel Working Papers*, 692. Institut für Weltwirtschaft, Kiel.

International Monetary Fund. http://www.imf.org.

—— *Annual Report*. Washington, D.C.

—— *Balance of Payments Statistics*. Washington, D.C.

—— *Direction of Trade Statistics*. Washington, D.C.

—— *International Financial Statistics*. Washington, D.C.

Jones, R.W., P.B. Kenen (eds.) (1984). *Handbook of International Economics*. Amsterdam: North-Holland.

Kindleberger, Ch.P. (1973). *The World in Depression 1929–1939*. London: Lane.

Klepper, G. (1998). Trade Implications of Environmental Taxes. In: P. Michaelis, F. Stähler (eds.), *Recent Policy Issues in Environmental and Resource Economics*. Heidelberg: Physica: 49–101.

Klodt, H., J. Stehn, A. Boss, K. Lammers, J.O. Lorz, R. Maurer, A.O. Neu, K.H. Paqué, A. Rosenschon, C. Walter (1994). Standort Deutschland: Strukturelle Herausforderungen im neuen Europa. *Kieler Studien*, 265. Tübingen: Mohr.

Koop, M. (1997). Trade, Foreign Direct Investment, and Multinational Enterprises in a General Equilibrium Model. *Kiel Working Papers*, 833. Institut für Weltwirtschaft, Kiel.

Kornai, J. (1980). *Economics of Shortage*. Amsterdam: North-Holland.

—— (1982). *Growth, Shortage and Efficiency. A Macrodynamic Model of the Socialist Economy*. Oxford: Blackwell.

Krueger, A.O. (1996). *The Political Economy of Trade Protection*. Chicago: University of Chicago Press.

—— (ed.) (1998). *The WTO as an International Organization*. Chicago: University of Chicago Press.

Krugman, P.R. (ed.) (1986). *Strategic Trade Policy and the New International Economics*. Cambridge, MA: MIT Press.

—— (1989). *Exchange-Rate Instability*. Cambridge, MA: MIT Press.

—— (1990). *Rethinking International Trade*. Cambridge, MA: MIT Press.

—— (1991). *Geography and Trade*. Leuven: Leuven University Press.

—— (1994). Competitiveness: A Dangerous Obsession. *Foreign Affairs*, 73 (2): 28–44.

Krugman, P.R., M. Obstfeld (1997). *International Economics, Theory and Policy*. 4th edition. Reading, MA: Addison-Wesley.

Langhammer, R.J. (1995). Regional Integration in East Asia: From Market-Driven Regionalisation to Institutionalised Regionalism? *Weltwirtschaftliches Archiv*, 131 (1): 167–201.

—— (1998a). European Integration Deepening and Widening: Implications for Asia. *Kiel Working Papers*, 892. Institut für Weltwirtschaft, Kiel.

—— (1998b). Europe's Trade, Investment and Strategic Policy Interests in Asia and APEC. In: P.D. Drysdale, D. Vines (eds.), *Europe, East Asia and APEC*. Cambridge: Cambridge University Press: 223–253.

—— (1998c). Regional Integration APEC Style: Are there Lessons to Learn from Regional Integration Style? *Kiel Working Papers*, 869. Institut für Weltwirtschaft, Kiel.

Langhammer, R.J., U. Hiemenz (1990). Regional Integration among Developing Countries. *Kieler Studien*, 232. Tübingen: Mohr.

Lindbeck, A., P. Molander, T. Persson, O. Petersson, A. Sandmo, B. Swedenborg, N. Thygesen (1994). *Turning Sweden Around*. Cambridge, MA: MIT Press.

Long, N.V., H. Siebert (1991). Institutional Competition versus Ex-Ante Harmonization: The Case of Environmental Policy. *Journal of Institutional and Theoretical Economics*, 147 (2): 296–311.

Lorz, O. (1996). Capital Mobility, Tax Competition and Lobbying for Redistributive Capital Taxation. *Kiel Working Papers*, 779. Institut für Weltwirtschaft, Kiel.

—— (1997). Standortwettbewerb bei internationaler Kapitalmobilität: Eine modelltheoretische Untersuchung. *Kieler Studien*, 284. Tübingen: Mohr.

Low, P. (1995). Market Access through Market Presence. In: OECD, *New Dimensions of Market Access in a Globalizing World Economy*. Paris.

McKinnon, R.I. (1982). Currency Substitution and Instability in the World Dollar Standard. *American Economic Review*, 72 (3): 320–333.

MacNeil, I.R. (1978). Contracts. Adjustment of Long-term Economic Relations under Classical, Neoclassical, and Relational Contract Law. *Northwestern University Law Review*, 72 (6): 854–905.

Maddison, A. (1982). *Phases of Capitalist Development*. Oxford: Oxford University Press.

—— (1992). *Dynamic Forces in Capitalist Development*. Oxford: Oxford University Press.

Magee, S.P., W.A. Brock, L. Young (1989). *Black Hole Tariffs and Endogenous Policy Theory: Political Economy in General Equlibrium*. Cambridge: Cambridge University Press.

Mankiw, N.G. (1995). The Growth of Nations. *Brookings Papers of Economic Activity*, (1): 275–326.

Marshall, A. (1890). *Principles of Economics. An Introductory Volume*. London.

Maurer, R. (1998). Economic Growth and International Trade with Capital Goods: Theory and Empiric Evidence. *Kieler Studien*, 289. Tübingen: Mohr.

Meltzer, A.H. (1998). Asian Problems and the IMF. Testimony. Prepared for the Joint Committee. February.

Messerlin, P.A. (1989). The EC Antidumping Regulations: A First Economic Appraisal, 1980–85. *Weltwirtschaftliches Archiv*, 125: 563–587.

Minton-Beddoes, Z. (1995). Why the IMF Needs Reform. *Foreign Affairs*, 74 (3): 123–133.

Mundell R.A. (1961). A Theory of Optimum Currency Areas. *American Economic Review*, 51 (4): 657–665.

Mussa, M. (1997). IMF Surveillance. *American Economic Review*, 87 (2): 28–31.

Myrdal, G. (1956). *An International Economy*. New York: Harper.

National Institute of Statistics, Geography and Informatics. *Mexican Bulletin of Statistical Information*. Aguascalientes.

Nelson, R.R. (1956). A Theory of the Low-Level Equilibrium Trap in Underdeveloped Economies. *American Economic Review*, 46 (5): 894–908.

Nicolaides, P. (1994). Towards Multilateral Rules on Competition. The Problems in Mutual Recognition of National Rules. *World Competition*, 17 (3): 5–48.

Norheim, H., K.-M. Finger, K. Anderson (1993). Trends in the Regionalization of World Trade, 1928 to 1990. In: K. Anderson, R. Blackhurst (eds.), *Regional Integration and the Global Trading System*. New York: Harvester Wheatsheaf.

North, D. (1990). *Institutions, Institutional Change and Economic Performance*. Cambridge: Cambridge University Press.

Nugent, N. (1994). *The Government and Politics of the European Union*, 3rd edition. Basingstoke: Macmillan.

Nunnenkamp, P., E. Gundlach, J.P. Agarwal (1994). Globalisation of Production and Markets. *Kieler Studien*, 262. Tübingen: Mohr.

Obstfeld, M., K. Rogoff (1996). *Foundations of International Macroeconomics*. Cambridge, MA: MIT Press.

OECD. http.//www.oecd.org.

—— *Economic Outlook*. Paris.

—— *International Trade by Commodities Statistics*. Paris.

—— *Main Economic Indicators*. Paris.

—— *National Accounts*. Paris.

—— *Short-Term Economic Indicators, Transition Countries*. Paris.

Olson, M. (1969). The Principle of 'Fiscal Equivalence'. *American Economic Review*, 59: 479–487.

—— (1982). *The Rise and Decline of Nations. Economic Growth, Stagflation and Social Rigidities*. New Haven, CT: Yale University Press.

Ostry, S. (1995). New Dimensions of Market Access: Challenges for the Trading System. In: OECD, *New Dimensions of Market Access in a Globalizing World Economy*. Paris.

—— (1997). A New Regime of Foreign Direct Investment. Group of Thirty. *Washington Occasional Paper*, 53.

PlanEcon (Annual Reports). *Czech Economic Monitor PlanEcon Report*.

Popper, K.R. (1945). *The Open Society and its Enemies*. London: Routledge & Kegan Paul.

Prebisch, R. (1950). *The Economic Development of Latin America and its Principal Problems*. United Nations Publications, Economic Commission for Latin America, II G.2.

Rauscher, M. (1997a). *International Trade, Factor Movements, and the Environment*. Oxford: Clarendon.

—— (1997b). Environmental Regulation and International Capital Allocation. In: C. Carraro, D. Siniscalco (eds.), *New Directions in the Economic Theory of the Environment*. Cambridge: Cambridge University Press: 193–238.

Rawls, J. (1971). *A Theory of Justice*. Cambridge, MA: Belknap.

Rogoff, K. (1996). The Purchasing Power Parity Puzzle. *Journal of Economic Literature*, 34 (2): 665–668.

Romer, P.M. (1986). Increasing Returns and Long-Run Growth. *Journal of Political Economy*, 94: 1002–1037.

Sachs, J. (1994). The IMF and Economies in Crisis. Presented at the London School of Economics. July.

—— (1997a). Limits of Convergence. Nature, Nurture and Growth. *The Economist*, 14 June. London.

—— (1997b). Power Unto Itself? *Financial Times*, 11 December.

Sachverständigenrat zur Begutachtung der gesamtwirtschaftlichen Entwicklung. Annual Reports. Stuttgart: Metzler-Poeschel.

Samuelson, P.A. (1954). The Pure Theory of Public Expenditure. *Review of Economic and Statistics*, 36 (4): 387–389.

Scheide, J. (1998). Central Banks: No Reason to Ignore Money. *Kiel Discussion Papers*, 316. Institut für Weltwirtschaft, Kiel.

Scheide, J., R. Solveen (1998). Should the European Central Bank Worry About Exchange Rates? *Konjunkturpolitik*, 44 (1): 31–51.

Scherer, F.M. (1994). *Competition Policies for an Integrated World Economy*. Washington, D.C.: Brookings Institution.

Schumpeter, J.A. (1934). *The Theory of Economic Development. An Inquiry into Profits, Capital, Credit, Interest and the Business Cycle*. Cambridge, MA: Harvard University Press.

Schweickert, R. (1994). Exchange Rate Based Stabilisation: Lessons from a Radical Implementation in Argentina. *The World Economy* 17 (2): 171–189.

Seidel, M. (1997). Between Unanimity and Majority. Towards New Rules of Decision-Making. In: H. Siebert (ed.), *Quo Vadis Europe*? Tübingen: Mohr: 47–66.

Siebert, H. (1983). *Ökonomische Theorie natürlicher Ressourcen*. Tübingen: Mohr.

—— (1987). Foreign Debt and Capital Accumulation. *Weltwirtschaftliches Archiv*, 123: 618–630.

—— (1989). The Half and the Full Debt Cycle. *Weltwirtschaftliches Archiv*, 125: 217–229.

—— (1991a). A Schumpeterian Model of Growth in the World Economy: Some Notes on a New Paradigm in International Economics. *Weltwirtschaftliches Archiv*, 127 (4): 800–812.

—— (1991b). German Unification, The Economics of Transition. *Economic Policy*, 13: 287–340.

—— (1991c). The Integration of Germany – Real Economic Adjustment. *European Economic Review*, 3: 591–602.

—— (1991d). *The New Economic Landscape in Europe*. Oxford: Basil Blackwell.

—— (1993). Internationale Wanderungsbedingungen – Erklärungsansätze und Gestaltungsfragen. *Schweizerische Zeitschrift für Volkswirtschaft und Statistik* 129 (3): 229–255.

—— (1994). *Aussenwirtschaft*. 6th revised edition. Stuttgart: Gustav Fischer.

—— (1995). Eastern Germany in the Fifth Year. Investment Hammering in the Basement? *Kiel Discussion Papers*, 250. Institut für Weltwirtschaft, Kiel.

—— (1996a). On the Concept of Locational Competition. *Kiel Working Papers*, 731. Institut für Weltwirtschaft, Kiel.

—— (1996b). Trade Policy and Environmental Protection. *The World Economy: Global Trade Policy*, 1996: 183–194.

—— (1997a). *Weltwirtschaft*. Stuttgart: Lucius & Lucius.

—— (1997b). Die Weltwirtschaft im Umbruch: Müssen die Realeinkommen der Arbeitnehmer sinken? *Aussenwirtschaft*, 52: 349–368.

—— (1997c). Reintegrating the Reform Countries into the World Economy. *Kiel Working Papers*, 829. Institut für Weltwirtschaft, Kiel.

—— (1998a). An Institutional Order for a Globalizing World Economy. In: K. Jaeger, K.-J. Koch (eds.), *Trade, Growth, and Economic Policy in Open Economies – Essays in Honour of Hans-Jürgen Vosgerau*. Berlin: Springer: 331–349.

—— (1998b). *Economics of the Environment Theory and Policy*. 5th revised edition. Berlin: Springer.

—— (1998c). Labor Productivities and Labor Costs in Euroland. *Kiel Working Papers*, 866. Institut für Weltwirtschaft, Kiel.

—— (1998d). The Future of the IMF – How to Prevent the Next Global Financial Crisis. *Kiel Working Papers*, 870. Institut für Weltwirtschaft, Kiel.

—— (1999). What Does Globalization Mean for the World Trading System? In: WTO, *The Global Trading System at Fifty*. The Hague: Kluwer.

Siebert, H., I. Collier (1991). The Economic Integration of Post-Wall Germany. In: *American Economic Review*, Papers and Proceedings, 81: 196–201.

Siebert, H., H. Klodt (1999). Towards Global Competition: Catalysts and Constraints. In: OECD, *21st Century Economic Dynamics: Anatomy of a Long Boom*. Paris.

Siebert, H., M. Koop (1990). Institutional Competition: A Concept for Europe? *Aussenwirtschaft*, 45: 439–462.

—— (1993). Institutional Competition versus Centralization: Quo Vadis Europe? *Oxford Review of Economic Policy*, 9 (1): 15–30.

Siebert, H., J. Eichberger, R. Gronych, R. Pethig (1980). *Trade and Environment. A Theoretical Enquiry*. Amsterdam: Elsevier.

Singer, H.W. (1950). The Distribution of Gains between Investing and Borrowing Countries. *American Economic Review*, 40 (2): 473–485.

Sinn, H.-W. (1996). The Subsidiary Principle and Market Failure in Systems Competition. *CES Working Paper*, 103. Munich.

Sinn, S. (1992a). Saving–Investment Correlations and Capital Mobility: On the Evidence from Annual Data. *Economic Journal*, 102: 1162–1170.

—— (1992b). The Taming of Leviathan: Competition among Governments. *Constitutional Political Economy*, 3: 177–196.

Snape, R.H. (1998). Reading Effective Agreements Covering Services. In: A.O. Krueger (ed.), *The WTO as an International Organization*. Chicago: University of Chicago Press: 279–295.

Solow, R.M. (1956). A Contribution to the Theory of Economic Growth. *Quarterly Journal of Economics*, 70: 65–94.

Srinivasan, T.N. (1998). Regionalism and the WTO: Is Nondiscrimination Passé? In: A.O. Krueger (ed.), *The WTO as an International Organization*. Chicago: University of Chicago Press: 329–349.

State Statistical Bureau, People's Republic of China. *China Statistical Yearbook*. Beijing.

Statistics Bureau, Management and Coordination Agency, Government of Japan. *Statistical Handbook of Japan*. Tokyo.

Statistics Canada. http://www.statcan.ca.

Statistisches Amt der DDR. *Statistisches Jahrbuch der Industrie der Deutschen Demokratischen Republik*. Berlin.

—— *Wirtschaftsbereich Industrie, Produktion und Auftragsbestand*. Berlin.

Statistisches Bundesamt. *Produzierendes Gewerbe* (Fachserie 4, Reihe 2.1/ Reihe S. 17). Wiesbaden.

—— *Volkswirtschaftliche Gesamtrechnung* (Fachserie 18). Wiesbaden.

Stehn, J. (1997). Grundfragen einer Osterweiterung der Europäischen Union. Unpublished Paper.

Stoeckel, A., D. Pearce, G. Banks (1990). *Western Trade Blocs: Game, Set or Match for Asia–Pacific and the World Economy*. Centre for International Economics, Canberra.

Stolpe, M. (1995). Technology and the Dynamics of Specialization in Open Economies. *Kieler Studien*, 271. Tübingen: Mohr.

Summers, R., A.W. Heston (1988). A New Set of International Comparisons of Real Product and Price Level Estimates for 130 Countries, 1950–1985. *Review of Income and Wealth*, 34 (1): 1–25.

—— (1991). The Penn World Table (Mark 5): an Expanded Set of International Comparisons, 1950–1988. *Quarterly Journal of Economics*, 106 (2).

Tangermann, S. (1997). Reforming the CAP. A Prerequisite for Eastern Enlargement. In: H. Siebert (ed.), *Quo Vadis Europe?* Tübingen: Mohr: 151–179.

Thünen, J.H.v. (1826). *Der isolierte Staat in Beziehung auf Landwirtschaft und Nationalökonomie*. Hamburg: Perthes.

Tiebout, C. (1956). A Pure Theory of Local Expenditures. *Journal of Political Economy*, 64: 416–424.

Tobin, J. (1978). A Proposal for International Monetary Reform. *Eastern Economic Journal*, 4: 153–159.

Tumlir, J. (1979). Weltwirtschaftsordnung: Regeln, Kooperation und Souveränität. *Kieler Vorträge*, 87. Institut für Weltwirtschaft, Kiel.

—— (1983). International Economic Order and Democratic Constitutionalism. *ORDO*, 34: 71–83.

US Census Bureau. *International Data Base*. http://www.census.gov.

US Department of Commerce. *International Trade Administration*. http://www.ita.doc.gov/tradestats.

Viner, J. (1950). *The Customs Union Issue*. New York, London: Stevens.

Williamson, J. (1983). *The Exchange Rate System. Policy Analysis in International Economics*. Washington D.C., Cambridge: MIT Press.

—— (1996). A New Facility for the IMF. *International Monetary and Financial Issues for the 1990s*, 7: 1–9.

Willms, M. (1993). Costs and Benefits of European Monetary Union. In: Centre International d'Etudes Juridique et de Droit Comparé, *European Monetary Union. Legal Foundations and Economic Implications*. Luxembourg: 97–111.

—— (1995). *Internationale Währungspolitik*. 2nd revised edition. Munich: Franz Vahlen.

World Bank. http://www.worldbank.org.

—— *Global Development Finance* (previously: *World Debt Tables*). Washington, D.C.

—— *Global Economic Prospects and the Developing Countries*. Washington, D.C.

—— *World Data*. Washington D.C.

—— *World Development Indicators*. Washington D.C.

—— *World Development Report*. Oxford.

World Economic Forum (1998). *The Global Competitiveness Report 1998*. Davos.

World Trade Organization. http://www.wto.org.

—— *Annual Report*. Geneva.

—— (1995). *Regionalism and the World of Trading System*. Geneva.

Index